STRAY

BREAKING FREE, FALLING HARD, GROWING STRONGER

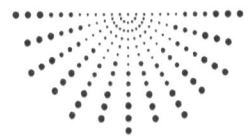

SHANNON O'BRIEN

Edited by Eldes Tran

Cover design by 100Covers

For rights and permissions, please contact:

Shannon O'Brien

shannon.obrien.author@gmail.com

Published by **RoamLight Publishing**

Paperback ISBN: 979-8-9933497-0-1

eBook ISBN: 979-8-9933497-1-8

First Edition

❀ Formatted with Vellum

CONTENTS

PROLOGUE

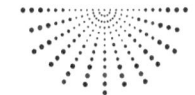

I stood on a jungle trail in Bolivia, mud clinging to my ankles and panic rising in my throat. The sun dipped low in the sky, monkeys howled in the distance. I was hopelessly lost.

I'd wandered off the path while volunteering at a wildlife refuge, thinking I could find a shortcut back. I couldn't. The jungle swallowed sound, the trees looked identical, and I hadn't brought a flashlight. I hadn't told anyone where I was going. There was no map, no phone signal, no other humans around.

For a few long minutes, I froze, imagining spending the night out there—sleeping in the dark, alone, with all the things that crawl and hiss and bite. My stomach twisted.

Then something within me shifted. I took a breath, and another. I started listening—*really listening*. I remembered the way the sun moved when I had hiked out earlier, the direction the river should be, the bend in the trail where I'd first veered off.

I found my way back before nightfall. No grand rescue, no dramatic collapse—just quiet relief and a bit more trust in myself than before.

That moment wasn't the most dangerous I've faced, nor even the most transformative. But it was the first time I realized that I could get myself out of the woods.

We all have defining moments scattered within our life story.

"Aha" moments.

Moments that change everything.

Forever.

More often than not, these moments are born from hardship.

Life's hardships can knock us straight to the ground, curled into a fetal position. We are left battling demons, anxiously attempting to crawl out of a dark hole, desperately trying to find our way out and back into the light.

Going through such struggles also provides opportunity.

For hope.

For resilience.

Struggle grants us opportunities to learn.

To rise stronger.

With more resolve. And wisdom.

The summer after I graduated high school, I entered one of those defining chapters. A dark one that profoundly shaped my outlook and attitude toward life.

My ex-boyfriend and dear friend, John, lost a battle with himself. He took his own life in the summer of 2006.

The shock was seismic. It shattered the foundation beneath me.

But in the wreckage, something fierce awakened. I became obsessed with living life fully—doubly, in his honor. To not take any moment for granted. To say yes. To feel everything. To wring every drop of meaning out of this short time we're given.

That thirst—to live wide open—led me to travel.

It began in South America, just after university. I could have never guessed that the six-month journey would launch me into a life living abroad. It's been fifteen years and counting.

My wildest imagination could have never conjured up the mad adventures I would experience, the loves I would become enamoured with, the dangers I would behold, the traumas endured, and the profound friendships forged. It would all rewire my sense of what matters.

The deeper I ventured into the world, the more it reshaped me. Not in grand, cinematic moments, but through quiet truths whispered along the way. That living simply often feels the richest. That gratitude softens even the hardest days. That struggle is not the end, but the beginning of something more meaningful.

I learned to protect the relationships that matter, to welcome perspectives different from my own, and to chase balance instead of perfection. And above all, I've come to believe that this world, and the people in it, are more kind and beautiful than we're often led to believe. These are truths that have rooted themselves in me, shaped by years of wandering, discomfort, connection, and reflection.

Come—walk beside me onto these paths. Let's seek the lessons hidden in the everyday. Let me take you across the world, simply because it is there.

Stories don't end—they only lead us forward.

So here's to the journey. To the strange and beautiful detours.

1

BEHIND PRISON WALLS

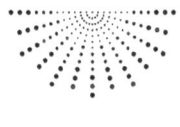

BOLIVIA

"*We* could disappear."

Dane's eyes flicked toward me, the afternoon sun glinting off his chestnut hair. We were sprawled across a weathered bench in the courtyard at University of California, Santa Cruz, legs stretched out, soaking in the warmth of spring. Seagulls wheeled overhead, their sharp cries cutting through the steady pounding of feet against a rubber running track. The track circled a soccer field perched high on a hill, overlooking the foggy ocean below.

"Disappear where?"

"South America." I rested my chin on my hand, my freckled arms crossed over my knees as I gazed toward the sequoias towering at the edge of the courtyard. Their dark trunks stood stark against the bright blue sky.

Dane shifted, his broad shoulders settling deeper into the bench. "And what about these damn university degrees we've busted our asses for over the past four years?"

I sat up straighter. "You know the job market's crap. The whole world is still recovering from the 2008 financial crisis. No one's handing out dream jobs."

"Thanks for the hope on this fine, sunny day."

I ignored his sarcasm. "I want to learn more about the world. I don't want to get old without venturing beyond my comfort zone and chasing some unique adventures."

"Fair enough." Dane drummed his fingers on the armrest. "Why South America?"

"Because it's not Europe." I said it without flinching. "Every American goes there to 'find themselves' between museum tours and overpriced hostels. South America's wilder. Less curated."

I paused, surprised by how fiercely I felt about it. "And let's be real, our menial budgets would stretch so much further down there. We could live off beans and take bus rides, spend maybe a grand a month each, and still see volcanoes and ancient cities."

Dimples carved into Dane's cheeks. "Go on."

"We could hike through the Amazon and stand on top of Machu Picchu. It's one of the seven wonders of the world!" The words tasted electric in my mouth.

"We could club in Buenos Aires," I added quickly, as if afraid the idea might lose him. "They party all night long!"

"And you got the funds for this?"

"I've been hoarding all the money I've made coaching gymnastics." I pushed a strand of dark blonde hair behind my ear. "And I know you have savings too."

"I must admit, we make most excellent wingmen for one another," Dane said with a mischievous glint in his deep brown eyes. "I'm not opposed to a few beautiful South American women in my life."

"And who knows," I paused dramatically, placing a hand on my forehead pretending to swoon, "maybe we'll stumble upon some beautiful South American men along the way, too. I'm single for the first time in five years, you know."

"I'll believe it when I see it," Dane joked back. "But yeah, sounds like a plan."

When you're young, with no real obligations, sometimes that's all it takes—a dream, a bit of courage to do something different, and enough cash to get you started. I felt lucky to have a best friend by my side too.

Over the next few months, we picked out backpacks, broke in our hiking boots, and dog-eared the pages of a trusty *Lonely Planet.* We were off before we knew it—six months through Peru, Chile, Argentina, Uruguay, and Bolivia—chasing adventure.

One month into our trip, having made our way to La Paz, Bolivia, Dane and I sat with a cup of tinta, or coffee.

"You know, Shan," Dane stretched his legs out in front of him, ankles crossed, "I've been thinking about this 'gringo trail' we're on. It just connects all the major tourist hotspots."

I took a sip of my coffee. "It's hard to get off it!"

Dane winked. "Well, the places along the gringo trail are popular for a reason. Machu Picchu, the Mayan ruins—they're all incredible destinations. But we gotta be missing out on something by sticking to this well-worn path that every tourist follows, right?"

"For sure." His point took shape in my mind. "There's so much more to South America than the highlights. Like when the locals invited us into their homes for meals at Isla del Sol. Those were some of the most memorable experiences we've had so far."

"Exactly! Lord knows I will never forget eating guinea pig in that random guy's house!"

"Hahaha! Weirdest 'delicacy' *ever.*"

"And remember when we spent that whole day just wandering around the neighborhoods in Lima?" Dane's eyes brightened as he recalled the experience. "We got to see real street life—fresh fruit lining the roadside, local markets with all that traditional pottery."

"Everyone was super friendly."

"Yes!" Dane's gaze turned distant, as if replaying the scenes in his mind.

"And I loved the music everywhere. Andean flutes and drums blending with the city noise. So cool."

Dane's tall frame relaxed as he nodded, his oversized jacket slipping off one shoulder. "This is the kinda stuff you can't find on the gringo trail."

I jumped up from my chair, throwing my arms in the air. "Yeah, fuck all the upscale bars and chain restaurants too!"

Dane laughed. "OK, well, let's make sure we keep doing that. Just keep our eyes and ears open for unique experiences, talk to backpackers and locals, get their advice, and see where it takes us."

"OK. Sounds good. In fact, let's make this a new travel rule!" I said. "We have to say yes to every adventure that falls into our laps."

"I can say yes to that." Dane raised his hand for a high-five. "We can start by asking around the hostel to see if anyone has some interesting recommendations."

Our trip through South America occurred before the days of everyone carrying cellphones in their pockets. Dane and I were particularly behind the times. We found it unnecessary to drag along our Nokia phones, which had nothing on them but Snake. Buying a SIM card in each foreign country was definitely not on our agenda. Our only internet access was through communal computers in hostels. Every few days, we lined up with the other backpackers, waiting to use the desktop computer. When it was our turn, we'd be given thirty to forty-five minutes, no more.

Dane and I were not yet aware of YouTube vlogs or comprehensive online guides with tips to help people plan their explorations. We also lacked the abundance of travel blogs outlining step-by-step directions to every possible adventure. Instead, we relied heavily on word of mouth to get around—gathering advice from other backpackers along the way.

One afternoon, Dane and I lounged at the hostel, sinking into a pair of sagging beanbags in the communal hangout area. Around us, other backpackers dozed on weathered couches marked with cigarette burns and mysterious stains. Cyril, our newfound friend, regaled us with tales.

"You guys have to visit San Pedro Prison while you're in La Paz," Cyril insisted, his thick Afro bouncing up and down as he nodded with excitement. "It's a must-do experience, trust me."

Dane and I exchanged skeptical glances, unsure of what to make of Cyril's enthusiasm.

"A tour of a prison...? Where the hell did an idea like that come from?" I asked.

"They began a few years ago, thanks to an inmate named Thomas McFadden," Cyril explained. "He got caught in the La Paz airport attempting to smuggle five kilos of cocaine. Got thrown into the prison penniless, desperate to make a dime."

"So he dreamed up the idea of prison tours, eh?" Dane concluded.

"Yup. Smart idea, right? Charge the backpackers to visit him. Share the cut with other inmates so they support the plan. Genius. Must be that African-born British side of him!" Cyril teased, proudly dusting off his shoulders, touting his own heritage.

I squinted at him, as if better focus might somehow rearrange the facts. "OK, getting the other inmates on board by sharing the profits makes sense, but how the hell did he get prison officials to agree?"

"You must be new to Bolivia." Cyril's voice dripped with sarcasm. "Everything is corrupt as hell, girl! The prison guards, like most Bolivians in power, are corrupt. Of course they're open to a deal that lines their pockets! The guards take a cut of the money tourists pay."

"Clever. But isn't it...dangerous?" Dane voiced the concern that lingered in my mind.

Cyril brushed aside our nervous thoughts with a dismissive wave. "I was fine, wasn't I?" He gave a nonchalant grin as he adjusted the collar of his Nike shirt. "You'll be all right, mate. Live a little."

"Why the hell would we want to spend time in a prison though? That's my nightmare!" I fired back. The whole thing sounded like a precarious power balance, carefully orchestrated to benefit those at the top.

"Trust me, it's not your usual tour. Hell, the Lonely Planet advertises it as 'the world's most bizarre tourist attraction'!"

I picked at a frayed seam in the beanbag. "I do love bizarre things..."

"All right, let's do it!" Dane sat up a bit straighter. "How do we sign up for this tour?"

"The only way to get into the prison is to hang in the park outside of it, Plaza San Pedro. Chill there until someone approaches you. It feels weird, but just do it."

Soon enough, Dane and I were loitering in the park, sticking out like neon signs in a dimly lit alley. Old men in battered hats and oil-stained jeans lounged on the graffiti-covered benches or played dominoes under the shade of the sparse trees. Rusted swings hung by one chain at the nearby playground. Screws jutted out of the slide. We were the only gringos in the park, drawing shifty gazes from the weathered individuals around us, exchanging money for plastic baggies. Their appearance mirrored the worn-out surroundings—ragged clothes, dirt-crusted bodies, and watchful eyes that scanned every passerby with cautious calculation.

It did not take long for a man to approach us. "¿Quieren visitar la prisión?" he asked, his voice low and gravelly.

Dane and I shared a glance before Dane responded in Spanglish. "Uh, sí, we want to see."

The man nodded and stated matter-of-factly, "OK, twenty dollas cada uno."

"Twenty?" I echoed, my voice tinged with disbelief. Twenty dollars was what we usually spent for an entire day's food and accommodation.

Dane's brow furrowed as he took in the man. "Amigo, ten dollars? Diez? Por favor."

The man shrugged nonchalantly, unwilling to budge on the price. "It's a special tour, amigos. You no get this anywhere else."

"OK, OK, lo haremos," Dane relented.

With a satisfied nod, the man gestured for us to follow him. "Vamos," he said, leading us across the street and through a set of gates into the prison compound.

We were ushered into a small entry office—a concrete room with a metal desk and barred windows. As we stepped inside, two guards in neatly pressed, military-style uniforms walked toward us. Despite their shorter stature, the prison guards exuded an air of intimidation, emphasized by the guns hanging from their belts. Their expressions were devoid of any hint of welcome.

I shifted uncomfortably, suddenly feeling acutely aware of the weight of the passport in my hand.

"Passports and payment," one of the guards demanded, his voice sharp and commanding.

"Passports?" Dane asked. "Por que?"

"We keep 'til you go."

Alarm set in. It's a general rule of thumb to always keep your passport close by when traveling. "Dane, you sure about this?" I whispered.

He sighed, eyes scanning the room with apprehension. "We're here already.... Let's just do it?"

I shrugged, and with trembling hands, I reluctantly handed my passport to the guard. Dane followed suit, his grip steady, sliding the passport across the counter as if he didn't have a second thought.

In exchange for our money and passports, the guards scrawled a number on our arms. Then, they led us down a hall and through more towering, rusted gates. Three other tourists waited.

We introduced ourselves. Patrick and James, two friends from Ireland, stood side by side—both pale and freckled, with fiery red hair. A horrendous sunburn marred James's shoulders, his peeling skin like that of a snake.

Marc, a solo traveler from Belgium, had wavy brown hair that fell effortlessly over his forehead, framing his face. His thick, black-rimmed glasses contrasted with his sharp blue eyes. A faded U2 shirt and well-worn hiking boots hinted at little concern for appearances.

Once through the gates, we entered a broad outdoor courtyard where hundreds of people milled about. The sounds of chatter and laughter were interrupted by the occasional shout. Some rowdy men played a game of soccer on a sprawling cement area. Others gathered casually exchanging pleasantries. A group of children ran around playing together. Stationed in a corner, young boys were shining shoes. I wrinkled my nose at the scent of their shoe polish mixing with dust that hung in the air. Women worked at food stands embellished with oversized Coca-Cola signs, while mangy dogs and cats slept lazily beneath tables. The wind whipped a national flag on a high tower, its red, yellow, and green bands faded from years of exposure to the elements. Everyone wore street clothes. There wasn't a guard in sight.

Three men approached. The first towered over the others. His muscular frame filled out his black tank top, veins bulging and tattoos inked on every inch of visible skin, including his shaved head. He wore combat pants, which accentuated his commanding presence.

The other two men, shorter, but no less imposing, carried themselves with a rough demeanor. Their strides were purposeful, each step resonating with an air of authority. The first man sported a thick mustache that matched his long brown ponytail. The second had short, spiked hair and piercing green eyes. His sleeveless shirt, emblazoned with skulls, clung to his chest. Tribal snake tattoos coiling around jaguars and bloody spears covered his thick arms.

This man introduced himself. "Hey, what's up, amigos? I'm Juan Carlos, your guide for today. Call me JC." He sauntered forward, gesturing for us to follow. His movements were fluid, body language oozing self-assuredness.

"When will we enter the prison?" I asked.

"You're in it!" He laughed. "This prison's not like the ones you know, sweetheart. We run ourselves."

"What do you mean *we*?" James chimed in.

"We. The prisoners. We run ourselves in here," JC shot back.

"You're a prisoner?!" I blurted out in disbelief, quickly trying to take back my words which might have offended him. "I mean...you're a prisoner and our tour guide? We don't have guards as a tour guide?"

"Woman, there are not ANY guards inside this prison," JC snarled. "Like I said, we run ourselves in here. We have our own rules, our own government systems. Only guards we got guard the outside, making sure we don't get out. Look around, no one here is shackled. We're free to roam inside."

"But...there's kids inside?" Marc shifted his weight from one foot to the other. "And the women, are they prisoners, too? I thought this was a men's prison?"

"All the prisoners are men, but we're allowed to bring our families in with us."

"But how do the kids go to school and live a normal life inside a prison?" I pried.

"Women and kids can come and go as they please. Hell, kids make it to school everyday. And after, they just return to their dads here," JC responded.

"Is that how you guys get supplies for all your shops? The women and kids just bring it in with them each day?" Marc asked, as though piecing together the details of this strange world.

"You got it. It's also how we can get goods out to sell. I'll show ya," JC said, with a cheeky wink.

"I don't get it," Dane continued. "Why would the government have kids and women in a prison?"

"The Bolivian government believes this system could work. Inmates have to work and be responsible. They're not cut off from their families and societies like most bullshit prison systems are. With this system, inmates are less likely to re-offend if we get released."

"And that works?" Patrick replied cautiously.

"Fuck if I know!" JC chuckled. "But I'll take the freedom we get compared to most prisons! Come, let me just show ya."

JC led us around the communal spaces of the prison. The two other inmates shadowed us, acting as unofficial bodyguards. A sense of unease gnawed in the pit of my stomach. The absence of guards within the prison made me feel vulnerable. When I initially agreed to this tour, I didn't realize that we'd be entering a prison with no real security.

However, as I glanced at the women and children going about their daily lives, a small sense of relief washed over me. Their presence provided a semblance of normalcy amidst the harsh reality of our surroundings.

As we wandered the grounds, I was shocked that the prison was functioning as an independent society. It wasn't just a building—it was a sprawling compound surrounded by high walls, with distinct sections both outside and inside. A city within the city of La Paz. They had restaurants, churches, small businesses, like a photocopy shop, and stalls selling dishware. There were handicraft workshops, a gym, a seamstress, even a bar and billiard hall.

The inmates had established their own rules, a political system, and even a sophisticated economy based on the jobs they'd created. To afford the necessities of life—food, clothing, housing, and medicine—they worked and earned within the walls.

"Where are the prison cells, though? How do you get locked in them at night if there's no guards inside?" Patrick asked.

"When I said we don't have pig guards in here, that's what I meant. We don't get locked in cells. Hell, we lock ourselves in our rooms to try to keep the danger out!"

"I don't get it," Dane said.

"Look, when you get thrown in this hell hole you better bring cash with you. You buy accommodation from an outgoing inmate. Lock, key, and an official property title deed is drawn up and all. We got eight sections in the prison, and no two cells are the same."

"What's the difference between them?" I asked.

"Think of 'em like suburbs. We got a five-star section, which is where the wealthy drug lords live. Those apartments are BIG, carpeted, fully furnished. They got bathrooms, views, hell, even a flat-screen TV. People can pay as much as thirty-thousand dollars for one of them. More modest men, like myself, might just have a simple room. Money talks. Just like in the outside world. You don't got dinero in here, you don't got nothing."

"But what if you don't have money?" Dane prodded.

"We got slums. Dark, dirty slums filled with evil. I'll show ya. There can be five men crammed into holes of a room we call coffins. Those only cost a few hundred dollars. But hell, we got homeless just sleeping outside, too. This damn city sits at 3,600 meters above sea level. It's one of the highest cities in the world. Can you imagine how cold that shit gets at night? In the winter? Homeless freeze to death sometimes. Or worse.... You don't got no home, you don't got no protection. That is the worst fate."

"OK," I responded, "but if you have a bit of cash for housing outside the slummy area, then this place doesn't seem *so bad*, yeah? Everyone seems to get along, doing their thing?"

"Woman, you have no idea. This place is filled with nothing but pain and violence. It's haunting, *especially at night*. You're here in the daytime, sweetheart. Everyone's on their best behavior. At night, the drugs are out, the addicts. People will do *anything* for a fix. This place at night, it's a hell you better pray you never know. Especially you." JC pointed menacingly at both Dane and me. "We HATE Americans in here. You guys are the reason this shit facility is overcrowded. We're only meant to have two hundred fifty, and there's more than two thousand!"

My eyes dropped to the ground as JC ranted, heart beating fast as his words circled in my mind.

"Americans are the first we knock out. Your goddamn government's stuffing us in here like cattle. The War on Drugs bullshit. YOU AMERICANS ARE THE ONES BUYING ALL THE DAMN DRUGS! We're just supplyin' it. Going about pointing all the fingers at the dealers, when all you Americans are the fucking crackheads using it. I wouldn't be selling that shit if it weren't for the scumbag Americans buying it."

"War on Drugs?" Patrick pressed. "What the hell does that mean?"

A sharp crash sounded from the far side of the yard. I flinched. A group of inmates were wrestling over a plastic bottle, shouting, their movements wild and aggressive.

JC barely glanced at the chaos before turning back to us, his face hardened. "Back in '71, President Nixon kicked it off. Called drug trafficking a national security threat."

James pressed, "And...?"

"Over four decades, a trillion dollars down the drain," JC said. "Production, supply, trafficking—ain't gone down. Domestic demand? Higher than ever. What a waste o' cash."

Marc shook his head. "Wait, so they poured all this money into stopping drugs, but nothing's changed?"

"Exactly, bro." JC nodded. "They point fingers at dealers and producers abroad instead of looking at their own country and its people."

"You know," Patrick chewed lightly on the inside of his cheek, "historically, prohibition policies rarely work. Why doesn't America see that?"

"Good question, mate." JC shrugged. "Maybe it's easier to blame than to change."

James added, "Meanwhile addiction, homelessness, mental illness —it's all through the roof in America. Wouldn't it make more sense to focus on those?"

In the corner of my eye, a prisoner sat crouched in the dirt, carving deep lines into his forearm with a shard of metal. I tore my focus away and tried to shake off the image before finding my voice. "Like Einstein said, you can't keep doing the same thing over and over, expecting different results."

"Yeah, man. The U.S. has been doin' just that. And here we are, stuck in this prison, feelin' the consequences of their failed policies."

JC continued walking, leading us from the open courtyard into the prison's slum district. We followed closely, little ducklings in a row, our footsteps echoing through narrow, maze-like alleys.

Cells branched off the twisting corridors. The labyrinth of despair disoriented me. Around each corner, the stench of rancid urine and vomit burned my nostrils. A bitter taste coated my tongue and curled at the back of my throat. Every breath felt like swallowing something foul. It became increasingly difficult to focus on anything else. I didn't want to offend anyone by holding my nose, but the smell was unbearable.

Darkness filled the damp and moldy halls. Flickering light bulbs cast eerie shadows on decaying walls, emphasizing the bleakness of this forgotten corner of society. Grotesquely oversized rats scurried across the grimy floor. Addicts lay sprawled, staring up at us with hollow gazes, their arms and legs potholed with scars from shooting up.

My fear heightened as a realization intruded my mind. I was winding through all of this at the back of the line—the only woman in the group. I imagined my tour rounding a corner and me disappearing, snatched and pulled into the dark depths of the building.

Dane must have picked up on my tension because he whispered to me, "Hey, are you OK?"

I hesitated, torn between masking my fear and acknowledging it. "I'm...I'm really scared," I admitted in a whisper.

Without hesitation, Dane asked, "Want to switch places?"

Grateful, I accepted. Dane slowed until I passed him and then followed along behind, a shield at my back.

We continued to follow JC through the maze of hopelessness. "Scared, sweetheart?" he asked me condescendingly. "Don't you worry. Ain't no one going to touch you lot. If they do, they'll be killed. You tourists coming in here bring us a lot of money. We need it. We can keep doing this as long as no one gets hurt. Everybody knows not to touch the tourists. We all benefit from having ya."

With that reassurance, I relaxed...slightly. However, a few years after my visit, I learned that a female tourist from Australia was raped in the same prison. This led to the tours being canceled. And if JC was right, the perpetrator was probably murdered in some horrible way.

My shoulders dropped as tension melted when we wound our way out of the seemingly endless hallways of misery in the slum area. Emerging into the light of day, we entered a spacious courtyard dominated by a drained swimming pool. JC directed us to circle around it. Its steep concrete walls were darkly stained and pocked with blunt indentations.

"This is an important piece of our community: La Piscina, which means 'pool' in Spanish," JC explained. "You do something wrong, you'll end up in here."

And....? I thought to myself but did not dare say aloud.

"Like child rapists," JC continued, "you get put in this prison for raping a child and you will immediately get thrown into this pool, after we stomp ya and whip ya with an electrical cable. We all gather round and throw rocks at ya til you're dead. You should see the fuckers begging for their lives, trying to climb their way out. No chance."

The weight of the pool's history became clear. The dark stains that marred the walls were blood, silent remnants of the brutal and unforgiving life within the prison. It was shocking how nonchalantly JC could speak of such communal killings.

"Look, we gotta!" JC said, as if trying to redeem and explain himself. "You saw, many of us got our own kids in here. They get to run around safe and be kids. No one dare touch 'em. But then you get a child rapist in here? Hell no. We can't risk that shit. They just got to go."

In some ways, I suppose the prisoners' skewed logic made sense. However, I struggled to understand the order in which they considered crimes acceptable or unacceptable. We'd been told the two "bodyguards" with us were inmates serving time for murdering multiple people. And to their peers, somehow they were considered OK compared to another man with a different crime?

JC continued, "Look, you judge us for crimes we've done, but one thing we got going for us is respect for children. Hell, even if some inmates are fighting, when a child comes passing by someone will yell out "Niño!' which means child. The guys will stop brawlin' until the kid's gone, then get back to it. We want to keep our families with us, yo. It's one thing we agree on. But shit, enough of that," a mischievous grin spread on his lips, "we're wrapping up this lovely little tour, but let me take you to one last spot."

He led us into a bare room with white floors and walls. A long table stood in the center, ringed by metal folding chairs. The one I sat on had a slight wobble, matching the day's vibe.

"All right, team, so what can I get ya? Alcohol? Marijuana? Cocaine? What do you want?"

"*Excuse me?*" Dane asked.

JC and his murdering mates burst into laughter. "Boy, we make it inside the prison! Hell, we got some of the best cocaine in the goddamn country! Cheaper and purer than anywhere in the world!"

"But...how...?" I persisted, voicing Dane's confusion.

"Remember, our women and children can come and go freely, right? Well, they bring in the supplies we need and also smuggle the shit out for sale! I'm telling ya, we got some of the best cocaine in Bolivia, and therefore the planet."

This made sense, considering Bolivia was the world's third-largest cocaine producer, and most inmates in San Pedro Prison were there for smuggling, trafficking, and manufacturing drugs.

"Well then, I think it's best we try some!" Patrick called out.

It shouldn't have surprised me. Experimenting with cocaine was a common activity for backpackers in Bolivia. Within the city of La Paz, one could even stumble upon cocaine bars, where you could peruse a menu of different types to try. The servers would deliver it to your table, alongside your drinks, and you could casually sit and snort lines as if it were nothing more than sipping on a fresh vodka tonic.

"Yeah sure, why not? When in Rome, right?" Marc joined in. "Give us each a twenty bag, mate."

Dane and I sat idly as JC and our bodyguards railed up line after line of cocaine. Conversation flowed, as it often does between people on cocaine.

James leaned forward, elbows on the battered table. "You ever lost someone close to you?"

JC wiped his nose with the back of his hand. "Yeah. My brother. Overdosed when he was twenty-two. Was my best friend, man. After that..." He shrugged, a raw, hollow look flashing across his face. "Kinda stopped givin' a shit about anything."

Patrick jumped in, "I get that. My cousin...a drunk driver took him out. Only seventeen."

The bodyguard across from me picked at a crack in the tabletop. "Ain't nobody escapes loss. Whether it's death, divorce, bad blood." He tapped two fingers against his temple. "It leaves marks up here."

Their stories reminded me that we all start with similar hopes and dreams, but life, in all its messiness, has a way of throwing curveballs, taking us down paths we could never predict.

"Ever feel like life just...sideswiped you?" JC said. "Like you were on one path, then—*bam*—something hits, and you're somewhere you never thought you'd be?"

I laughed. "Story of my life."

The bodyguard muttered, "Ain't it all of ours?"

Over those hours, I heard pieces of myself in their stories—bad luck, screwups, the longing for something better. Our lives were worlds apart, but the gaps between us felt smaller than I expected. At the end of the day, we're all just trying to make sense of where we ended up, and why. We all want to connect and get through the day without being crushed by the weight of it all.

We sat around that table with a sense of genuine openness, a mutual desire to understand and be understood. To have someone empathize with you is a different type of intimacy. It is a rare and beautiful form of connection. One that transcends the barriers of social status, background, and circumstance.

In that fleeting connection, we were just humans—fragile, flawed, and yet somehow whole. For that brief moment, everything else faded, and I understood that even in the most unlikely places, amidst the chaos and the mess, we all crave the same thing: to be seen, to be heard, and to be understood. And maybe, just maybe, that's enough to keep going.

2

A COLCA CANYON
MISADVENTURE

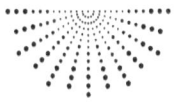

PERU

*F*or weeks Dane and I soaked up city vibes in La Paz, which included a fair share of over-the-top nights partying. Needing a breather and a dose of nature, we decided our next stop would be a more wholesome one, which our bodies would thank us for. We chose Colca Canyon, in southern Peru.

Colca Canyon was famed for being a colorful Andean valley, home to exotic animals such as the condor and the world's largest hummingbird. Many tourists flocked to Colca Canyon via bus tours. Upon reaching designated viewpoints on the canyon's peak, the buses stopped, and hordes of tourists piled out to admire the condors. With wingspans stretching up to ten feet, those graceful avian giants soared effortlessly into the air on the thermal updrafts permeating the canyon. Their dark plumage contrasted beautifully against the azure blue sky, while their distinct white collars and feathered crests added elegance to their appearance.

Dane and I, always aiming to be even more intrepid travelers, decided to hike in the canyon instead of taking the stereotypical bus tour. A local man told us it was possible to spend a day hiking to the bottom of the canyon, sleep in a lush, palm-lined oasis on the Colca River's edge, and hike out the next day. This was all the information we had, and I believed this was all the information we would need. On a crisp and sunny morning, we hauled our oversized packs onto our shoulders, left the town of Cabanaconde, and headed toward the oasis on foot.

From the top of the canyon, we gazed out on the vast expanse before us, adorned with rugged cliffs and breathtaking landscapes that stretched toward infinity. The sunlight painted a kaleidoscope of colors, illuminating the canyon's contours and revealing its sheer grandeur. Humility washed over me. Standing before such magnificence, I recognized how insignificant I was in the vastness of it all, and how nature deserved my highest respect.

With a mix of eagerness and anticipation, we embarked on the steep descent into the heart of the canyon. Its rocky walls plunged deep into the earth as layers of sedimentary rock revealed the passage of millennia. As we continued down the trail, the air grew noticeably warmer, and the gentle breeze carried the faint scent of earth and dry soil.

Arriving at the peaceful oasis, I threw my arms in the air. "Look at this place, Dane! We have it all to ourselves!"

The canyon walls embraced us, providing a sense of shelter and seclusion from the outside world.

Dane leaned back against a nearby tree, a proud smile spreading across his face. "I know, right? Just us and nature. A little paradise all to ourselves. Told ya; it pays off to stray from the well-trodden tourist paths."

"Touche, dude. Let's make some food. I'm starving."

Under the twinkling stars and the flickering glow of our campfire, we rustled up a humble dinner of two-minute noodles and chugged our water before settling into our sleeping bags for the night. The gentle chirping of crickets provided a soothing lullaby as we settled in, surrendering to the embrace of the star-studded darkness above.

The next day, the sun rose, spreading soft warmth across the rugged landscape. We rose early to begin our ascent up the steep walls of the canyon via a trail on the opposing side. Before we had taken off, locals informed us we'd need to ascend about 1,000 meters, which should take about four to six hours. Hundreds of trails led up the canyon, each zigzagging in switchbacks. The sharp turns and loops would help us climb the steep slopes more gradually, ultimately heading for the peak.

I overconfidently said, "They all go to the top, so it shouldn't really matter too much which one we take. Let's try this one!"

We wound our way up a thin goat trail. Each step demanded caution as we carefully navigated the uneven terrain. Dry bush plants poked at my legs and a rock stubbornly wedged in my shoe. Every step was a reminder of its presence, a sharp, jarring discomfort pressing into the arch of my foot. As we paused to catch our breath, I took in the surrounding scene—the sharp contrast of the dark shadows cast by the canyon walls against the bright, sunlit rock; the rich, earthy colors of the terrain, ranging from deep reds and browns to pale yellows and whites; the silence, broken only by the occasional call of a condor soaring overhead. Three hours later, we found ourselves three-quarters up the canyon, with no sign of civilization.

"Looks like we must have taken the wrong path, Shan," Dane said.

There were no other connecting paths. The only thing to do was head back down the canyon, find the correct path, and start again.

My enthusiasm for our hike dimmed as we made our way downward, navigating the loose rocks in a zigzag pattern until we returned to the depths of the canyon.

Back at the bottom, we gazed up at the canyon walls, towering with a quiet power, shielding the mysteries of the land above. With the impact of a tidal wave, we realized there were hundreds of paths weaving their way up and around the canyon walls. None of the routes had markings, and each one looked like a narrow, barely discernible path. None appeared more worn or accessible than the others.

"This damn pack is killing me." Dane sank to the ground. "It's gotta weigh at least twenty-five pounds."

I slumped to the ground next to him, rubbing my shoulders. "What the hell were we thinking bringing everything inside our backpacks on this hike? We should have left the stuff we wouldn't need at the hostel and just picked it up after."

"Noted for our next hike.... We gotta admit, we have no idea what we're doing. This is a first for us." Dane pulled out a crumpled brochure, our only pathetic excuse of a map, from his pocket. The brochure, showing an obscure drawing of the trail, was never meant to be used as a map. "Exhibit A. This 'map' doesn't tell us shit."

Our hopes of a clear path crumbled like ancient stone, leaving us to face our harsh reality, a daunting trek ahead, with no clear route to guide us through the canyon.

"It's fine," I said, trying to keep things positive as we wallowed in our stupidity. "We really just need to get to the top. We can just take one of these trails and figure it out from there."

"Shan, that's what you said the first time."

"Any other suggestions?"

I was met with silence.

"All right. Let's try this one," I said, pointing to another trail. "We don't have all day."

We pulled our packs back on and headed up another trail.

Our pace slowed as we maneuvered lethargically up the switch-backs in the ever-intensifying midday sun. I chugged my water without reservation. It helped fuel me during the ascent. Following Dane's lead, I tried to keep my mind fixated on positivity, despite the heavy pack on my back feeling more like a cumbersome boulder with each step. The straps dug into my shoulders, making me acutely aware of how sore and chafed I was. Sweat dripped down my back, soaking through my shirt.

Two hours later, we reached the top. My heart dropped in my chest. The trail ended at the canyon's summit with no signs of civilization in any direction. We gazed upon a beautiful, desolate wilderness. However, desolate wilderness was what we were desperately trying to escape. Our water bottles were almost empty, mirroring the emptiness gnawing at our bellies. Ill prepared for the demanding journey, our monstrous packs held nothing to help relieve either thirst or hunger. Each step became an agonizing reminder of our hubris and unpreparedness. Our weary feet were now covered in developing blisters, like battle scars etched on our soles.

I wanted out. Now.

But back down the canyon we needed to go. Our trial-and-error search continued.

It became a loathsome guessing game.

We would wind our way down to the canyon floor, wander aimlessly for a bit, peering up at the endless succession of trails. We'd choose one, force ourselves back up, only to find it was another wrong trail. Back down, we'd go to repeat the entire process again.

And again.

And again.

"This is useless, Shan," Dane gasped, wiping the sweat from his brow. "We gotta move smart. Let's just get back to the oasis and return the same way we started."

I glanced around, my eyes struggling to adjust to the intense brightness. "Yeah, but we've been wandering for almost five hours, Dane. We've lost the original trail."

Dane scanned the maze of paths before us, each one a faint, winding track imprinted into the dry, rocky landscape. "You're right. Every path looks the same," he said, his face flushed with exhaustion. "How are we supposed to figure out which one leads back?"

I clenched my fists, kicking a loose rock with my boot. "I don't know. We're in the middle of nowhere, and all these trails just blur together."

We'd have to keep with the original plan, finding our way up a path that could lead us out of the canyon and to civilization. Surely one of these damn paths would afford us a view of the nearest village or town.

Right...?

I lost count of the number of times we trudged up and down those canyon trails, but my body did not. It had been several hours since we had run out of water, and we had eaten nothing that day except a small cereal bar in the morning. My lips were cracked and dry, my tongue thick, swollen almost, as if my body was holding onto any last drop of moisture it could find. With each labored step, with each failed attempt on a trail gone wrong, I grew weaker, physically as well as mentally. Tired, to the marrow.

A human body can only go about three days without water, but dehydration begins to break you long before that. My head pounded, a constant throbbing as it strained to push blood through my body running on fumes. Muscles cramped unpredictably, knotting up as if protesting each step.

We were moving slower now, dragging our feet. The canyon walls, once vibrant with earth tones and shadows, were starting to blur, the colors dulled by my mind's hazy filter. If we didn't find water soon, the physical toll would shift from discomfort to something more dangerous. I could feel it coming, inching toward me like a predator, waiting for that last bit of energy to run out.

Trudging up yet another trail, we reached a point where the remote canyon sprawled endlessly before us, its vastness disappearing into the horizon. I plummeted to the ground, descending like a fallen star. Dane collapsed next to me. We sat in silence for a long while, a defeated and foreboding silence.

My mind spiraled at the gravity of our situation. Our impulsive decision to embark on this ill-fated journey had been shrouded in reckless naiveté. We were in the middle of nowhere. We had informed no one of our plans or whereabouts. No one would know we were missing. No one would come looking for us. We had no food. Hunger gnawed at my core like relentless vultures. We had no water. My throat was as dry as autumn leaves, my lips cracked and parched. The fiery sun beat down on my pale skin, increasingly dehydrating me with temperatures in the mid-nineties.

In that bleak realization, I began to lose hope. Completely. My mind resigned to the fact that this was it. An ill-prepared trek would be the end of my story. It was time to admit defeat.

Memories from my brief twenty-two years of life flashed through my mind, like scenes played from an old film projector: playing with my sister in the backyard as a child, lounging by the pool as a teenager on a mission to get a tan, and roaming the mall with my middle school friends, laughing over inside jokes.

"Dane, I'm losing hope." The words spilled out of my lips like sweet relief, until Dane's shocked and terrified eyes fell upon my weathered face.

"NO, SHAN." His command was more of a desperate plea. "You cannot! We cannot. We're going to get out of here, OK? DO NOT LOSE HOPE ON ME." He blinked back tears. "Hope is all we have, Shan. *We have nothing else.*"

There is an Italian proverb that states, "Hope is the last thing ever lost," and with Dane's desperate plea to keep the hope, I was determined to do my best.

We needed a better plan than just pushing ourselves in vain up and down these exhausting canyon paths.

I joined Dane in scanning the horizon, my eyes squinting against the glaring sunlight. My heart sank as we saw nothing but the endless expanse of rocky terrain.

Dane's voice broke the silence. "Wait! Over there!" He pointed toward a distant spot on the canyon floor.

I followed his gaze and squinted. "What is it?"

"Look closely," Dane urged. "There's a small village."

At first, I couldn't see it, but then it slowly came into focus. The dwellings expertly camouflaged themselves, blending seamlessly into the rocky landscape. Fashioned from rock and clay, they appeared as an extension of the earth.

"How did we miss that?" I asked, astonished.

Dane shook his head, a mix of relief and amazement on his face. "They've built it to blend in. It's like it's part of the canyon."

Hope sprung like a dandelion on a spring day.

"We just need to make it there! They can give us some food and water and lead us in the right direction! We're going to make it!" I shouted in exhausted relief.

Perched on top of the mountain with a bird's-eye view of the village, we meticulously calculated the direction we needed to go and estimated how long it might take. With renewed energy, we descended the canyon walls and headed toward the village.

As we reached our destination, our spirits soared with a sense of accomplishment. The village was composed of roughly thirty rustic dwellings, each one to two rooms in size. The rooftops took shape with a delicate intertwining of sturdy sticks and skillfully woven palm leaves, providing shelter and protection from the elements. All we needed to do was find someone to explain our situation. *Everything was going to be OK.* Sweet, sweet relief washed over me like a comforting embrace from a long-lost friend.

We meandered through the maze of houses. The first home had a coating of dust, cobwebs hanging from the ceiling. The next had an overturned table and a nest of birds that took flight the moment I poked my head in.

"Hellllooooooooo," Dane yelled out with gusto. "Someone? Anyone...?"

The response was an unsettling silence that swallowed his words whole.

We continued our inspection, moving cautiously from one silent home to the next. The third house we entered had broken window panes. A musty odor hung in the air.

In the fourth house, a forgotten chair faced the wall, its wood warped and splintered with age. An old, tattered jacket was draped over the back.

I turned to Dane, my mouth an O of horror. "Oh, no!" I wailed. "This place has been abandoned!"

As my cry echoed through the canyon, we heard a rustling nearby. I spun around quickly to find an ancient couple materialize from a hut down the shaded path. The man and woman had deep wrinkles, weathered from a lifetime of exposure to the sun. Their bodies stooped with age, they moved with a slow, labored gait, the old woman finding stability with a stick she leaned on, supported also by the man's arm.

Why were they the only ones there? Did the whole village leave, but these two were too old and weak to walk out? Were they left behind for this reason? Maybe they'd lived their whole lives there and refused to leave with everyone else? I'll never know, but I was certain I'd never been so happy to see another human. We raced to the couple, anxiously yammering in Spanish, begging for water and directions out of this godforsaken place. We received a response in Quechua, the native language of the Andean people in Peru.

We did not speak or understand Quechua.

But we had played charades many times before.

Dane and I broke out into a dramatic act, holding our throats and panting to display our need for water, yanking out our water bottles and holding them upside down to show they were empty, waving our hands in front of our faces and pulling our shirts in and out to display the heat we were feeling. I am certain this elderly couple understood us. Language aside, our message was clear. **We were desperate for water.**

They met our pleas with straight faces. "No. Andan ustedes." In Spanish, this means, "No, you go."

Dane winced. I burst into tears, and jumped back into a more desperate version of our charades game, now on my hands and knees, literally begging for water.

"NO, Anda tu," the man repeated, with no remorse or sympathy in his eyes. He grabbed his wife's arm, and they slowly hobbled back home.

Crushing despair washed over me. A lump formed in my throat, the kind that chokes your breath and brings a burning sting to your eyes. The world around me blurred, my vision clouded by the unending flood of tears. I couldn't believe it—how could they turn us away? How could a human witness such desperation and ignore it? My heart pounded, every beat amplifying the fear that had taken root deep inside me.

I collapsed onto the dusty ground, my knees buckling under the weight of hopelessness. My hands clenched into fists, pounding the earth in frustration.

Dane's eyes were heavy with sadness, his face lined with worry. Despite the storm of emotions visible on his face, he remained steady.

He silently extended a hand toward me, his grip firm as he pulled me from the ground. He controlled his voice, yet I could sense the strain behind it. "We got this, Shan. We're going to keep going."

I hesitated, still trembling with despair, but his words anchored me. With a shaky breath, I reluctantly wiped the tears from my face, trying to swallow the lump in my throat. I forced myself to gather whatever strength I had left, nodding to Dane as we prepared to carry on.

As nightfall approached, we figured it was a good idea to take rest and set up camp on a flat portion of the canyon valley floor. The stars illuminated the night sky like a comforting blanket, their gentle light streaming down upon us. Lying in my sleeping bag, I stared up, desperately hoping for a shooting star—a sign I could wish on for a safe way out of the valley. Of course, a star never shot by in the sky. I feared this was a dangerous omen.

The next morning, we woke early, packed our things, and carried on. My body continued to lose strength. Small steps became increasingly labored, and my legs felt as heavy as anchors dragging through the depths of an endless ocean, impeding my every move.

I began to collapse intermittently under the oppressive weight of my pack. The first few times, I attempted to stop it from happening, stuttering a few steps but then picking up my feet. As I grew weaker and weaker, though, I surrendered to the battle, allowing my body to slump into a heap on the dirt. Sometimes, I would lie there on my back, the gritty texture of the dirt seeping into my clothes and skin. In those moments, I felt utterly defeated, and found it difficult to contemplate getting back up. But despite the overwhelming fatigue, a flicker of determination remained, compelling me to summon the strength to push myself back onto my feet and continue the journey.

Norman Vincent Peale once said, "Negative thinking definitely attracts negative results." Keeping this in mind, I knew I needed to ground my mind in positivity, to push out the voracious flood of negative thoughts flowing in. I needed purpose, inspiration, a reason to keep fighting. That purpose came to me with thoughts of my loved ones, my dearest friends and family. I simply had to see them again, enjoy their company, revel in the comfort of a deep embrace. This couldn't be the end. Memories of cherished times with my loved ones kept me going.

Up, down, and up again. The mountains and hills in this canyon seemed to have no end.

But my body did.

"I...I can't," I panted, eyeing the path twisting upwards into the sky.

"Leave your bag here. I'll come back for it after we get you up there."

"You can't, Dane. That's not fair."

"Shan, look at me." His hands were firm on my shoulders. "Leave it here. I'll push you up. We're making it to the top. Together."

I nodded, letting the pack fall from my shoulders. As I took a step forward, my legs wobbled, like they'd forgotten how to hold me up. Dane moved behind me, planting his hands firmly on my back.

"Just keep your eyes on the trail. One step, that's all you've got to think about."

I nodded again. I took a step, and he pushed. Another step, another push. The path was steep, uneven, the loose rocks slipping beneath our feet. Dane kept pushing, silent, his breaths just as labored as mine.

Halfway up, my knees buckled. Sweat trickled down my neck. Salt burned my cracked lips.

"You good?" he asked, moving beside me.

I managed a nod, though it felt more like a lie than anything else.

"We'll get water soon." He sounded like he was trying to convince himself as much as me. "But first, we get to the top."

Another step, another push. Then another. The sun beat down like it had something personal against us. As it baked the ground I could feel the heat radiating through the soles of my boots. Yet, Dane's hands on my back were steady, grounding me, forcing me to keep moving.

We finally reached the summit. I sank down immediately, my limbs buzzing.

"You stay here," Dane said, already starting his way back down. "I'll grab your pack."

I wanted to tell him to take a break, to rest before going back, but the words stuck in my throat. I watched him disappear down the trail.

He returned with my pack slung over his shoulder, his face twisted with exhaustion. He forced a smile as he dropped it beside me.

"You're a superhero, Dane."

"I wish."

Hours passed and the pink hues of twilight descended upon the canyon floor, our fear of camping another night took hold. It was not the camping itself which intimidated us; it was the lack of food and water. By that time, one and a half days had passed without either. And we were filling our days with rigorous exercise, hiking up and down the canyon walls under the blistering sun. I wondered how much more we could take. However, we had made a silent agreement not to speak our fears aloud. We intended to keep the negativity in our heads to ourselves.

As I reached the pinnacle of exhaustion, a faint whistling sound drifted through the canyon, like a distant lullaby. *Could my ears be deceiving me?* I forced my trembling legs forward once more and strained my ears. No, there it was again. Then, a man appeared, leading a donkey around the bend. He stuttered to a halt, eyes widening. His brows furrowed, and he blinked several times. He appeared to be as shocked to see us as we were to see him.

Dane and I exchanged desperate glances before Dane finally spoke in Spanish. "Hello, sir. We are so happy to see you. I'm Dane, and this is Shannon."

The man studied us for a moment. "I am Luis."

I jumped in, my voice cracking with urgency. "Please, we need your help." My hands clasped together in the prayer position in front of me. "Desperately!"

Dane ran a hand through his disheveled hair, gripping the back of his neck, as if trying to hold himself together. "We've been lost for two days…. We haven't had food or water…."

"We need somewhere to rest," I whispered, my voice barely audible as tears welled up in my eyes. "We need help getting out of the canyon, please."

Luis's expression softened. "You look like you've been through hell. My home is not far from here, just a few kilometers. You can come with me."

A wave of relief washed over me. "We would be so grateful," I managed to say, my voice quivering as I clenched my fists to keep from breaking down.

Luis gave a small nod, his eyes kind but serious. "Tonight, you will sleep under a roof, next to a fire. I will feed you. There is a truck that comes tomorrow at 7 a.m. You can ride that truck out of the canyon."

"OK! There is a truck that comes every day at 7 a.m.? Excellent news!" Dane responded.

"No. There is a truck that comes once per week. It brings supplies for people like me who live in the canyon. It will be here tomorrow at 7 a.m.," Luis corrected.

In all the misfortune we had recently experienced, which we admittedly brought upon ourselves due to lack of experience and being grossly unprepared, we found it to be unbelievably good luck that we happened to be there at the exact time for a once-a-week truck.

"Oh my God! Yes! Thank you! We have to get that truck in the morning! I'm not even sure I could walk out of here in my current state," I admitted sheepishly.

Analyzing my state, kind-hearted Luis continued, "I will send my mother with you in the morning. She will make sure you don't get lost on the way. It's about a two-hour hike. Be ready by 5 a.m."

"Thank you," Dane said, his voice thick with emotion. "Thank you so much."

Luis waved a hand, dismissing our gratitude. "No need to thank me. Let's get you out of here to see your family. They must be worried about you."

Luis led us back to his modest home, a simple adobe structure built right up against the canyon walls. The interior was dimly lit, with a small fire crackling in a corner hearth. The scent of smoke mingled with the musty aroma of the clay walls, creating a comforting atmosphere despite our exhaustion. With no other homes in sight, the silence of the canyon pressed in.

For dinner, Luis served us plates of rice and beans. The moment the food touched our lips, we devoured it like wolves tearing into their first meal after a long, harsh winter. Luis's hand paused midair, his fork hovering as he stared at us. Without a word, he set down his own cutlery and disappeared for a moment, returning with a massive jug of water and two cups.

"Here," he said, setting it in front of us.

We poured the water into our cups and began chugging mercilessly. Water spilled down my chin as I gulped. Luis chuckled, shaking his head, then scooped more rice and beans onto our plates.

"Thanks," I gasped between mouthfuls, wiping my mouth with the back of my hand. Dane nodded vigorously beside me, too busy shoveling food to speak.

As we finished, Luis's eyes turned to the ground. "I'm sorry I don't have an extra bed for you. You can use mine."

Dane shook his head. "No! We would never! We have our tent with us and can sleep comfortably in that."

"We're beyond thankful for your help," I added.

A faint smile tugged at the corners of Luis's mouth. "OK. I will see you in the morning, then."

After setting up our tent, Dane and I quickly succumbed to sleep.

The next morning, when we first set sight on Luis's seventy-six-year-old mother, a pang of distress washed over us. We were concerned that this elderly woman, wearing her traditional attire, wouldn't be fast enough on the trail to lead us to the truck on time.

As we embarked on the journey, it became obvious that Luis's mother had not only grown up hiking through this canyon, but had never stopped. The way she moved on the trails, with such speed and agility, was truly astounding. She protected her feet with nothing more than hojotas, sandals she made from recycled tires. The worn rubber gripped the rocky terrain with a confidence we could only envy. We laughed at ourselves, trying to keep up with an old woman in colorful polleras. Each skirt was a different color—rich reds, deep blues, and earthy browns—layered one on top of the other.

Two hours later, we finally made it to the truck's stopping point.

Dozens of others did, too. Local farmers dispersed throughout the canyon ventured to this point once a week, their donkeys following, in order to collect needed supplies for the week. Each of them was equally surprised to find two sun-stricken gringos covered in dirt, climbing into the back of the truck.

Squeezed in the truckbed's corner, among locals and produce, Dane and I turned to each other and simultaneously let out a deep sigh of relief.

"I can't believe we made it out of that godforsaken canyon," I gasped.

Dane nodded, his face breaking into a wide grin.

"I really could not have done it without you, Dane. Seriously, pushing me up those hills like that. There's no doubt in my mind. You saved my life."

We embraced, Dane's arms tightening around me with a desperate, grateful energy.

"Never again!" I mumbled into his shoulder, half-laughing, half-serious. "We'll never be this unprepared in nature again."

He pulled back slightly, holding my shoulders. "**Never.** Next time, we bring maps, food, gallons upon gallons of water—hell, a satellite phone!"

"Deal. But...my God, no more treks for a while, please."

"Fine by me!"

We sat there, grinning like fools, the wind whipping around us as the truck bumped along the road.

As Terry Pratchett once said, "We live and learn, or, perhaps more importantly, we learn and live."

3

THE CALL OF THE WILD

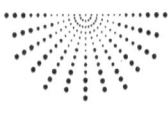

BOLIVIA

*E*veryone has a first love. You know, that man or woman you become completely inebriated with. That person whose eyes you can drown in. The one you imagine you'll spend the rest of your life with.

And then it ends.

The flames of my first love, my highschool sweetheart, extinguished when I realized that my six-foot-four dream man had zero interest in travel. All it took was a plane ticket, and he went running.

Well, I guess I was the one running...off to South America. My lost love chose to stay put at his mom's house.

At the time, it seemed unimaginable I'd be attracted to another man. My boyfriend and I had been together for five years, and he was the only man I had ever been with. What would life be without him? How do I flirt and interact with other men? Where does love go when it's gone?

These questions were left unanswered as Dane and I settled into our trip in South America.

After two months on the road, we stepped through the creaky wooden door of our hostel and out into the streets of Arequipa. The vibrant energy of the city hit us immediately—vendors calling out their wares. "Queso fresco!" a woman yelled as she balanced a woven cloth full of goods on her back. "Cabezas de cabra!" another shouted, displaying an assortment of goat heads, their hollow eyes staring lifelessly from a metal tray. Another vendor waved a handful of dried llama meat, enticing passersby with promises of its chewiness and savory flavor. The hum of traffic mixed with the clang of pots and pans from makeshift food stalls and the chatter of other travelers bargaining for textiles or tiny, intricately carved Andean figurines.

"Hold on," I said, stopping abruptly.

Dane paused, turning to look at me with a raised eyebrow. "What's up?"

I pointed at a small, weathered poster taped to the door. The images were faded, but clear enough—monkeys, pumas, and jaguars stared back at us. The text was in Spanish, advertising an opportunity to volunteer at an animal refuge called Comunidad Inti Wara Yassi (CIWY), a nonprofit organization located deep in the Bolivian jungle.

"Check this out," I said.

Dane leaned in closer, squinting at the poster. A slow grin spread across his face. "This...sounds amazing."

I nodded. "Yeah. I mean, I've been thinking...maybe we've had enough of the partying every night in La Paz. It's been fun, but..."

Dane's eyes lit up. "I've been feeling the same way, but I didn't want to say anything because I thought you were having too much fun."

"What? I've been over it for a while! I didn't say anything because I thought *you* were having too much fun."

Dane barked out a short, incredulous laugh. "Looks like the universe knew we needed a push."

"Let's get some more information, though. Come on. Let's go check out their website." I grabbed his arm, yanking him back into the hostel.

In the small computer room, Dane and I plopped down, side by side, on rigid wooden chairs that creaked under our weight. I leaned forward, narrowing my eyes at the monitor as I scrolled through the information about CIWY. "This place seems legit. Their main goal is to rescue, rehabilitate, and care for wild animals that have been seized from illegal trafficking. They're really focused on ending animal trade too, with educational programs and community events."

Dane nodded, his eyes glued to the screen. "Sounds like they're doing some good work, rescuing animals from markets, circuses, restaurants, and even private residences."

"I wonder how they go about that."

Dane pointed to some small print on the screen. "Apparently the Bolivian police bring a lot of the animals in. And others are turned in voluntarily by people who had irresponsibly kept them as pets."

"A pet monkey is a truly idiotic and cruel idea."

Dane continued reading. "Well yeah, cuz it looks like after all the interactions with humans, these animals can't survive in the wild anymore. They don't know how to, haven't built the skills. They have to learn from their own species, you know? Or it looks like some of them just come to CIWY too messed up from horrible conditions."

I sighed, feeling a pang of sadness as I read about the animals' suffering. "Malnourished, parasites, broken bones, psychological trauma... Humans suck dude. These poor animals have been through hell."

"But it's amazing that CIWY is stepping up since the government can't handle it."

"For sure." I leaned back in my chair, crossing my arms, deep in thought. "They've got three locations in Bolivia. My vote would be to go to their first sanctuary, Parque Machía. It's their headquarters. And it's in the Pre-Andean, Amazonian rainforest! Just look at all the animals they care for—over four hundred of them, from pumas to spider monkeys. Even a black bear!"

"Machía," Dane repeated.

I had already switched screens to Google Translate. "It means 'mountainous terrain' in Yurcare, the indigenous language."

"Interesting. So, what do you think, Shan? Ready to trade city life for something totally different?" Dane playfully nudged me in the ribcage. "Something that actually feels like we're making a difference?"

I met his gaze. "Yeah, I am. You know I'm always up for random things."

"Let's do it then."

A spark of excitement danced in my chest. "Let's do it. Monkeys and pumas, here we come!"

4
INTO THE JUNGLE

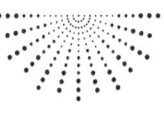

BOLIVIA

My chest tightened with anticipation as we stepped off the bus at CIWY. The warm, humid air wrapped around us, a stark contrast to the cool, mountainous breeze of La Paz. The refuge was surrounded by dense jungle, with the sounds of birds and animals echoing from all directions. It felt surreal, like I'd stepped into the pages of a nature documentary, but the sweat forming on my brow and the dirt beneath my boots reminded me this was real. I was here, about to embark on something unlike anything I'd ever done before.

After a quick orientation, I was introduced to the director, Marcus, who during a one-on-one meeting assigned me my role at the animal refuge. Marcus seemed as much a part of the jungle as the monkeys and other wild animals he cared for. With long, ratty brown hair tied into a man-bun and clothing so ripped and tattered it seemed to be held together by sheer willpower, he exuded an untamed energy. Dirt streaked his hands and arms. I wondered how many years he'd spent in this unforgiving environment. It was hard not to feel awe sitting across from someone who clearly lived and breathed this jungle existence.

He leaned back in his chair, arms crossed over his chest as he studied me with amber-flecked eyes. His sun-creased face cracked into a half-smile as he scratched at the edge of his scruffy beard. "You'll have some local staff showing you the ropes—been working here longer than I have. The animals are like family to them and they know how to train the volunteers."

"That's great, thank you."

He leaned forward, resting his forearms on his knees. "They'll meet you up at the spider monkey enclosure every morning at 7:45 a.m. You'll have to hike up into the jungle, about forty-five minutes, depending on how fast you move."

"No problem, I can manage that."

His eyes narrowed slightly. "Couple things to keep in mind, sometimes the wild monkeys get a little...territorial. If you've got fruit on you—or anything that *looks* like food—they'll come after you. They've got no shame about it, either." His mouth curled into a wry grin. "They've been known to ambush tourists. Just keep your head down and don't make eye contact if they start circling."

I forced a laugh, but my stomach tightened. *Ambush tourists?* That didn't sound exactly... comforting. Was this really a good idea? I glanced toward the jungle beyond the clearing, dense and dark beneath the midday sun. Too late to back out now.

Marcus rubbed his palms together, dirt flaking from his fingertips. "Anyway, the local staff will take care of you. Just don't be surprised if the monkeys test you a bit at first." His smirk widened, showing slightly yellowed teeth. "But hey, nothing like earning the respect of a monkey, right?"

I smiled nervously, unsure if he was joking. He pushed himself to his feet, brushing his hands on the ripped knees of his cargo pants. "You'll be fine," he said over his shoulder as he headed toward the next person.

After my meeting, I found Dane slouched on a broken plastic chair, flicking mosquitos off his arms. "Dane!" I shouted as I approached him. "I got spider monkeys! I'm so stoked!" My voice dropped a bit. "Although, I was kinda bummed I didn't get placed with a puma. How badass would that have been?"

Dane raised an eyebrow. "Why didn't they put you with them?"

"He said they never place women with the pumas. Apparently it's like the cats know we're weaker, and they'll mess with us more—pouncing and stuff. Can you imagine? It sounds terrifying. To be honest, I'm fine missing out on that."

I noticed the mischievous grin spreading across Dane's face. "So, what about you? Where did they place you?"

"I got placed with the black bear!"

My jaw dropped. "A bear? Are you serious? What the hell are you gonna do with a bear?"

"His name's Baloo, like from *The Jungle Book*. He was rescued from a circus. And get this—he literally rode in a seat on the bus to get here."

I stared at him in amazement. "Imagine being a passenger on that bus! Ha! But Jesus, you're going to be working with a bear? That's insane! What are you supposed to do with him?"

"My main job is to feed him in the mornings and evenings. But the best part? During the day, we take him on walks."

I blinked, trying to process what he just said. "Wait, what? You're going to walk a bear through the jungle? Like, on a leash or something?"

Dane nodded, looking even more excited. "Yeah, pretty much! He's on this verrrryyyy long leash. Me and another volunteer just follow him around. One of us in front, one behind, just, you know, strolling through the jungle with a bear."

I burst out laughing at the absurdity of it all. "That's wild! But why two volunteers? I mean, what's the other person even for?"

Dane rolled his eyes. "For safety, obviously. If Baloo decides to do something unpredictable, we've got to be able to manage him. The thing's huge! The other guy's been here for a month already. He can show me the ropes."

I shook my head. "You're really going to be walking a bear. I can't believe it."

Dane shrugged, his grin never fading. "Neither can I. I think we're in for one hell of an experience here."

5

A LOVE STORY AMIDST MONKEYS AND MOUNTAINS

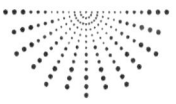

BOLIVIA

The first time it happened, I heard a sharp chattering echoing from the trees. Before I could process the sound, a blur of fur shot down from the canopy above. I froze, heart pounding, as the capuchins descended. Their cries were sharp and frantic, a mix of screeches and whoops that vibrated through the air. One landed on my shoulder, its small, clawed hands gripping me with surprising strength. Its fur was damp and matted, smelling faintly of musk and the sour tang of fermented fruit.

Another capuchin tore at the bag on my back, filled with fruit that would serve as breakfast and dinner for the spider monkeys. I twisted, instinctively clutching the straps tighter. But when a third monkey lunged forward, baring teeth that gleamed like tiny knives, my courage cracked. Those teeth—impossibly large for such a small face —were capable of slicing through my skin and bone with ease.

"OK, OK! You win!" I yelled, my voice shaky as I let the bag drop to the ground with a thud. The monkeys swarmed it instantly, hissing and snarling at one another in a frenzy. I stumbled back, tripping over a root and landing hard on the damp trail.

From my spot on the ground, I could only watch as the capuchins tore open the bag with efficiency. Their little hands—dexterous and quick—rummaged through the fruit, flinging aside anything less appealing in favor of the juiciest pieces. The aroma of crushed passionfruit and split pineapple filled the air.

The capuchins took turns flashing their teeth at me, a clear warning to stay back. Their eyes darted between me and their prize, as if daring me to challenge them. I stayed put, my pulse pounding in my ears, waiting for them to finish.

When they finally scampered off, their bellies full and their shrill calls fading into the canopy, I crawled forward to assess the damage. The bag was a tattered mess, most of the fruit gone, with only a bruised mango and a few squashed bananas left behind.

I sighed, hoisted the remains onto my back, and continued my trek to the spider monkey enclosure, the oppressive tropical heat bearing down like a wet blanket. My shirt clung to my back, my skin slick with sweat. Each breath felt thick, the air more like steam than oxygen. The distant calls of the spider monkeys urged me on, cutting through the hum of cicadas and the steady drip of moisture from the canopy above.

It wasn't the last time the capuchins ambushed me. Each encounter was a chaotic mix of adrenaline and frustration, my reflexes sharpening with every attack. But no matter how fast I tried to outpace them, the little thieves were always one step ahead, their cleverness reminding me of who truly ruled this jungle.

The twenty spider monkeys that lived at Parque Machía during this time were a tight-knit unit. They slept cuddled together within two large cages. Each morning, after releasing them from their cramped nightly quarters, I faced what quickly became the worst part of my day: cleaning the rancid cages. The entire ground was a swamp of wet, runny excrement, streaked with half-digested fruit seeds. Sticky puddles of urine lined the floors and clung stubbornly to my boots. The stench was beyond horrific—thick and sour, it lodged itself to the back of my throat. Armed with buckets, mops, and brooms, I scrubbed and scooped, trying to restore some semblance of cleanliness. Gagging, I had to fight the urge to vomit with every pass of the mop. It was messy, disgusting, and unavoidable.

Meanwhile, most of the spider monkeys raced into the jungle, exploring and frolicking freely. These "semi-wild" monkeys always returned to the base camp for mealtimes and bedtime. They knew that the camp provided a safe space where their needs were met.

Due to injury, trauma, aggression, or a lack of survival knowledge, a few of the monkeys were not given the option to freely roam the jungle. CIWY had concerns that these monkeys might get killed, lost, or severely injured if allowed to wander the jungle without supervision. As an alternative, they gave these monkeys a harness to wear. It could be clipped onto various ziplines arranged in an intricate maze amongst the rainforest trees.

The monkeys didn't wear their harnesses overnight, but they were ready and eager to have them put on when we opened their cage each morning. It reminded me of dogs getting excited at the sight of their leash—they knew it meant playtime was about to begin.

As a volunteer, my task was to clip the monkeys onto a zip line, which allowed them to swing and play among the trees at their leisure. Each zip line offered a different experience: some dipped steeply, others swung wildly, and a few were higher or longer, connecting different sections of the rainforest canopy. They were like a jungle gym for the monkeys, strung between the trees in elaborate paths.

The monkeys had strong opinions about which line they wanted, and they weren't shy about communicating their preferences. If one zip line lost its novelty, they would let me know, calling out insistently or tugging my arm toward a new direction. Sometimes they'd climb onto me, chattering in frustration until I caught on to what they wanted. Over time, I became attuned to their signals and could anticipate their moods and needs.

All the magic happened in this "*work*." During these hours, I was free to lie on the dirt floor of the jungle, or maybe hang loosely in a tree. Life slowed down. There were no tasks to attend to, no screens to distract, literally nothing to do but lounge around, admiring these wild creatures in their natural habitat. I jokingly dubbed myself "Jane Goodall," a title I carried with pride as I settled into life among the monkeys. They quickly identified me as a person who loved and cared for them, and they therefore showed me love and respect.

On my third day, I developed a genuine connection with one of the monkeys for the first time. CIWY staff had named him Jorge. He ambled toward me, black fur rippling slightly with each step. His dark eyes locked onto mine. Then, he stopped, tilted his head, and extended a tiny hand toward me. It was a wrinkled, leathery thing, with wiry hairs sprouting along the knuckles and nails that were surprisingly human-like.

I hesitated for a moment, unsure if this was truly happening, before gently reaching out and sliding my fingers around his. The grip was firm but delicate, his palm warm and damp. We walked together, hand in hand, toward a new zip line. His other hand occasionally brushed the ground as he swayed beside me. Each step we took together felt like an unspoken pact, a tiny moment of interspecies understanding. My heart swelled with a mix of awe and tenderness.

When we reached the zip line, Jorge released my hand and climbed onto the platform with ease. But for a moment, before he leaped into the trees, he turned back, his eyes meeting mine one last time. I stood there, rooted to the spot, marveling at the quiet magic of how two vastly different worlds could connect.

Before I could snap out of my moment, two monkeys leapt down from the canopy, landing light on their feet. Without hesitation, they scrambled up my legs and clambered onto my shoulders and head, seeking a free ride to the next zip line. Their chatter, a chaotic series of clicks and squeaks, filled the air as they settled in.

In that moment, I realized just how deeply these untamed creatures had accepted me into their world. Over the days that followed, other monkeys grew comfortable enough to hitch a ride as well, their antics becoming part of my daily routine.

The first time I met Pablo, he bounded toward me, eyes wide, his tiny hands reaching for my arm. Before I could react, he was on me—climbing up my leg, his little claws digging into my skin as he scrambled up to my shoulder, his body light and quick like an acrobat.

He tapped my head lightly, then my shoulders, and finally my stomach. I doubled over at the unexpected tickles. A mischievous glint shone in his expressive eyes. Then, as if to reward himself, he let out a wild cackle, his shrill voice bouncing off the treetops. The sound was so infectious, I couldn't help but laugh along with him.

Pablo stayed close, hopping from my shoulders to my back, using me like a playground. I found myself immersed in the true essence of "monkeying around," a term that felt wholly appropriate in the presence of this young monkey. With each playful interaction, Pablo taught me the joy of living in the moment and embracing the simple pleasure of laughter.

Katinga, another cheeky youngster, propelled herself onto me without warning. Her tiny limbs wrapped around my arm as she clung on with unrestrained joy. She squirmed, urging me to grab her arms, legs, or tail and spin her in dizzying circles. Her laughter erupted in cackling bursts. I tickled her armpits, and she shrieked with glee, sending us both into a fit of giggles that echoed through the trees.

One gentle soul, a monkey named Isabella, had a round, swollen belly, full of the new life growing inside her. One afternoon, she approached me slowly, her midsection swaying with each step. Without hesitation, she collapsed into my lap, her back pressing against my outstretched legs, arms draped limply at her sides. A deep human-like sigh escaped her lips. She reached out and stroked my ankle, her fingers tracing gentle circles against my skin.

"Oh, Isabella," I murmured, running my fingers through the fine hair on her head. "You're going to be such a good mama, you know that?"

She tilted her head slightly, dark eyes locking onto mine. It was as if she was listening, trying to understand the meaning behind my words.

I let my hand drift down, gently tracing the contours of her swollen stomach. She exhaled again, this time with a deeper release, her whole body softening under my touch. She shifted slightly, her small fingers wrapping gently around my wrist as if to say, *keep going.*

"You'll take such good care of your little one," I whispered. "You already know how to love, don't you?"

Her gaze remained fixed on me. It was clear that we both felt a deep connection and mutual gratitude, despite our language limitations. Expressing our emotions verbally was an impossibility, yet the emotional resonance between us was undeniable. In those tender moments, we communicated beyond words.

I also had a unique connection with Ignacio, a monkey who usually shunned most of the human volunteers. I heard numerous stories of his aggression toward anyone who attempted to interact with him. With his razor-sharp teeth, he had inflicted injury on many, resulting in the need for stitches put in by the local veterinarian, the closest thing they had to a doctor.

Ignacio's aggression wasn't just random—it was rooted in the abuse he had suffered before coming to the sanctuary. He had been kept as a pet by a family who mistreated him, and it left lasting scars on his psyche.

I don't know why Ignacio chose me as a trusted companion. He often approached me to hold hands, hurtle up onto my shoulders, or sit with me amongst the trees. I felt honored that he trusted me. His serene, compassionate eyes spoke of resilience and completely captivated me.

One afternoon, Ignacio went missing.

Mateo was the first to reach me, his eyes narrowed in concern. He was one of the full-time caretakers at the sanctuary, but unlike most of the staff, he hadn't just *come* to the jungle—he *belonged* to it. Short and sinewy, with sun-darkened skin and black hair cropped close to his scalp, Mateo had a lean body built by years of climbing trees, hauling sacks of fruit, and moving through the jungle like it was second nature.

He'd grown up there—literally. The older staff said he'd been abandoned as a toddler near the sanctuary gates and raised by the staff alongside the animals. He was more comfortable in trees than on the ground, barefoot more often than not, and impossibly attuned to the forest around him. The monkeys weren't just animals to him—

they were his siblings. He moved like something out of *The Jungle Book*, a real-life Mowgli who'd never left the pages.

"He wouldn't just go," Mateo said, scratching at the faint scar curved along his cheekbone. "Ignacio always comes back. He knows the routine."

"He could be caught on something," someone muttered.

Mateo exhaled sharply. "Something's wrong."

His deep-set brown eyes flicked between me and the other two volunteers. Then he pointed at me. "You're coming."

"Me?" I blinked.

Mateo crossed his arms over his broad chest. "You're the only one he'd go to if he's scared. You feed him. You play with him. He clings to your head like you're his mother."

"I guess that could be true…" I mumbled.

Mateo slung a machete across his back and gestured for me to follow. "Let's go. If he's hurt, we don't have time."

After hours of aimless wandering, shouting Ignacio's name repeatedly into the treetops, we almost gave up our search. It was at this moment that we noticed rustling leaves in a mango tree, not too far off in the distance. It was Ignacio perched high on a swaying tree branch. When he caught sight of us, he let out a soft coo.

With a burst of energy, he leaped from his arboreal perch. Bounding toward us with unrestrained enthusiasm, he danced around our feet. His agile body sprung up and down in jubilant leaps, as if he couldn't contain his delight at our presence. Moved by his genuine display of affection, I reciprocated, squatting down to his level. We met eye to eye. In a tender moment of connection, he wrapped his slender arms around my neck in a heartfelt embrace. Overwhelming pride filled me as his warm arms held me close.

When I stepped back to take a closer look, I noticed raw wounds on his back and legs. Singed patches of fur revealed burns that had eaten through his skin and left the membranes below exposed in at least ten places. His injuries were severe—open, red, and dangerously susceptible to infection. He whimpered softly when I gently cradled him, doing my best to avoid his burns.

Later, I learned the horrific truth: during his adventure, Ignacio had become entangled in electrical wires carelessly strung through the jungle foliage. The wires had scorched the right side of his body, leaving me face-to-face with the devastating reality of habitat destruction. I was grateful the refuge had skilled veterinarians who treated his burns. Within weeks, Ignacio was back to his usual self. But the memory of those wounds—and the fragility of his world— never left me.

On an average day, at around 4 p.m., after I'd spent most of my time bonding and playing with my monkey friends, it was time to cut up fruit for their dinner. This had to be done inside the cage where they slept, to avoid being mobbed by eager monkeys who would snatch up every piece before I could cut and distribute it evenly.

As I sliced the fruit, the monkeys gathered around, watching my every move with rapt attention. Slender fingers wrapped delicately around the bars of the cage, as their hungry gazes followed the progression of the knife, tracking the juicy slices of fruit as they tumbled into a bowl. Periodically, Isabella would release her grip to extend a tentative hand toward me, her expression filled with bitter-sweet yearning.

As I cut the fruit, I often thought about how amazing it was that the monkeys who freely roamed the jungle each day always knew the exact time to gather and eat. As if following some shared timetable, these monkeys emerged from the dense foliage at precisely the antici-pated mealtime.

Once I cut the fruit into bite-sized pieces, I placed it inside various food trays. Then came the real challenge—hoisting the trays into the trees before the monkeys got to them first.

The trays were attached to a rope-pulley system designed to keep them just out of reach until they were fully suspended in the treetops. In theory, this method was meant to mimic the natural foraging process, ensuring the monkeys had to climb and retrieve their meals as they would in the wild. But in practice, it became an all-out battle of speed and cunning.

As soon as I grabbed hold of the rope, the monkeys sprang into action, their sharp eyes locked onto the ascending prize. Some scrambled up the trunks, ready to launch from the branches in desperate leaps toward the trays. Others, the wise old veterans of this daily contest, lingered below, watching with calculating stares, waiting for the perfect moment to strike.

More than once, a particularly daring monkey would leap into the air, fingers outstretched, attempting to snatch a tray before it reached its final height. Sometimes they succeeded, latching onto the edge and clinging for dear life as the tray swung wildly, sending bits of fruit raining down like a tropical jackpot for the monkeys below. Other times, their reach fell short, and they tumbled back into the foliage, only to try again.

"You little bandits!" I tightened my grip on the rope and yanked hard to outpace their advances. "At least let me get it all the way up first!"

By 5:30 p.m., my work for the day wrapped up. I slung my empty pack over my shoulders and began to trek down the mountain. The path was a maze of slippery roots and moss-covered rocks, each step demanding my full concentration and balance. I moved carefully, aware that one misstep could send me tumbling.

With each challenging step, I marveled at the primeval surroundings. The thick canopy overhead filtered golden sunlight into fragmented beams, like stained glass, casting complex patterns of light and shadow that danced across the undergrowth. Cicadas buzzed in the distance, a constant hum beneath the occasional shrill cry of exotic birds. One of the wild monkeys that ambushed me on my morning trek to the enclosure, crouched on a thick branch, its tail twitching. Others lurked in the canopy, barely visible through the dense leaves, watching, waiting.

After reaching camp and taking a cold shower, it was time for dinner. Evening meals were always a highlight because all twenty volunteers lounged around a long wooden table, sharing stories from their day.

These cherished hours were the same hours that I began to fall for a handsome Australian named Noah. Was it his piercing blue eyes that shot through my heart? Was I attracted to his thick, manly beard that perfectly outlined his soft, pink lips? Maybe I liked that he appeared to be a risk-taker? The man was assigned to work with a puma no less! His confident demeanor, coupled with the image of a puma on a leash, was something that made him irresistible to me.

"What the hell do you do with a puma on a leash all day?" I blurted out.

Noah grinned. "Ah, mate, it's like takin' a dog for a walk. Only, in this case, the puma's definitely the one in charge."

I raised an eyebrow. "So, you just walk him around?"

He nodded. "Yeah, but the leash is verrrryyy long. Helps me keep up with his pace. He's quick, dartin' under logs, through trees, hoppin' over roots. I have to stay on my toes."

"Isn't it hard to keep up?" I asked, imagining the agility and speed of a puma compared to a human.

"Hard? Bloody oath, it is!" Noah laughed. "I'm definitely staying fit."

"You most certainly are." I immediately regretted my forward comment. As a cover-up, I attempted to continue probing. "Aren't you scared of him though?"

"Not too much, mate," he said with a prideful shake of his head. "Sanko's chubby and a lover at heart. And he's not exactly wild. Grew up in captivity. The sanctuary doesn't think he'd survive in the jungle on his own. So, I take him for walks to keep him active and healthy. I'd like to think he appreciates it!"

"Sure he does, but he's still a wild cat!" I said.

Noah shrugged, a glint of humility in his eyes. "I do get a bit jumpy when he decides it's playtime. That's when he pounces on me. Next thing I know, we're rollin' down a hill intertwined with one another! Dangerous stuff, that. One swipe of his paw could do some serious damage."

"It'd be a shame if he messed up that handsome face of yours," I said, blushing.

Noah's grin widened as he looked at me with a twinkle in his eye. "Ah, you think I'm handsome, eh? Don't worry, I'll keep safe. Wouldn't want to disappoint you."

I looked away, my cheeks warm.

Danes eye's flicked back and forth between Noah and me with amusement. "You want to hear a story about pouncing and outrunning an animal? Get this."

The table quieted as Dane began his tale. "So today I was walking in front of Baloo, just like any other day. Nate was behind, and everything seemed fine. Then, out of nowhere, I hear Nate behind me yell, 'RUN!'"

Noah and I exchanged wide-eyed glances.

"So, what do I do?" Dane continued, his voice full of suspense. "I run my ass off, of course! I'm leaping over fallen logs, sliding through mud, getting whacked in the face by vines—just booking it as fast as I can. But you know I can't outrun a bear..."

"Holy shit, Dane." My heart pounded just from listening. "What happened?"

Dane grinned, clearly enjoying the attention. "Next thing I know, I feel this massive weight slam into me, and I'm on the ground. Baloo's got his mouth around my head!"

The room collectively gasped, and Noah shook his head. "Mate, that's insane. What did you do?"

"I just lay there," Dane said, his voice dropping to a more serious tone. "I tried to stay calm, taking deep breaths, not wanting to make any sudden moves. Keep in mind that Nate is just another volunteer, just about as clueless as me. The idiot suggested hitting Baloo on the ass to scare him off!"

Nate shrugged from across the table.

"But I'm like, 'No way, man! You're going to piss him off!'"

I could hardly believe what I was hearing. "And then?"

Dane shrugged, as if what he was about to say was no big deal. "So, I just lay there, trying not to freak out. After what felt like hours..."

"It was just a few minutes!" Nate chimed in.

"It felt like hours, dude. But yeah, Baloo just let go and walked off, like nothing ever happened."

"Unreal." Noah let out a low whistle. "You've got balls, mate. I thought my puma was tough, but damn."

As the conversation shifted, my thoughts wandered back to Noah. "Will you be joining the drinks tomorrow night?"

"If you're there, darlin', I will be sure to." Noah winked.

My heart fluttered. "Sweet. I'll be there for sure."

The next evening, I stood in front of the mirror, peeling off my ratty volunteering shirt and changing into a white tank top. The thin fabric clung to my skin, outlining my cleavage with intention. I adjusted the straps, stared at myself, and tilted my head.

"What's a girl to do when she's been out of the dating game so long she doesn't even know the rules anymore?"

The mirror had no answer. Just my own uncertain eyes stared back.

I turned to my backpack, half-zipped in the corner of the room, and fished out a plastic bottle tucked beside rolled-up socks. I unscrewed the cap and sniffed: vodka. Sharp and sterile.

Back in front of the mirror, I raised the bottle and tipped it to my lips. "To liquid courage."

The first shot burned. The second one, less. By the third, I could feel a warm prickle rising in my chest, dissolving the anxious knots in my stomach. I studied my reflection. My eyes looked different now—less guarded.

Maybe that's why they called it spirits. The vodka provided the spirit of bravery I needed.

"All right," I said aloud. "Let's go."

The bar was a short walk from the refuge—a local watering hole already buzzing with voices and the infectious rhythm of cumbia. I stepped inside and scanned the dimly lit room. A group of volunteers sat clustered around a sticky wooden table, plastic cups in hand.

Then I saw him.

Noah leaned back in his chair, one arm draped over the backrest. For a moment, I watched him—adoring the way his eyes crinkled when he laughed.

I took one final swig from the bottle I'd smuggled in my bag, then tucked it out of sight. My feet moved before I'd fully decided.

"Noah," I called.

He looked up.

I slipped into the seat beside him. "You know, I've been wanting to tell you something for a while now..." The words tumbled out before I had a chance to overthink them.

He looked up from his drink. "Yeah? What's that?"

Warmth crept up my neck, but the vodka dulled any self-doubt, letting me lean in just a little closer. "I think you're incredibly attractive."

His grin widened, playful mischief in his eyes. "Oh, is that right? Well, aren't you a charmer?"

The graze of his fingers on my arm lit up my skin like a match to paper. All I could focus on was the intoxicating energy between us.

The night spun on, drinks flowed, and our banter rolled effortlessly.

"So you're telling me," Noah said, grinning, "you *voluntarily* ate a tarantula?"

I raised a brow. "It was roasted. And there was peer pressure. Don't act like you wouldn't do it."

"Mate, I panic when a huntsman shows up in my house. I'm not built for jungle snacks."

Later, sitting on the curb outside, our knees touched and neither of us moved away.

"Your Spanish is actually decent," he said, nudging my shoulder.

"And your English is passable." I smirked. "For an Australian."

Laughter, easy and unfiltered, slipped between us.

At some point, we shared stories instead of trading jokes. He told me about the time he nearly hit a kangaroo while driving. I told him about hikes through the redwood trees in Big Sur.

"You ever get homesick?" I asked.

"Sometimes. But I like it here. I like..." His voice trailed off, eyes flicking to mine. "This."

I didn't need to ask what he meant. His hand was already closer than it had been a moment ago. Mine met it without thinking.

"It's strange," his fingers absentmindedly traced the label on his bottle, "I feel like I've known you longer than a few weeks."

I nodded. Shoulders leaned in. Breath mingled.

He looked at me—really looked—and smiled softly. "You're trouble, aren't you?"

"Only the good kind."

And just like that, something shifted. There was no fanfare. No dramatic pause. Just a quiet gravity pulling us together, closer and closer, until there was no more space between us. His lips were on mine, soft but demanding, as if he couldn't wait any longer. And I didn't want him to. My fingers curled in his shirt without thinking. His hand slid to the small of my back, and I leaned in like I was falling, only I didn't care where I landed. I melted, the whole world blurred, until it was just us, lost in the rush of the moment.

The rest of the night was a whirlwind of lips and hands and tangled sheets, a beautiful blur that left me breathless and wanting more.

Later, when the adrenaline had faded and we lay tangled up in each other, there was an ease between us, as if this was how it was always meant to be.

"Doesn't feel like I have enough time with you," I murmured into the curve of his shoulder.

He turned to face me. "So let's not stop here. Let's do some travels together when we're done with our six weeks of volunteering."

"Really?" I said. "Continue heading south into Chile and Argentina?"

"I'd love nothing more."

And so, my first travel love affair began.

When the day arrived, I found Dane sitting on a bench just outside the volunteer quarters, his hands resting on his knees as he looked out at the jungle. The evening air was thick with humidity, and the sounds of the forest buzzed around us. I hesitated for a moment before approaching, unsure how to bring it up.

"You sure you don't mind if I take off with Noah?" I asked him.

Dane turned to me, stretching his arms along the back of the bench. "Of course I don't mind. We always said we weren't tied to each other's side for the whole trip, right? Besides, I'm planning to stay another month here at CIWY anyway. I know you're done with the place."

"I've had such an amazing time, but six weeks is enough for me. I can't stand one more day of cleaning out that cage filled with shit." I bit my lip, feeling a mix of relief and guilt. "I just don't want you to feel like I'm ditching you or anything."

Dane shook his head. "Not at all! I'm excited for you! It's about time you got involved with a new guy, isn't it? Someone different from that damn high school sweetheart you couldn't seem to get over."

"Yeah, it feels good."

"Go let loose, have a good time with him. You deserve it."

A wave of gratitude washed over me. I leaned in and wrapped my arms around him. Dane returned the hug, pulling me close. We stayed like that for a moment, the sound of the jungle filling the space between us.

"Promise we'll meet up again? And please stay in touch! Share your adventures!"

Dane pulled back slightly, looking me in the eyes. "You bet."

I stood up, feeling lighter, and gave him a final nod. "Take care of yourself, Dane."

"You too." He leaned back on the bench with a lazy wave. "Go have some fun, Shan."

6

WANDERING HEARTS

BOLIVIA, CHILE & ARGENTINA

*T*he journey Noah and I shared led us to the surreal landscapes of San Pedro de Atacama, Chile, where we navigated otherworldly salt lakes in a rugged four-wheel vehicle. For miles on end, the earth lay parched and cracked, its surface etched with hexagonal patterns of dried salt. This vast expanse, once the floor of a prehistoric sea, was an ocean of white, frozen in time. It hummed with an eerie stillness, interrupted by the occasional jagged rock or the faint rise of a distant hill. The desolation was mesmerizing. The sheer emptiness of the horizon stirred a profound sense of wonder within me.

Amidst this stark, lunar-like terrain, we spotted a solitary cactus standing tall on one of the random hills. It was an ancient cardón, its thick, spiny arms reaching skyward. The cactus' skin was a muted green and cracked in places from the dry heat. Tufts of yellowish needles poked out. It looked impossibly resilient, as if it had been standing there for centuries, weathering the harshness of the desert.

With a mischievous grin, Noah reached into his bag and pulled out his signature aviator sunglasses and black trucker hat. He raised an eyebrow and handed them to me. "I think this cactus needs a makeover," he joked.

I laughed, taking the items and carefully placing them on the cactus. Noah chuckled as I struck various poses, taking selfies with the cactus as if it were him. His smile stretched wide, just enough to show that crooked bottom tooth I secretly adored. It was those little quirks, that unpretentious Aussie charm, that had drawn me to him in the first place.

Somewhere along the border between Bolivia and Chile, the landscape shifted again—sand swallowed the edges of the road. The dunes emerged slowly at first, then rose up like mountains, golden and rippling in the sun.

Time to sandboard.

Much like snowboarding, sandboarding involves strapping a board to your feet and gliding down a steep slope—in this case, a vast expanse of shifting sand instead of snow.

The board trembled beneath my feet as sand whipped across my face. My heart pounded, thrill taking over as I sliced through the dunes. Free. Flying. Wind roaring in my ears. No thoughts. Just the pure thrill of surrendering to gravity and letting the desert carry me.

Then came the trudge back up the dune. Every step was a battle as the soft sand swallowed my feet, dragging me down. We paused halfway up, panting as heat radiated off the sand.

Noah caught his breath. "It'll be worth it, sweetheart. We gotta work for the fun!"

With that, we pushed on, each step feeling a little easier as we neared the top.

On the next run down, Noah and I tumbled into one another, collapsing in a heap, sand covering every inch of us.

He grabbed my face and pulled me in close for a kiss. In those carefree moments, nothing mattered but the feel of him, the warmth of his lips on mine.

"Noah, look at us." I laughed, brushing sand from his cheek.

He pulled me close for a kiss on the forehead. "Who cares about the sand? All that matters is the fun we're having here, together."

Later that night, as we sat in a restaurant, Noah lifted his beer. "Cheers to finding the cheapest meal in town!" He grinned as we clinked glasses over bowls of caldo de pollo, a simple chicken soup with corn, noodles, and a squeeze of fresh lime. It was the kind of no-frills meal that filled our bellies without emptying our pockets. With barely enough funds to scrape by, we stretched every dollar as far as it would go—because the longer we could make our money last, the longer we could keep traveling.

I stared down at my soup, watching the oily broth glisten under the dim yellow lights. Another bowl of caldo, another plate of rice, another day of eating the same local meals that had once felt exciting but now just tasted like routine. I missed variety. I missed food that didn't come with bones floating in the broth. I missed fresh salads, burgers dripping with melted cheese, pasta that wasn't overcooked. Something as simple as a real coffee—strong, not instant—felt like a cruel fantasy.

Noah slurped his soup, oblivious. He didn't seem to mind the repetition, the cheap meals, the endless search for budget-friendly accommodations. I envied that about him, his ability to accept things as they were and move on.

The chatter of locals filled the restaurant, along with the clatter of spoons against ceramic bowls. The thick smell of fried dough and boiled chicken lingered in the air. It should have felt comforting, familiar by now. Instead, it pressed down on me, suffocating. I pushed my spoon through the broth, appetite gone.

The next afternoon we trudged through the heat, our heavy back-packs dragging on our shoulders like sacks of wet sand. My feet scuffed against the pavement, each step heavier than the last as we passed guesthouse after guesthouse—too expensive, too dingy, too far from the attractions. A tension built that I couldn't shake. Finally, I stopped short. "This is ridiculous! We've been walking for over an hour. Can't you just pick a place already?" I huffed, wiping the sweat rolling down my temple.

I knew it wasn't Noah's fault, but I couldn't stop the anger from spilling out. "You always take so long deciding, and we end up in the worst places anyway!"

Noah glanced at me, his expression soft. He didn't flinch, didn't rise to my temper. Instead, he gave a small shrug. "Sorry, darling. Why don't you make the call? I'm happy to stay wherever you want. We'll find something soon, I'm sure."

His readiness to let me lead felt empowering. I liked having control, being the one to decide while he simply went along with it. But beneath that comfort, a small voice inside me whispered unease. Sometimes it seemed like he never voiced what he truly wanted—always folding to my wishes without question. It made our relationship feel unbalanced, a one-way street paved by his silence.

But right then, all I saw was his steady calm.

We finally chose a room—a tiny space with just a bed, four walls, and a creaky ceiling fan. It was enough.

"Doesn't matter where we end up." Noah's hand slid into mine, giving it a small squeeze. "As long as you're here."

To him, I could do no wrong. Under his gaze, I felt invincible.

I didn't yet see the shadows that can grow in too much light.

The next day, my stress melted away as we boarded a bus to Valparaíso, Chile. We marveled at the street art that adorned every alley and staircase, transforming the city into an open-air gallery.

As we wandered down a narrow, graffiti-lined street, one mural stopped me in my tracks. It depicted a mother, her features twisted in grief, clutching the lifeless body of her child. The muted, gray tones of the child's limp form contrasted starkly with the vibrant reds and oranges that radiated from the mother's tear-streaked face. The anguish in her eyes felt raw. It was hard to look at, but even harder to look away.

I interpreted the artist's message as a silent plea for attention to the suffering that so often goes unnoticed—a reminder of how fleeting life can be, and how precious the moments are that we share with those we love.

We moved on, passing a vibrant mural of a farmer herding goats across a hill at sunset. The deep greens and golden hues were peaceful, idyllic. The brushstrokes depicted the simplicity of a calm, rural existence. Stillness. I wondered if that kind of a quiet life, with a home base, would ever call to me. For now, it lived only in art.

And then, there were the more political murals—like one showing a clenched fist breaking free from chains, its bold lines in black and red striking a defiant tone against the gray walls of a crumbling building. These works felt like a shout for change, for justice. The fierce passion they conveyed depicted the revolutionary spirit of a country that has endured both struggle and triumph—and refuses to let either be forgotten.

Murals here were more than just decoration; they were a form of public expression, rooted in Chile's history. During the dictatorship of Augusto Pinochet, murals became a tool for resistance. Artists used the streets to defy the regime and express political dissent. Over time, these works evolved into a powerful means of telling the country's stories, from struggles with inequality to celebrating cultural identity.

The city's eclectic charm ignited my appreciation for the creativity of humanity. Valparaíso's murals were more than just art. They were mirrors of the human condition—our hopes, our fears, our joys, and our pain.

After hours of wandering the streets, we needed a break from the walls and alleys. We chose to relax in a grassy park. Noah, ever the music lover, whipped out his travel-size JBL speaker and set it on the ground. "You've gotta hear this track," he said, grinning as he played an underground rock band called *The Dark Angels.* I lay back in the grass with my head in his lap, sun warming my face.

"You're staring again," I teased, pretending to be annoyed. He had this way of looking at me—puppy-dog eyes gazing right into my soul.

"Can't help it," he said, not breaking eye contact. "You're kind of my favorite view."

A sweet warmth spread through me. It wasn't just the words; it was the way he said them. His admiration was so obvious, so genuine, that I couldn't help but feel a deeper connection every passing day. His devotion and our shared wanderlust drove us forward, into the next city.

In Santiago, the capital of Chile, the local market bustled with energy. Noah and I wandered through the narrow aisles. Stalls overflowed with colorful fruits, vegetables, and handmade crafts. Vendors called out in rapid Spanish.

"Hay cocos! Mangos frescos!" one shouted, gesturing toward a pyramid of ripe fruit.

"Vende fresas, todo fresco!" another yelled, waving a basket of berries in our direction.

A fellow backpacker told us to check out a tucked-away drinking hole known for its famous terremoto cocktail. The place was easy to miss—no flashy signs, no stylish decor—just long wooden tables and benches forcing strangers to sit together. We squeezed into a table shared by locals, who greeted us with smiles.

The crowd was a mix of thirty-somethings who seemed to have made the bar their second home. Three guys with messy hair and band-logo tees clustered around a table, their laughter rising above the chatter. One sported a Los Bunkers shirt—a nod to the iconic Chilean rock band known for blending British rock influences with politically charged lyrics. His friend wore a snapback cap, slightly tilted to the side. A tattoo of a Chilean flag peeked out from under his sleeve. The woman sitting next to them, with long dark hair and bold red lipstick, looked like she'd just stepped out of a scene from a telenovela. She wore a leather jacket that had clearly seen better days, but she carried it like it was the trendiest thing in the room.

A waiter soon placed two huge pint glasses in front of us, the drink's milky yellow color shimmering under the dim light. "What is that?" I asked, my eyes widening in surprise.

Noah leaned in, looking equally intrigued.

"Alcohol with ice cream?" I raised my eyebrows. "How perfect!"

The scoop of pineapple ice cream floated on top, slowly melting into the pipeño, creating a frothy, creamy layer. I lifted the glass to my lips, taking a tentative sip. "It's fizzy!"

"Apparently that's from the wine's carbonation." Noah swallowed, and then stuck his tongue out to lick the remnants of ice cream stuck to his mustache. "Sour aftertaste, ey?"

"Yeah. But smoother than I expected. Just a...yeasty kick at the end."

Noah chuckled, wiping his mouth with the back of his hand. "Nothing like a tropical dessert with a punch. You wouldn't even know it's strong."

A local sitting across from us leaned in, clinking our glasses with a toast. His short stature and thick, graying beard framed a face full of warmth and mischief. "That's why they call it terremoto. It's so strong, but you don't feel it at first. The ground starts shaking later!" He mimicked a swaying motion, causing everyone at the table to burst into laughter.

We spent the afternoon practicing our Spanish, stumbling through conversations with the locals. Drinking terremoto after terremoto, the lightness of the atmosphere lulled me into a carefree bliss.

But as the locals had warned, the drink caught up with me. It hit me all at once. Suddenly swaying, my head spun as the world tilted.

"I need to sit down," I mumbled.

"You are sitting, darlin'."

I pushed my chair back and made a beeline for the bathroom.

Dirty tiles, flickering fluorescent lights, and the unmistakable smell of mildew hit me as I stumbled inside. I collapsed to my knees in front of the toilet, hugging the bowl, heaving. My hands slipped on the grimy edges. My knees were soaked in mysterious wetness from the floor.

I returned to the table disheveled and defeated. Noah greeted me with a reassuring smile. "We've all been there. Let's get you back to the hotel."

By the next morning, the headache had faded, replaced with laughter as we recounted the previous day's misadventures.

That was the beauty of our travels—each moment, no matter how messy, was a shared experience that brought us closer.

We didn't let the lingering taste of terremoto slow us down. A few days later, we found ourselves in Mendoza, Argentina. Fresh mountain air filled my lungs as the towering Andes loomed in the distance, their snow-capped peaks gleaming in the bright sunlight, their sheer mass a stark contrast to the flat, arid valley below. Small, whitewashed adobe buildings dotted the landscape, blending with the terrain.

We rented bicycles, ready to explore the region's famed wineries. The air shimmered with heat as we pedaled, our tires crunching over the dry dirt roads. The sun-drenched vineyards stretched out before us, their rows of grapevines perfectly aligned, a patchwork quilt of emerald greens and sun-kissed purples. Rustic cellars lined with aging barrels welcomed us with generous pours of the region's signature, Malbec. Its velvety richness coated my tongue. The deep, full-bodied flavor was so smooth I couldn't resist buying a bottle at each stop.

Noah plopped the bottles into the wicker basket attached to his bike. "We'll drink as we ride!"

And so we did—cycling through the vineyard-lined roads, casually sipping Malbec straight from the bottle, feeling an intoxicating blend of freedom, wine, and sunshine. In these moments, the world felt perfect.

But as the vineyards faded behind us, the pulse of city life called again, leading us to Buenos Aires. We settled into a small, sunlit apartment tucked above a narrow street. There, the pace of life picked up, and with it, a strange yet beloved local delicacy awaited us: fernet con coca. A dark, aromatic liqueur made from a mix of herbs, roots, and spices. Fernet is intensely bitter on its own but becomes a staple in Argentina when mixed with Coca-Cola.

Noah eyed his glass warily, the bitter herbal liqueur swirling with Coca-Cola. "Are we really drinking this?"

I took a hesitant sip. The fernet's sharp, medicinal bite caught me off guard. "It's...different," I said, scrunching my nose.

Noah took a gulp, his face contorting in surprise. "It tastes like cough syrup!"

"Kinda disgusting, huh?" The sharp flavor clung to my tongue.

"Maybe it's better mixed with red wine? I hear that's a thing..."

Noah gave the drink another go, this time mixing the fernet with red wine. He handed me the glass. I took a big gulp.

"Somehow this is even stranger!" I extended the cup in Noah's direction.

"I think I'll stick to the beer," he said with a grin.

The parties in Buenos Aires didn't start until after 2 a.m. By the time we hit the dance floor, I was buzzing from the strange concoction.

The bass thumped, rattling the scuffed floorboards beneath our feet. Neon lights flashed overhead, casting streaks of electric blue and hot pink across the swaying crowd. Heat thickened the air, mingling with the scent of sweat and spilled drinks. Bodies pressed together, moving to the hypnotic pulse of reggaetón and cumbia. The crowd constantly shifted and bumped as people jostled for space. The DJ, perched high above the sea of dancers, loomed in shadow, his booth lit so the turntable gleamed through the haze.

Noah threw himself into the rhythm of the music, ignoring the crowd packed tightly around us. He didn't care that his moves were over the top—dramatic spins, exaggerated hip thrusts, and wildly swinging arms. His laughter cut through the pounding beat, carefree and contagious.

At first, I danced with hesitation, my shoulders tight and my hands awkwardly wrapped around my drink. But Noah, with his complete lack of inhibition, became impossible to resist. He reached for me and pulled me into the thrumming heart of the dance floor.

"Come on, Shan!" he shouted over the music, spinning me like a salsa dancer before breaking into a ridiculous moonwalk that made me double over.

I couldn't help but admire him. He moved as if the rest of the world didn't exist. I let his energy carry me, shedding my self-consciousness. I mimicked his silly moves—flailing my arms and even attempting an awkward robot dance. We stumbled into each other, giggling like kids at recess.

When the rhythm shifted to a slower sultry beat, Noah pulled me close, his hands finding my waist. Our bodies swayed together, his forehead brushing against mine, and for a moment, the frenzy of the room faded into the background. I tilted my head to look at him, our eyes meeting in the kaleidoscopic glow of the lights. In that instant, no words were needed. I rested my head against his chest, letting myself fall deeper into the moment, the sound of his heartbeat syncing with the music.

Crisscrossing South America with curiosity, Noah and I grew closer with each new place we discovered.

Until the day came when our hearts were overfilled with love, yet our bank accounts were empty.

It was time to go home.

Back to "the real world."

After six months of nothing but leisure and adventure, it was time to make money again.

"I know you've always wanted to visit Southeast Asia, Shan, and that's right near me! If that's the plan for your next trip, you have to stop in Australia to see me first," Noah casually suggested, as we lay entangled in each other's arms the morning he would depart.

"I'd love to," I responded, as my heart burst with fireworks of excitement at the hope of a future of more love and adventures. "I'll head home and start saving some money." But then hesitation crept in. "But I'm scared it'll take me too long to save up, and the connection between us might fade, being long distance and all."

Noah squeezed my hand reassuringly. "Don't worry about that. We can stay connected with video calls. You won't need to save too much money either, just enough for the plane ticket. You can stay at my place for free. It's beautiful. You'll love it."

I smiled at the thought of living in the Northern Beaches in Sydney, but concerns still wracked my mind. "I'd need money for more than just the ticket. What about food, touristing around, drinks, whatever? All of that costs money. And there's no way you're paying for everything."

"You could get a one-year holiday working visa." Noah's inviting tone wrapped around me like the first rays of morning sun, soft and promising.

"What's that?"

"It means you could live and work in Australia for a year! The wages are pretty high, like twenty dollars an hour. You could have money for living and fun, but you could save too. WE could save for more travels *together*."

"*We*. I love the sound of we," I murmured in a dream-like state. My mind drifted, imagining a life I hadn't considered until then. *We.* It wasn't just me anymore, navigating the world alone. "I had no idea working holiday visas even existed!"

"Yep. It'll be perfect. And I promise to be the best tour guide, showing you the beauty of my country." Noah's eyes beamed with sincerity.

"That sounds amazing. I can't wait to see Australia with you."

Noah leaned in, his voice soft and comforting. "We'll make it work, Shan. South America is just the beginning of our adventures."

I nodded, my heart full of hope and love.

The future stretched out before us, uncertain yet filled with promise. I didn't know what challenges lay ahead or how our relationship would evolve, but one thing was certain: I was determined not to let fear hold me back. I didn't want to be burdened with regrets or what-ifs. The horizon beckoned, and I was ready to meet it.

7

DOWN UNDER BEGINNINGS

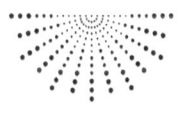

AUSTRALIA

𝒩 oah and I had spent ten months apart, holding on to our relationship through late-night phone calls and blurry video chats. Then, *poof*, we went from being worlds apart to living together in the same space, navigating what it meant to be in a "serious relationship."

Not just any space, though. We were sharing his bed, in his child-hood room, *in his parents' house.*

"You know, where I'm from—it's crazy expensive," Noah said. "Paying rent? It's a feat I just couldn't face yet. So, I still live at home. Most of my mates do."

I couldn't hide the initial judgment in my expression. I moved out of my parents' home at eighteen. "I guess it makes sense...I can see how close your family is."

Noah gave a sheepish laugh. "Yeah, the family's tight. It works. Plus, I'm saving to buy my own place one day...when the time's right."

It was different from my experience, but there was a quality I admired—the closeness, the way his family fit together in that house. The constant hum of activity, laughter, and the occasional sibling argument shouted down the hallway. I could see the value in being part of something that felt so constant and comfortable. I was swept into the rhythm of their lives, unofficially adopted into a big Australian family.

His parents' house was in the Northern Beaches of Sydney, a sun-drenched stretch of coastline that felt worlds away from the bustling city center. The Northern Beaches wasn't just a suburb—it was a series of picturesque beach towns, each one carrying its own charm. There was Manly—Noah's hometown—with its bustling ferry terminal and lively cafés; Dee Why, known for its relaxed, family-friendly vibe and rock pools; and Avalon, an almost bohemian enclave surrounded by lush greenery and golden sand.

The culture was all about sun-soaked afternoons, barefoot strolls, and an easygoing lifestyle that revolved around the ocean. People greeted each other with casual smiles and "How ya goin'?" as if everyone knew one another. Surfers jogged to the waves before work, their boards tucked under their arms, while tanned locals sipped flat whites at beachfront cafés. It was the epitome of the Australian dream.

Grace, Noah's mom, had short, curly brown hair that bounced like it had a mind of its own. Her eyes were always twinkling with a kind of mischief and joy that could cheer up even the grumpiest person.

Despite having fully grown children, Grace insisted on continuing every stereotypical 1950s housewife duty. She did all the grocery shopping, cooked every meal, washed every dish, scrubbed the bathrooms, cleaned the floors, folded the laundry, and vacuumed the carpets. She was a one-woman show. An absolute superstar as care-giver of the household, and she did it all with a smile.

What stood out to me most was that Grace never asked for—or expected—help. For me, this was awkward. I had long since learned to care for myself, cooking my own meals, cleaning up my own mess, and juggling the responsibilities of independent living. These were skills that Noah and his siblings, having never left home, clearly hadn't yet had the chance—or need—to develop.

Between my two jobs—coaching competitive gymnastics and rolling burritos at a trendy Mexican café—I helped out as much as I could. But Grace always seemed one step ahead of me. She'd swoop in to wipe down a counter before I'd even noticed the crumbs, or finish a pile of ironing I'd barely registered existed.

Her effortless efficiency left me wondering about the unspoken expectations in their household. Was this what Noah would expect from a partner one day?

Up to this point, I hadn't been able to get a sense of how Noah functioned in a home. We'd only known each other in transit—living out of backpacks, bouncing between hotels and hostels where someone else cleaned up after us. It was a lifestyle that masked a lot of the daily responsibilities that reveal how someone really lives. Seeing him in the house he'd grown up in, surrounded by routines he'd never had to think twice about, left me with a quiet unease.

Noah's eldest sister, twenty-two-year-old Ella, was the beauty of the family, with long, silky brown hair, olive-tanned skin, and voluptuous curves. She had a genuine heart, with nothing but sincere intentions.

One evening, as we lounged in the living room, I let out a frustrated groan. "You wouldn't believe what my boss did today. He scheduled another pointless meeting during lunch. Who does that? I swear, it's like he gets off on ruining everyone's day." I grabbed a handful of chips, shaking my head. "And you know what it was about? The *precise* amount of filling we're supposed to put in the burritos. Like, down to the gram. As if anyone's out here measuring black beans with a damn scale."

Ella glanced up from a cup of tea, her expression calm but curious. "Maybe he just wants consistency for his customers. Don't forget how lucky you were to find a job at that restaurant a week after arriving here."

"You're right... But damn, I think it's his favorite pastime to micromanage people and suck the joy out of every moment."

Ella chuckled softly but shook her head. "Shan, come on. Maybe he's under pressure."

I sighed, slumping back into the couch. "Yeah, or he just likes being terrible."

Ella smiled. "Or maybe he needs someone to remind him how to be better. A little kindness can go a long way, you know."

Her optimism was disarming, often causing me to pause and reconsider my perspective. "You're too nice for your own good, you know that?"

"Maybe," she said with a playful shrug, "but it doesn't hurt to try."

Noah's middle sister, Olivia, was a kindred spirit—uncompromisingly blunt and honest. Strikingly beautiful like her older sister, she had long, toned legs, tan skin that deepened in the summer, and a slender frame with curves in all the right places. Her wavy brown hair framed a face that was both sharp and delicate, with high cheekbones and hazel eyes that held an amused glint, always ready to challenge or tease.

Curious if an outfit made you look fat? Wondering if the dish you made had too much salt? Need perspective on a decision you were mulling over? If you asked Olivia, she would tell you the truth, whether you liked it or not. We enjoyed spending time together, indulging in one glass of wine after another, and lounging on the outdoor sofa in their sun-drenched backyard.

Both Ella and Olivia openly welcomed me into their home as an honorary third sister. I was free to rummage through their closets for an outfit, to take part in long venting sessions about boys who intended to break their hearts, or to cuddle in pajamas, melting our brains watching mindless chick flicks.

Sprawled on the couch in Olivia's hoodie and Ella's fuzzy socks, I balanced a bowl of popcorn on my chest. Ella muted the TV mid-scene and sighed.

"The guy I went on a date with last night told me I was 'intimidating in a good way.' What does that even mean?" she groaned, flopping dramatically against the cushions.

"It means he's a coward," Olivia said, mouth full of popcorn. "Next."

I chimed in from under the blanket we shared. "You want me to fight him? Because I'll fight him."

Both girls laughed, and Ella reached over to squeeze my arm. "God, I'm so glad you're here."

Olivia nodded. "Seriously. You're like the sister we didn't know we were missing."

In that moment—with mascara smudged under our eyes, limbs tangled on the couch, and the scent of butter and borrowed perfume in the air—I felt it. I *was* one of them.

On a sunny November afternoon, Noah's family gathered on the back deck, everyone barefoot and relaxed, drinks in hand. A speaker played Fleetwood Mac softly in the background as Grace emerged with a tray of cold beers and a bowl of chips.

Noah's dad, Phil, leaned back in his plastic chair. "I tell ya, this is the life. A cold drink, a warm breeze, and a family that won't shut up."

"We learned from the best," Olivia shot back, grinning. "You never shut up either."

"I only talk because no one else says anything interesting." He pointed a finger at her with mock seriousness.

Noah groaned. "You *literally* told that same joke last weekend."

"That's the secret to being funny," his dad raised his thick gray eyebrows, "repetition. Eventually, someone laughs."

Everyone cracked up. Grace rolled her eyes fondly and nestled into her seat beside him, her hand resting lightly on his knee.

Conversation flowed easily—old stories, running gags, Olivia teasing Ella about a childhood haircut gone wrong. Everyone chimed in, overlapping and giggling.

I smiled into my drink, my chest filled with the deep, settled comfort of being in a place where everyone was exactly where they wanted to be. They were so natural with one another. Genuine friends, always happy to spend time together—at the beach, at a party, in a restaurant, or just having drinks at home. I'd never seen a family quite like it. I'd fallen in love.

Noah caught me watching them and leaned in. "Pretty great, huh?"

I nodded. "You guys are amazing."

I meant it. They were the most harmonious, drama-free, connected family I had ever encountered.

I hadn't grown up with a mother I could have casual cocktails with. I didn't grow up in a household known for socializing with friends. I didn't grow up in a family so tight-knit that we chose to spend the majority of our free time together. I appreciated every moment with Noah's family. I was thankful to be a part of it.

Even Noah's best friends became completely entwined with my life. As he buried himself in his university studies, working toward a degree in sound engineering, there were many days I enjoyed hanging out with his friends. It didn't matter if Noah was around or not—I was included, always part of the circle.

The crew happened to be all guys, but that didn't bother me in the slightest. They felt like brothers. I'd grown up surrounded by mostly male friends. Inside jokes circled between us like a shared language, long benders filled with rolling-on-the-floor giggles ensued. There was never pressure to perform or impress—just the freedom to be one of the gang.

Friday nights carried an unspoken rule, that everyone in town had to be out, *to be seen*. Bouncers guarded the entrances to bars, arms crossed and expressionless, scanning each face for any signs of tipsiness. With a curt shake of the head, they would refuse entry to anyone who showed signs of having a few too many. We always managed to make it through the long line and into the bar like it was our rightful place.

"I got the first round!" Steve yelled, his wavy brown hair flopping into his eyes as he spun around with a grin. His skinny frame weaved effortlessly through the crowd like a kid on a sugar high.

Ciaran grabbed Steve by the collar and pulled him back playfully. "Slow down. We got all night, mate."

Ciaran was one of Noah's best friends, and so, by default, slid into being mine as well. It helped that we had the same sense of humor—and weirdly, the same last name: O'Brien.

The pub was packed, as always. Somehow, Ciaran spotted a free table in the far corner.

"There," he said, placing a hand on my back to guide me through the crush of people. "Let's claim it. I'll hold the perimeter."

"You make it sound like war," I joked.

"Pub's a battlefield." He winked. "Never forget it."

There was a lightness to him that I clicked with immediately—banter without effort, comfort without thought.

I shook my head, smiling.

We sank into our chairs just as a group of girls strutted by, their heels clicking like metronomes. They looked like they'd stepped out of a nightclub promo shoot—tight, short dresses clinging to every curve, hair blown out, lashes thick, lips glossed to perfection. The pub wasn't fancy—wooden stools, sports on the TV—but they moved through it like it was a runway. I caught my reflection in the darkened window beside us, tugged self-consciously at the loose hem of my top, suddenly wishing I'd picked something flashier.

"Oi, you want ciders or stick to beer?" Steve shouted across the table.

"Cider's good, cheers," I called back, shaking off the insecurity. The guys never noticed what I wore, anyway.

By the time the first round landed, our voices had risen a few notches, and the second round was already being debated.

I struggled to keep pace. Every time I drained my glass, a fresh one landed in front of me like clockwork. Around the table, no one slowed down—they clinked glasses and moved through rounds like it was a sport. I pushed through, matching them drink for drink, hoping no one could tell how hard I was working to belong.

Another pub, another round of drinks. My head spun while my fingers felt sticky with condensation from the pint in my hand.

As the night wound down, Noah's mates and I inevitably ended up at a kebab shop. Fluorescent glow buzzed overhead as we spilled inside.

"Oi, pies are the superior choice," our mate Oscar declared, elbowing Ciaran in the ribs as we stumbled into the queue. His eyebrow piercing caught the light as he leaned over the counter.

"Mate, that's borderline treason," Steve said. "Aussie nights end in kebabs."

Oscar scoffed. "You lot have no taste. Meat pies are elite—pastry, beef, gravy, a cornerstone of Aussie comfort food!"

Ciaran nudged me. "Team kebab, right?"

We spilled onto the curb with greasy paper bags steaming in our hands. The boys sunk onto a bench like marathoners who'd made it to the final stretch—sweaty, loud, and half-delirious. Meat juice and garlic sauce covered our faces. No one cared. The street was half-deserted now, just a few scattered drunks and the occasional speeding taxi.

"Remember when Steve tried to dance on the bar?" Oscar snorted, choking on a bite of his pie.

"I didn't *try*—I *succeeded*," Steve protested, licking tzatziki off his thumb.

Oscar nearly spat out his food. "You also pulled the fairy lights down with you, rock star." Pastry flakes stuck to the corners of his mouth. "Beach day tomorrow?"

"Absolutely," I said, picturing the saltwater washing away the remnants of another big night. "I'll drag Noah away from his studies."

"I'll bring the speaker," Steve added. "But only if I get control this time."

"God, no," Oscar groaned. "You played that same Arctic Monkeys song five times last week."

"Because it's a banger!"

The boys started bantering again. Steve flicked a bit of lettuce at Oscar, who retaliated by squeezing a line of garlic sauce onto Steve's shoe. Ciaran threw his head back in a belly laugh, his broad shoulders shaking as he handed me the last chip from his tray without a word. I took it, grinning, sauce still on my fingers.

Steve caught my eye across the bench, and raised his meat pie in a mock toast.

Everything about this crew was a beautiful mess—sticky hands, loud mouths, ridiculous decisions—it felt like home.

In the morning, Noah and I pulled into the car park, the tires crunching over loose gravel as the scent of sunscreen filled the air. He missed out on most Friday nights, but we made a point to spend the days together whenever we could.

A cluster of local surfers crowded the lookout point. A few perched on the hoods of their battered vans and cars, legs dangling lazily, their wetsuits pulled down to their waists, exposing tan, salt-crusted torsos. Others shuffled barefoot in the sand, boards tucked under their arms, their eyes fixed on the waves like predators studying prey.

"Check out that A-frame," one of them called, pointing toward the break. "Mate, did you see the spit on that barrel?"

"Bloody oath I did," another replied, already waxing his board. "I'm out there. But who's that paddling out? Looks like a kook."

The group burst into laughter, a mix of camaraderie and territorial pride.

Surfing the Northern Beaches wasn't just a pastime, it was religion, and the car park was their sacred temple. The local crew treated the spot with a possessive reverence. "Locals only," was written in their glances as they sized up anyone unfamiliar.

Among them were the quintessential Aussie surfer dudes. Long, sun-bleached hair left to fall in unruly waves. Polarized sunglasses perched on sun-kissed noses. Flannel shirts hung loosely over broad shoulders, paired with boardies and bare feet, as if shoes were an affront to their way of life. Muscles, honed by years of paddling and carving through waves, flexed unconsciously as they moved.

I turned to Noah, who wrapped his arm around my shoulder. "Think they'd notice if I paddled out?" I grinned gesturing to the lineup.

"Not unless you drop in on one of their waves." His eyes followed the surfers with quiet admiration, as though part of him longed to be part of the tribe.

A surfer began paddling for a steep set wave. He popped up quickly, feet finding the board, but then hesitated—just for a second. But it was enough. The lip of the wave pitched forward, sucking his fragile-looking body over the edge with it. His board launched skyward as he disappeared into the churning water, completely engulfed. The whitewash eventually spat him out. He surfaced, coughing and shaking his head, barely clinging to his board as the next wave loomed behind him.

"Holy shit," I gasped. "That is not for me. I'm happy with my feet dug into the ground, thank you very much."

"They'd probably send me packing," Noah agreed.

"Barbie at mine tonight?" Steve suggested.

"Sweet as." The crew responded in unison.

"Not for me, unfortunately. I got work," Noah said, shrugging apologetically.

"As always," I moaned.

"No worries, we'll take care of her." Ciaran gave my shoulder a friendly pat. "She's one of the boys."

Every Saturday, the backyard of whoever's house we were at transformed into our gathering spot. Empty bottles glinted like broken green gemstones in the grass. The smoky scent of sizzling meat drifted around us. The grill was the center of it all. Its flames flickered as the sausages hissed, flinging bursts of grilled onion and juicy marinade into the warm evening air. Music played in the background from Australia's preferred radio station, JJJ. We danced, drinks in hand, dodging the occasional spill. Someone always ended up with beer on their shirt, laughing it off before reaching for another schooner.

"Oi—watch the cracks, mate," Ciaran called as I stepped toward the esky. The pavement was splitting apart, a thin weed clawing through as if determined to gate-crash perfection.

"Cheers." I steadied myself.

He shrugged. "Gotta look after you—we're connected by the liver, remember?"

Our running gag. Ciaran and I had become inseparable, joking that we were long-lost family—bound not just by blood, but by the same overworked organ. On especially spirited nights we'd lift up our shirts and press our sides together, right under the ribs. Grinning like fools, we'd declare our eternal pact to keep it (mostly) intact.

"Connected by the liver!" I yelled, while everyone else rolled their eyes.

Eventually the music faded and chairs scraped against concrete. The fairy lights overhead still glowed warm—but one bulb flickered faintly, pulsing in and out like it couldn't decide whether to belong or not. Buzzing from the evening spent with friends, I gathered my shoes and waved good-night, dragging myself back to Noah's.

On the surface, I had everything. Living on Sydney's Northern Beaches meant waking up to pristine white sands and the crashing waves of the Pacific. It was a lifestyle with a backdrop pulled straight from a postcard. But beneath the sun and saltwater, it felt like I was stuck in a narrative that wasn't entirely mine.

I enjoyed the life I had built for myself on the other side of the planet. *But did I build this life? Or just mold myself into someone else's?*

Manly, where we lived, had the charm of a seaside village with a gentrified, polished touch. White, upper class. Everyone there looked like they were born at the gym—tanned, toned, and impeccably dressed in trendy beachwear or sophisticated summer dresses. It was a world away from my home in Northern California, where things were more laid-back, and people didn't try quite so hard. I had to adjust to this sense of put-togetherness.

One Monday afternoon—like many before it—Noah and I stopped at our usual fish and chip shop. The familiar scent of fried oil greeted us as we pulled up.

Battered fish was our greasy, golden indulgence. Its crust gave way to delicate, flaky flesh, always perfectly tender. The chips, thick and hearty, soft and pillowy inside, were seasoned with chicken salt, an iconic Australian touch that gave them a savory, almost umami flavor.

We took our prize to the beach, the salt air mingling with the aroma of the fried feast. I suggested sitting in the sand, as I always did.

"Nah, I'm not sitting in the sand, Shan," Noah responded as he peeled back the brown paper our meal was wrapped in. Oil soaked through, leaving dark marks on the edges. "I grew up in the sand, don't need it sticking to everything anymore. Let's just sit up here in the car park."

I shrugged like it didn't matter, though inwardly, I was puzzled. How could he prefer a bench in the car park over the sandy comfort of the beach? It felt like a small, yet symbolic, disconnect between us. I felt a growing tension between my desire for independence and the reality of the life I was being drawn into.

The next morning followed a rhythm that had become all too familiar. Before the sun had even touched the rooftops, I was jogging toward the gym, compelled by the ultra-fit culture of Sydney that surrounded me.

The women inside—dressed in coordinated activewear, chiseled and glowing—carried an unspoken pressure for perfection. It wasn't just about fitness, it was about fitting into societal beauty standards. So, I pushed harder, determined to keep up, to be part of that world.

Afterward, I biked to my morning shift at the Mexican restaurant. By mid-afternoon, I was biking across town again, ponytail swinging, to coach at the gymnastics center.

That day, like most, ended with Noah's car waiting outside.

"Hey, darlin'. How ya going?"

"Day was long. I'm tired," I admitted, sinking into the seat after a quick peck on his cheek. "But it's over now. And the weekend will be back soon! Keen for some fun?"

"I've got to study heaps this weekend. Sorry, darlin'."

I shrugged. "Don't worry about it. I'll just hang with the boys."

Noah glanced at me, a smile spreading across his face. "I'm really glad you're in with them. Knew you'd fit right in."

As we pulled into his driveway, the house glowed. The warmth from the living room spilled out onto the porch. We walked in, greeted by his family sprawled comfortably on the couch.

"G'day!" his mom called out cheerfully. "Dinner's on the counter, fresh and hot."

I smiled. *I'm so lucky. Spoiled, really.*

Noah's hand found mine, giving it a gentle squeeze. "See? You're part of the family."

8
UNRAVELING ILLUSIONS

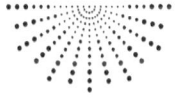

AUSTRALIA

*N*oah and I lay on the grass in his backyard, staring up at fluffy white clouds drifting across the blue sky. The Australian sun beat down on us, warming our skin, while a gentle breeze rustled the eucalyptus trees overhead, sending a shiver through the grass beneath us. A wind chime clinked—slow, hollow, offbeat. An occasional itch from the blades of grass against my legs was a small price to pay for the quiet tranquility of this moment.

Noah turned his head toward me, a serious look on his face. "Hey, I've been doing some research."

"Oh?"

"Yeah. I found out about this 'de facto relationship visa' thing. It's kind of like a marriage visa, but for serious couples. It might be our best shot at staying together after your one-year visa expires."

My heart skipped a beat as a cloud shaped like a giant turtle floated by. "What's involved with that?"

The cloud overhead morphed into the jagged shape of a shark, its open mouth stretched into a snarl. The breeze shifted, cool and sudden, brushing my skin with a chill that didn't match the weather.

"Well," Noah continued, his fingers tracing patterns on the grass, "it's not easy. We have to prove how serious and committed we are.

The application costs around $3,000. We'd need joint bank accounts, a timeline of photos showing our relationship, and personal letters from friends and family vouching for us. And we need to have lived together for at least a year."

"That sounds...intense. And expensive..."

"We'd split the cost," Noah continued. "We're each making almost thirty dollars an hour. We could pay it off in a week and a half of work."

I nodded, trying to process everything. "OK...but I just moved in. And my visa is only for one year. So we'd need to get on all this immediately?"

"Yeah. I think we should do it."

I forced a smile, trying to match his enthusiasm. "Yeah, we should go for it. Just so we have an option, you know?"

He reached over and squeezed my hand. "I knew you'd say that! We're going to make a future beautiful as, darlin'."

"Sure," I said, trying to sound more excited than I felt. "It'll be fun, right? Like a little project for us."

Noah laughed. "Yeah, exactly. A project. And it'll be worth it in the end."

The end. *Was this the end of my dating life?*

I couldn't shake the feeling of how serious and intimidating everything suddenly felt.

But a plan had been hatched.

I no longer allowed myself the space to gradually observe and experience the evolution of our relationship, to stay open to the different paths it might take.

Noah was overwhelmingly in love.

I loved Noah's love for me.

For us.

And so, I wrestled with my hesitations, shoving them into the far corners of my mind, compartmentalized. Instead of allowing questions to surface about what the future might hold for us, I forced myself to embrace the mindset that we were each other's future—no questions asked.

Every moment became an opportunity to collect "evidence" of our love.

However, with time, a lingering doubt continued to grow within me. This was only my second serious relationship. *How could I be sure Noah was "the one"?*

A few months after the visa talk, Noah and I sat across from each other at the kitchen benchtop, our dinner plates pushed aside. Above the fridge, a clock ticked forward, but its hands never moved.

Noah leaned in close, eyes sparkling with excitement as he gestured wildly with his hands. "Imagine this, darlin', we'll find a cozy apartment right by the beach once you've fully immigrated here. And then, we can adopt a small dog. Let's call him Schooner!"

A tight smile tugged at my lips, but inside, my mind was in a frenzy. My heart raced erratically, and my palms grew clammy. I had come to Australia to see where this travel love affair might take me, not expecting it to turn into a fast-track toward immigration and marriage. At twenty-four, I wasn't ready for such a commitment. It scared the hell out of me.

"You know," Noah continued, "we could really live anywhere. If you want to be closer to your family, we could move to the States. Or even somewhere else entirely. It doesn't matter to me, as long as I'm with you."

I swallowed hard, trying to ignore the tightening in my chest. "But you have your whole life here, Noah. Your friends, your family...they mean so much to you. I don't want to pull you away from all of that."

He reached out and wrapped his fingers around mine. "They'll understand, Shan. They just want me to be happy, and I'm happiest when I'm with you."

I looked down at our intertwined hands, his words only deepening the conflict inside me. "But what about what you want? It feels like everything is about me—where I want to live, what I want to do. Don't you have dreams of your own?"

Noah smiled, his eyes gentle. "My dream is to be with you. And if that means traveling the world or living in a different country, then that's what I want, too."

My hands fidgeted with the hem of my skirt. "It's just...I don't even know what I want to do with my life, Noah. I'm so confused about everything. How can I commit to a future with you when I don't even know who I am?"

"We'll figure it out together, Shan. We don't have to have all the answers right now. We just need to trust that we'll find our way."

I nodded, more out of a need to reassure him than out of any real conviction. The doubts remained, gnawing at me. I pushed them down, trying to focus on the love we shared instead. "Yeah...we'll figure it out."

But as we sat there in silence, the weight of my uncertainty lingered, a heavy presence I couldn't shake.

Noah squeezed my hand. He was the sweetest, most loving partner. Fully committed to me. I desperately wanted to feel the same certainty he did. So I played along, hoping my heart would eventually follow. I didn't want my fears and doubt to spoil the future he was so eager to build with me.

Two weeks later I called my sister.

I paced around the living room, phone pressed to my ear, as I tried to explain my feelings to Tara. "I just...I don't know. I'm feeling so anxious about Noah. I mean, I love him. He's the sweetest guy ever. He does everything to make me comfortable in his home. He prepares my favorite meals, spruces up our room with framed photos of my friends and family. He even bought sheets and pillowcases in my favorite colors."

There was a pause on the other end before Tara's voice came through, laced with exasperation. "He sounds amazing, really. What's the problem?"

I sighed, running a hand through my hair. "I know, right? But something just feels...missing. I can't explain it."

Tara's tone sharpened. "Are you serious? You're being an idiot. You're so picky. You don't even know what you want! Noah accepts all your quirks and flaws with such a big heart. He's even adopted your dream of traveling the world!"

I could almost see her rolling her eyes. "Yeah, I know. *How could I complain?*"

"Exactly. Don't overthink it."

I sat down, gripping the phone tightly. Tara's words echoed in my head. Despite the nagging feeling in the back of my mind, I pushed my doubts aside. "You're right. Thanks for the reality check."

"Just remember, not everything needs to be perfect to be right."

"Yeah, I'll try to remember that."

The year I spent in Australia with Noah flew by. We rocked out at music festivals with our friends, took overnight camping trips in the Australian bush, and road-tripped up and down the beautiful coastline, all while working hard, living cheaply in his family home, and saving money for another big travel adventure together.

My holiday working visa ended one month before Noah finished his degree, so I returned to California. I had to be out of the country while my de facto relationship visa was being processed. Noah planned to meet me, so I could show him all of the best parts of my home state.

Stepping onto my hometown soil, a profound realization struck me like an insect meeting its fate against a windscreen. Sudden and undeniable.

I realized I was an incredibly adaptable person. In Australia, I had built an exuberant new life—finding happiness, forming connections, and creating a sense of home. I discovered I could seamlessly assimilate into different lifestyles, patterns, and circumstances, becoming an integral part of the new environment.

However, my adaptive ability had pushed me headfirst into a life direction without my stopping to consider if it was the right path.

The vibrant whirlwind of Australian life had enveloped me. And I surrendered to it.

I hadn't taken time to pause and reflect on my choices, on whether I truly wanted to be part of this whirlwind, or whether I merely allowed myself to be swept away without question. I hadn't "minded the gap," paying attention to the space between where I stood and where I actually wanted to be.

The truth was, still in my twenties, I was adrift, caught in the ambiguous process of figuring out life: who I was, what I wanted, and where I belonged. It wasn't just about geography—it was about people, purpose, and the intangible sense of alignment I craved but couldn't articulate. I was navigating an experimental stage, testing the boundaries of my desires and curiosities.

The direction I was heading was simply the path of least resistance.

The serious relationship I had fallen into felt like an ill-fitting coat: warm and comforting in moments, but ultimately stifling, pinching in places I needed room to breathe.

This clarity only emerged when I separated from Noah. The truth came into focus, like a lens wiped clean of fog. I wasn't ready for a long-term committed relationship. And I didn't want to migrate across the globe to Australia.

I loved my life with Noah. I loved his friends, his family, his country—but I didn't love him as a life partner. On the contrary, I cared about Noah dearly, *as a best friend*.

I had been living a lie—one I'd partly convinced myself was true. It was a striking revelation about the complex nature of human belief, of how we can, at times, even deceive ourselves with our own fabrications.

Of course this revelation led to the unraveling of my relationship with Noah.

On Skype.

I stared at the screen, watching Noah's face as the call connected. He smiled when he saw me, his eyes lighting up in that familiar, comforting way.

My heart was crushed under the weight of what I had to say.

"Hey, Shan," he said, leaning closer to the screen. "What's up? You look...tense. Is everything OK?"

I forced a smile, but it didn't reach my eyes. "Noah, I...I need to talk to you about something."

He immediately straightened up, the smile fading from his face. "OK, you're scaring me. What is it?"

I took a deep breath, trying to find the right words.

They wouldn't come.

"I don't know how to say this," I began, my voice cracking. "I've been thinking a lot, and...I just...I can't do this anymore."

Noah's face contorted. "What do you mean? Can't do what?"

"I...I'm sorry. I'm so sorry," I whispered, the words choking in my throat. "I love you, I really do, but...I can't be with you anymore. It's not fair to you."

He leaned back in his chair. "What? Where is this coming from? Why, Shan? Please, just...let's talk it out."

What was I supposed to say? *Sorry, I don't love you like you love me. I'm not attracted to you enough for you to be the only person I sleep with for the rest of my life. I'm interested in seeing other people. I realize I've been lying to myself this whole time and this isn't what I want?* I couldn't hurt him more than I already was. I didn't want him to feel like our breakup was his fault.

Tears welled up as I shook my head. "I don't know what's wrong with me. Maybe it's because of my parents, the way their relationship is screwed up. I don't know how to have a good one. I'm sorry, Noah. I just can't do this."

His voice cracked as he spoke. "Shan, please. Don't do this. We can figure it out. We'll talk in person, work through it together. Just...don't end us like this."

I wiped my tears. "What's the point of meeting in person, Noah? I've already made up my mind. I can't keep lying to myself, and I can't lie to you anymore. This isn't what I want. I'm so sorry, Noah."

He stared at me, his eyes pleading. "Please...don't do this." Tears streamed down his cheeks.

I had to look away, unable to bear the sight of his heartbreak. "I'm sorry," I repeated, my voice barely audible. "I'm so sorry."

There was nothing more to say. This was the end of an era. One that I had built on a foundation of dreams and illusions.

The silence hung heavy between us, broken only by Noah's quiet sobs. And then, with a trembling hand, I ended the call, cutting off the connection and sealing the end of what we once had.

The universe really does work in mysterious ways. The unraveling of our story was not just an ending, but a prelude to a new chapter. And for me, that next chapter began in a place far removed from everything I knew.

After Australia, I craved a reset. Quiet. Stillness. A return to something elemental. I wanted to strip everything back—to live simply, away from the noise, the expectations, the pressure to *figure it all out*. That yearning is what brought me to Nepal.

9

A TEACHER'S TALE OF CULTURAL DISCOVERY

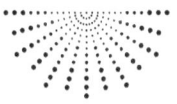

NEPAL

*W*hen I arrived at the remote village of Kaskikot, I immediately questioned my decision.

I found myself sitting on a rock, next to a one-lane dirt road, accessible only on foot. I had been introduced to my "foster family," an old man and woman who spoke no more than a dozen words of English. I was informed by the volunteer placement company through which I found this placement that no one in the village spoke English, except for a few teachers at the local school. However, they too only knew a few simple words or phrases.

I came to Nepal because I longed for simplicity. I thought that by living a more modest life, away from modern distractions, I'd create space for introspection and reflection. I believed I could find clarity in stillness.

But as I sat there, dusty and unsure, staring at the crooked wooden house I was meant to call home, I finally understood the idiom "Be careful what you wish for."

It was barely more than a shack, with dirt floors and walls that looked like they might give if I leaned on them too hard. Cooking was done outside. The woman of the house would gather wood for the fire. Each log carefully chosen and arranged, she'd painstakingly construct a stack, coaxing flames to life with gentle breaths.

The bathroom was a concrete block building, with a hole in the ground one squatted over. There was a bucket in the corner, filled with ice-cold river water to "flush" the squat hole, or alternatively to be used for a "shower." Every individual was responsible for retrieving their own water from the river if a shower was needed as none of the village buildings had running water. Some, like the home I was staying in, had electricity, which took the form of a single lightbulb hanging from the ceiling. No, there was no wifi.

What the hell have I gotten myself into?

I had always prided myself on the ability to "get off the beaten track," be adventurous and independent, but now I found myself alone, in a rustic village. I could communicate with no one, and I was simultaneously cut off from all with the outside world.

My host father strolled past, a short man with deep, weathered wrinkles etched from years of laboring under the harsh sun. He led two large buffalos by a weathered rope tied through their nasal passages. His kind smile, revealing a mouthful of missing teeth, spread across his tanned face as he proudly announced, "Walking buffalo."

Yup, just a casual afternoon walking buffalos, I thought. I began to understand the gravity of how different our cultural and life experiences were. *Damn, Shannon, you're always trying to be so cool and different from other people, but you've gone and pushed things too far this time,* I reflected. But there was no turning back. I had committed to one month in the village, living with locals and teaching at the school, and I intended to make the best of it. Or survive at the very least.

During my first few days, I found myself repeatedly frustrated, unable to express myself, ask for something I needed, connect with my host family or fellow villagers. I quickly decided I had to learn how to communicate in Nepali, or at least learn the basics for survival. Every time I found myself at a loss for words, unable to articulate my thoughts, I jotted down an entry in my notebook. I developed a detailed list of essential words and phrases to learn. Luckily, I had brought an English–Nepali translation book with me to help this learning process. I also found myself pointing to objects and asking whoever was nearby for the name, which I eagerly jotted down phonetically in my notebook immediately after.

Each morning, I set out on a dirt path winding up the mountain-side, surrounded by lush greenery that pulsated with life. The loose rocks beneath me shifted. The climb was demanding, my breath steady, yet labored, my cheeks flushed. Finally, the summit greeted me with a panorama that stole my breath away. I melted into the frame of a still life in a moving picture. Grandeur awed and moved me. Jagged peaks, layered atop one another, stretched into the horizon. Their sharp ridges blanketed in snow sparkled under the first light of dawn. The sun, a brilliant orb of yellow, peeked over the mountaintops, lighting up the snow-capped peaks in magnificent bright pink, orange, and yellow hues.

As the sun's beams cast a warm glow that kissed my face, I sat and quizzed myself on vocabulary, while sun rays mingled with the cool mountain air. I committed to learning five new words each day. Day by day it added up, and I was able to communicate and connect with the people around me. *We are social creatures and we need connection.*

I also took time on the top of the mountain to journal. This daily practice felt therapeutic. Writing became a means of connecting and communicating with myself. It was also a perfect way to reflect and process the endless cultural encounters I experienced each day.

At the end of my 5 a.m. hike, I stopped at the river to fill a bucket of ice-cold water for bathing. The women of the village carried those heavy loads with ease, leaning the bucket on their wide, child-bearing hips as they sauntered casually through the village, or maybe balancing it on their head. I never quite figured out how to do this with such style and grace, but I can't say I didn't try! Eventually, I made it back to my newfound home.

How does one bathe from a bucket? By dipping a cup into it and pouring it over your body, head first, then shoulders, and working your way down. The icy-cold Himalayan water zapped me into consciousness. I actually grew to enjoy it, after I learned to ignore the multitude of long-legged spiders lining the walls of the cement bathroom stall. They were the size of my palm, but I was told they presented no danger...

Breakfast took the form of dal bhat *every day*. That is the most typical meal for Nepali people. It is composed of white rice and lentils, commonly accompanied by a vegetable curry (tarkari), a mixture of spicy vegetables (pickles), and greens (sak). This meal is what sustained the members of my village on a daily basis. They (and now I) ate two plates of it every single day.

Lunch was not served.

Luckily, I was warned of this ahead of time, so I brought along an assortment of snacks, including nuts, cereal bars, and beef jerky.

One afternoon, as I walked home from school, one of the high-level English students raced up behind me. "What you eat?" she inquired as I chomped into my bits of beef jerky.

"It's called beef jerky," I responded.

"What beef?" she questioned further.

"Cow, beef is just another word for cow," I explained.

"COW!!? You eat cow?!!!" She screamed out in shock, her face turning ashen.

When I packed my beef jerky snack before moving to Nepal it never occurred to me that every person in the village would be Hindu, and for them, the cow is a holy animal that cannot be harmed. Legendary leaders such as Mahatma Gandhi have been quoted saying, "If someone were to ask me what the most important outward manifestation of Hinduism was, I would suggest that it was the idea of cow protection." Some scholars trace cows' sacred status back to one of Hindu's most important figures, Lord Krishna. He was said to have appeared five thousand years ago as a cow herder and is often described as "the child who protects the cows." Lord Krishna is also known by the holy name of Govinda, which means, "one who brings satisfaction to the cows." Throughout Hindu scriptures, the cow is referred to as the "mother" of all civilization, its milk nurturing the population. For Hindu people, cows are revered, and they roam freely. It can be considered good luck to gift them a treat such as fruit or bread. On the other hand, a person can be sent to jail for injuring or killing a cow.

And here I was munching on one...

"YOU ARE EATING GOD?!" the young student continued in horror.

My dumb-witted response carried on as well. "Well...it's not reaal-llllllyyyy God."

"COW IS NOT GOD?!" Eyes bulged, the young girl's jaw nearly dropped to the floor.

I quickly realized I was digging myself into a hole. It was time to make a quick escape. There was no need to crush a child's entire life's beliefs and teachings. I reminded myself, *You are a visitor in this place and must remain respectful of local beliefs and customs.*

"No, no, I'm sorry. I misunderstood your question. This is pig! Like oink oink, pigggggggg." *A white-lie never hurt anyone, right?*

"Oh, pig! Can I have some?"

"No." I was not about to indulge a child in naively eating a piece of her own God. I rushed off as quickly as I could in the direction of home.

10

CROSSING BORDERS OF DISCIPLINE

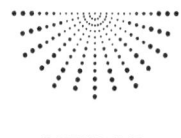

NEPAL

The slap echoed through the dusty classroom, startling the boys into stunned silence. Sita Ma'am, one of the teachers, stood beside me, hand raised in the air. Her golden bangles clinked as she turned to me with a satisfied nod. "You see, this way they learn respect."

I stood frozen, heart pounding.

Everything I knew about teaching collided with the reality in front of me. Hitting students was normal here, an accepted part of discipline. But in my world? Unthinkable. I came to Nepal to make a difference, to inspire change. Yet now, faced with Sita Ma'am's resolute expression and the obedient silence that followed, my confidence wavered.

When I first signed up to volunteer as a teacher in Nepal, I thought I was prepared for the differences. Cultural norms can be as varied as landscapes. People eat different foods, wear different clothes, practice different religions, speak different languages, and celebrate different holidays. I understood that. But I wasn't prepared for this—a classroom governed by fear rather than curiosity, by compliance rather than engagement.

I came to Nepal with a deep belief in the power of education. Volunteer Society Nepal had told me that nearly half the teachers in rural schools had little to no formal training. Due to this, the quality of education remained very low. The education system was based on old-school traditional methods: rows of students sat in silence, heads bowed, absorbing lectures and memorizing facts with little to no room for creativity or participation. Unlike the school system I was raised in, teachers frowned at questions from students. Commentary or responses from children on a topic were never asked for or appreciated. Just sit down, shut up, and listen to the teacher.

I worried about the future of these children, their potential stifled by an outdated system. Where was the collaboration and critical thinking? How would they become the globally minded citizens we needed?

I came with a plan, though. It wasn't just the students I aimed to reach—I wanted to inspire the teachers, too. I believed I could train teachers with concrete skills, which would lead to a more contemporary and engaging method of education. I wanted to leave a lasting impact.

But as I stood there in that classroom, with its bare cement walls and missing windows, a gnawing uncertainty blossomed. What if I was wrong? What if my ideas about modern teaching, about empowering students, didn't belong here?

The village school was nothing like I had imagined—just three sparse classrooms with no doors, and barely any materials. I found it particularly difficult to engage and manage a few of the more feral village boys in my classroom. Tanned, with dirt smudged on their cheeks, and brown eyes twinkling with mischief, these boys loved to race around the classroom like wild animals. These were farm kids, born to run free. They were used to the wide, open fields, not the musty classroom.

"Sit down, Bibek!" I demanded, trying to sound stern.

But Bibek, a wiry boy with scuffed knees, just grinned back, rocking side to side on his heels. "No tanks!"

His friends broke into a fit of giggles.

Across the room, Raju, another boy with a messy tuft of hair, raised his hand dramatically, only to slap it down on his desk with a loud smack. The others jumped at the sound, then burst into laughter again.

"Boys, enough! Your friends want to learn. You are not being fair to this class."

Bibek, the most excruciatingly defiant of them all, began making a series of exaggerated animal noises. Another round of laughter erupted.

Raju, doing his best to distract his peers, started tapping a beat on his desk, each tap louder than the last.

In Nepal, primary education was free and compulsory by law, which explained why the kids showed up each day, even though their parents didn't seem to care. I sighed, glancing at the door and wishing for a moment that their parents would come in to see their antics firsthand. But here, things were different. Most of my students' parents were illiterate farmers who had never gone to school themselves. To them, education seemed pointless—after all, their child would take over the family farm one day, just as they had. Why learn to read and write when you'd be working the fields until you died? Without parental support or respect for education, I had to manage classroom behavior on my own.

With hands smooshed to his face, Bibek let out a large farting noise.

My face flushed. I turned to see a small frame standing in the doorway, hands on her hips. It was Sita Ma'am.

"You! Why you no stop?" she scolded the boys, waving her hand for emphasis.

The boys exchanged quick glances and then went quiet.

Sita Ma'am huffed, her dark eyes filled with a mixture of concern and exasperation. "They not listen to you, yes?"

I nodded, feeling embarrassed. "They're...challenging. But I'm trying different ways to get through to them."

Sita Ma'am shook her head, clicking her tongue. "No, no! In

village, no try many ways. One way work." She raised her hand, giving a swift, illustrative slap in the air.

"In my culture we don't hit students, Sita Ma'am..."

"Good for them! They learn respect. They know you strong, no weak teacher."

"I—I can't do that, Sita Ma'am." I searched for words that wouldn't sound like I was judging her culture. "It's not...what I believe in. I want them to respect me, but not out of fear..."

Sita Ma'am frowned, her bright red shawl drooped with her shoulders. "You not hit, they not respect." She gestured toward the children. "You see? They wild now. You hit, they listen."

"I'll find another way I think, Sita Ma'am. But thank you."

Sita Ma'am threw her hands up in resignation. "You soft, you soft!"

She turned to the boys, her colorful kurta swaying. "Back to work! Now!"

The boys straightened up, exchanging nervous glances. Sita Ma'am shook her head at me one last time before leaving the classroom.

My struggles with behavior management persisted daily. I attempted to use every trick in my book to keep students engaged: games, songs, visual aids, partner and group work, but nothing seemed to interest or control a couple of the unruly boys in my class. They continued to do their best to entertain their peers with jokes and mischief. This kept the entire class from focusing or learning.

One afternoon, the principal of the school sat in the back of my classroom. He explained he wanted to observe my teaching, hoping to pick up some tips to pass onto the other teachers. That day, I was feeling especially worn out by Bibek. He continually refused to stop talking out of turn, despite my stern warnings. "Bibek, stop talking or I will kick you out of the classroom," I commanded.

"NO!" Bibek responded, in a direct challenge to my authority. He carried on sharing stories and giggling with everyone around him.

Frustrated and desperate to restore order, I pointed to the door. "OK, Bibek, time to go. Go outside. If you disrupt learning in this classroom, you are not welcome here."

Bibek's response came with a sharp shake of his head. "NO!" His jaw tightened. His shoulders squared as if readying for confrontation. His gaze hardened, daring me to challenge him further.

"NOW, Bibek! Get out of the classroom."

"NO!"

I needed to assert my power in the room, to show the other students that disrespect would not be tolerated. I'd had enough. I could not handle the disruptions while trying to teach. So, in a heated moment of unclear thinking, I stomped over to Bibek's desk, grabbed his arm firmly, and attempted to lead him out of the classroom.

As I yanked his arm, his body went limp.

My abrupt pull on his arm sent him flailing. His desk toppled onto the floor on top of him.

My body turned rigid, locked in place by shame and regret. Bibek quickly scrambled to his feet. "Ma'am, yes, ma'am. I sorry for talk. I go now. No talk tomorrow." His eyes stayed secured to the floor as he dashed out of the room.

The principal applauded from the back of the classroom. "Teacher! Very good! You finally use force! Children must sometimes be hit to understand what is right. I am proud of you!"

Proud? Of what? Assaulting a child? Back home, I would be fired for the same action. Now, my superior applauded me. I opened my mouth to respond, but closed it in shock and dismay. What could I say?

There is a fine line between respecting cultural norms that differ from our own, yet also standing up for the values and belief systems dear to our hearts. When is it necessary for a person to rise up and speak against a cultural norm that they believe to be unjust? And when is it time to accept cultural norms and those who strongly believe in them? If everything is a matter of perspective, how can we be sure our viewpoint is undeniably right?

My experience teaching in Nepal served as a poignant lesson in navigating this balance—understanding and respecting different cultures while also questioning norms that challenge my core values and beliefs. It taught me the importance of finding alternative strategies for managing classroom behavior without compromising my integrity. Ultimately, it reinforced that while cultural differences shape our worldviews, we must act according to our own moral compass. This experience helped bring me closer to mine.

11

A SLEEPOVER TO REMEMBER

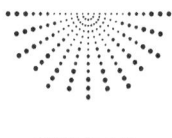

NEPAL

*T*he women at the river paused in mid-scrub, lifting their heads through thick lashes to glance at me. Their eyes sparkled with amusement as they watched me navigate a task that was second nature to them. Living in remote Kaskikot, I was a point of intrigue for the villagers. Most of them had not experienced many outsiders before. Every little thing I did or did not do captivated their attention. For example, when I ventured to the communal river to wash my clothes once a week.

One woman hunched over the river's edge, her arms lean but strong, lifted a soaked blanket and wrung it out with a quick twist of her wrists. Another repeatedly swung a heavy sari against the dry rocks, the impact loosening the dirt with each slap. Her movements were as fluid as the river itself. Their ease captivated me, the way they transformed the mundane act of washing into something almost artful.

I bumbled along, painfully aware of my own inefficiency. As I scrubbed the dirt from my clothes, my hands moved awkwardly through the water. My arms ached from wringing out a single shirt. My back stiffened from crouching on the uneven rocks. Shy stares broke into a chorus of innocent giggles. Occasionally, one woman flashed me a reassuring smile or nodded as if to say, "Keep trying." It was a subtle acknowledgment that, though I was an outsider, I was welcome there. Even if my clumsy hands didn't belong.

After finishing my task, I headed back to the village, only to find myself surrounded by a flood of children, their laughter skipping through the air like stones across water. They trailed behind me and flitted around like colorful butterflies. I felt like the Pied Piper leading this merry band of giggling kids through the village. I found joy in their companionship, though. Speaking Nepali with adults in the village intimidated me. I lacked confidence and was too shy. I felt much more confident practicing with the children.

One afternoon, as I sat under the shade of a tree, writing in my notebook, Gita sidled up beside me. She was a constant presence in my village life, my shadow. Communication was limited by our language barriers, but that didn't seem to matter to her. She reveled in simply being near me, watching my every move with intense curiosity and fascination.

She pointed at my pen, eyes wide with interest.

"Pen," I said, holding it up.

"Pen," she repeated. She then pointed to the notebook.

"Notebook," I said.

"Notebook," she echoed, her pronunciation deliberate.

We continued this game for a while, with Gita pointing at various objects around us—a bush, goat, grass—and me supplying the English words. When she had exhausted the immediate vocabulary, she switched roles, pointing at objects and giving me their Nepalese names.

"Dhoka," she said, pointing at a door.

"Dhoka," I repeated, writing it down in my notebook.

"Kopila," she said, touching a flower.

"Kopila." I jotted it down with a smile.

This mutual exchange of language became our daily ritual. Gita was as enthusiastic about practicing English as I was about practicing Nepali. A symbiotic relationship developed, and I looked forward to our sessions.

One evening, as the sun dipped below the horizon, casting a golden glow over the village, Gita and I sat outside, practicing our words. Her unique brown eyes, with a green tinge and yellow speckles, added a magical quality to her as she pointed at the sky.

"Sky," I said.

"Sky," she repeated, then paused. "Aakash," she added.

"Aakash." I enjoyed the way the word felt on my tongue.

"Good," she said in English, her confidence growing with each new word.

I looked at her, marveling at the colorful chura bracelets that adorned her slender wrists. "Gita," I said, pointing at her. "Very smart."

She blushed, looking down. "Thank you," she whispered.

The children weren't the only ones eager to practice English. The other three teachers at the school were just as enthusiastic. One woman, Ditya, was especially determined.

After wrapping up my lesson at school, Ditya approached with her usual warm smile. Her bangles jingled softly as she clasped her hands together. "Namaste, how...class?"

"Namaste, Ditya," I replied. "Class was good. The students are improving."

She nodded, her neatly tied bun barely moving. "Good. You...come...dinner with my family?" she asked hesitantly, her fingers playing with the tiny red beads of her tilhari, the gold pendant catching the light.

I hesitated, feeling a pang of guilt. Ditya had invited me to dinner every week for the past month, and each time I'd turned her down. I'd always blamed my long teaching days or my evening lesson planning. But her persistence was kind, not pushy, and I could see the effort she put into making me feel welcome. Besides, I thought it might be nice to have a change from my usual evening routine. Typically, I lay on a straw mattress on a rough floor, slapping at mosquitos that succeeded in breaching the defensive perimeter of my mosquito net.

"Ditya," I began, trying to find the right words. "I...feel bad. You've asked me many times. I should say yes."

Her face lit up with a mixture of surprise and joy. "Yes? You come? Family...happy!"

"Yes," I said, nodding in return. "I will come to dinner."

"Thank you, thank you," she said, her hands coming together again in gratitude. "You...see... Nepali home, Nepali food."

"I am looking forward to it," I replied, genuinely touched by her excitement.

As she walked away, the long, flowing skirt of her gunyu swayed gracefully, the rich maroon fabric a contrast against the village's earthy tones.

For Ditya and her family, it was clearly an honor to welcome me into their home. The whole hut had a humble, functional beauty. It was not pretending to be anything more or less than what it was. There was no furniture other than a single straw mattress on the ground, and a few worn wooden stools placed strategically around the open wood fire pit on the earthen kitchen floor. They provided seating while preparing meals. Two lightbulbs hung from the ceiling. One cast a warm glow over the kitchen area, and the other softly illuminated the combined space that doubled as their living room and bedroom.

In one corner, a simple coat rack stood—a rough wooden pole with a few pegs sticking out, where the family's modest collection of clothing hung. A couple of faded saris in dusty reds and soft browns, their hems tattered, hung next to a few thin shirts in washed-out greens and grays. Among them, tiny children's tunics in pale yellows and blues, patched at the elbows, dangled beside a lone shawl woven in a deep, shadowy blue.

Ditya busied herself in the kitchen. With practiced efficiency, she crouched low on the kitchen floor, using her hands to scoop rice into a battered metal pot from a woven basket. She placed the pot carefully over the earthen fire pit set into the floor. The scent of smoke mingled with the faint sweetness of the rice. Next, Ditya grabbed a rusted, blunt knife and sat cross-legged. With deliberate strokes, she chopped carrots and potatoes on an old wooden cutting board. She glanced up occasionally, meeting my gaze with a smile as I sat nearby, eager to help but unsure of my place in her kitchen.

"Please, how can I help?" I asked.

"No need. Sit, sit," she insisted, motioning to a low stool. "We talk."

I settled down. "Ditya, you cook with such skill. It's very different from how I cook at home."

She nodded, stirring a bowl of lentils. "Yes, here we use fire. You... in your country, how you cook?"

"In my kitchen, I have a stove and an oven," I explained. "Everything runs on electricity or gas. It's very convenient, but it doesn't have the same...charm as this."

"Electric...gas? No fire? How you get flavor?"

I laughed softly. "We use spices and seasonings, but I think cooking over an open fire adds something special to the food."

She smiled, her gold earrings catching the firelight. "Yes, fire is...life. Gives warmth."

As she continued to cook, the conversation shifted naturally. "Ditya, do you pray often?" I asked, noticing a small shrine in the corner of the room. A thin, fraying cloth in shades of crimson and gold draped the wooden platform. On top sat a faded statue of Shiva. Incense sticks that had long since burned out covered his serene face with a layer of ash. Around him were offerings: a few dried marigold petals, an ancient brass diya with soot-blackened edges, and a handful of rice scattered across the cloth. Above, a garland of wilted flowers hung from a peg on the wall.

"Yes, pray every day. Hindu...many gods. We pray for health, happiness, family. You?"

I hesitated, not wanting to offend her. "I'm not very religious. I believe in being kind and helping others, but I don't pray regularly."

Ditya looked at me with a mix of understanding and concern. "Western people...not so religious. I pray for you, for happiness."

"Thank you, Ditya. That means a lot to me."

She paused for a moment, then changed the topic. "You...have husband?"

I smiled, shaking my head. "No, not yet. I'm twenty-five and still figuring things out. In my culture, it's normal to wait."

Her eyes widened in shock. "Twenty-five? No husband? No family? Why?"

"I'm happy focusing on my own personal growth right now."

Ditya looked puzzled. "But...happiness? Family important. Who takes care of you?"

"I take care of myself," I said, smiling reassuringly. "I'm happy exploring the world and learning new things. Happiness comes in many forms."

Her brow furrowed in thought. "Different life," she said finally. "I start family at nineteen. Normal here. But...I pray for your happiness."

"Thank you, Ditya. I admire your devotion to family and your faith. We can learn so much from each other."

Dinner was eventually served. A spread of food, including gundruk (fermented leafy greens) and aloo tama (a curry made with potatoes and bamboo shoots), was placed in the middle of a woven mat on the floor. Ditya motioned for me to sit beside her and I obliged, settling in as her husband and their two children joined us.

Her husband, a quiet man with kind eyes, sat cross-legged across from us, while their son, restless with youthful energy, playfully nudged his sister before sitting down. The girl sat with a calm, attentive gaze, observing everyone as they arranged themselves. Ditya laid out plates. There were no utensils in sight. In Nepal it's traditional to eat with your hands, similar to Arab countries such as Morocco and many Asian countries such as Malaysia, India, Sri Lanka, and Indonesia.

"No forks?" I awkwardly asked.

"No need!" Ditya responded. "Eat more slow with hands. More calm. Better digestion. Please, eat." She gestured to the food.

Ditya's husband scooped up the rice and dal with his hands, expertly mixing the food into manageable bites. I observed his movements closely, trying to mimic the technique. He delicately bunched the rice together with his fingers, using his thumb to help push the food into his mouth. I followed his lead, hesitant at first but determined to embrace the experience.

"Only right hand," Ditya reminded me gently, her eyes warm with understanding.

I nodded, recalling the cultural significance. It is important to remember to only eat or pass food with the right hand. In countries such as Nepal, toilet paper is not commonly used. The left hand and some water are used to wipe oneself instead. So, for obvious hygiene purposes, it is only polite to use the right hand while eating.

I gathered a small portion of rice in my hand. I used my thumb to deposit the food into my mouth, being mindful not to stick my fingers all the way in, which I had learned was considered an unsightly display. Eating rice and dal with your hands is quite an art. Ditya nodded approvingly. "Very good."

"Thank you," I replied, feeling a sense of accomplishment. Since my arrival in Nepal, I gradually improved my skill through patience, observation, and a willingness to adapt to this cultural practice.

"You like buffalo milk?" Ditya's eyes sparkled, as if she had something special to share.

I smiled, recalling the rich and creamy texture and distinctively earthy and slightly sweet scent. I had come to *adore* fresh buffalo milk during my stay in the village. "Yes, I love it."

Ditya beamed, clearly pleased. "My family...we have buffalo!"

I raised my eyebrows, impressed. Buffalo ownership was a prestigious bragging right in the village since buffalos were worth a great deal of money. "Really? That's wonderful. Owning buffalo is a big deal here, isn't it?"

Pride was evident in her expression. "Yes, very important. Buffalo give us milk, help with farming."

Without another word, Ditya jumped up and hurried to a corner of the kitchen. She returned moments later with a large pitcher of buffalo milk and a cup. "You have," she insisted, pouring me a cup of the thick, flavorsome goodness.

"Thank you, Ditya. This is very kind of you."

She watched with satisfaction as I took a sip, the full-bodied liquid gliding across my tongue and coating it with a velvety texture. It was as delicious as I remembered, and I happily chugged glass after glass.

"You like much," Ditya said, her smile widening as she poured me another cup.

"I do. It's the best milk I've ever had."

Ditya laughed, a musical sound that filled the room. "Good. You drink as much you want."

Ditya continued to ask me one question after another while we ate. She worked as a translator through the entire dinner, relaying my answers to her family in Nepali. They wanted to know about my educational background, travels, hobbies, and family structure. Each time Ditya spoke, her husband and children listened attentively. Her husband nodded thoughtfully, while their son leaned forward with a growing smile, as if fascinated by the idea of someone from so far away sitting at their table. Even the young daughter, normally shy, perked up, her eyes widening as she listened intently.

"How many brother you have?" Ditya asked.

"None, just one older sister," I replied with a smile.

Ditya's face dropped in horror. She turned quickly to her husband, lowering her voice to a worried whisper in Nepali. Her husband suddenly straightened up. His dark brown eyes flicked from Ditya to me. His strong, veiny hands paused midway to his plate, fingers resting over the rice as he processed what she had said.

"You only have one sibling?" Ditya said, her voice filled with sympathy. "And it's a girl? There are only two girls in your family?"

"Yes..."

"Your poor mother!!!!" she cried out in shame.

In traditional Nepalese society, men are more highly regarded than women. Men make the rules, manage the finances, inherit everything from parents, and carry on the family name. If a woman is unable to bear a son, it is considered sad and shameful. Understanding this cultural difference, I chose my words carefully.

"Yes...but she's OK. She loves my sister and me very much, so she's fine...."

"Poor, poor mother. I will pray for her," Ditya responded in woe.

All I could say was "Thank you."

Ditya's husband continued to pour me glass after glass of buffalo milk. In Nepali culture, if a guest eats and drinks monumental portions, that means they enjoyed their visit. It is a compliment to stuff your face beyond capacity, and who was I to break social norms? Whenever my glass became empty, someone immediately filled it up to the brim again. It would have been rude to say no.

By the time we finished dinner, it was well past sunset. Ditya lived in a home nestled in the forest, a forty-five-minute walk from where I lived. It would be impossible for me to find my way home in the dark.

I hadn't realized that this dinner would be a sleepover.

Ditya had already taken this into consideration. She made previous arrangements for herself, her husband, and their two children to sleep in the same bed while I slept in the attic space.

"My children sleep there, but tonight for you!" Ditya exclaimed excitedly. "You must be careful climb ladder though," she added, pointing toward the flimsy rope ladder hanging from rafters above.

"I need the toilet though, please," I responded. "I drank way too much buffalo milk tonight!"

"Yes. Our gift to you. Toilet outside. My husband must take with you. He will check for snakes."

Armed with a flashlight, Ditya's husband guided me down a narrow dirt path, a hundred feet from the house. My bare feet squelched in the mud. The crisp night air was alive with the distant sounds of nocturnal creatures. The outhouse, as expected, was a simple cement block structure. I did my business quickly and then shuffled back inside.

Unfortunately for me, I have a *very* small bladder, and within minutes of retiring to bed, I needed to go again.

Back down the ladder I climbed. Ditya's husband woke up to grab his flashlight and escorted me back to the outhouse.

I was frustrated when, after wearily climbing up the ladder and getting into bed once more, I quickly woke up with an urgent need to relieve myself *again*. The realization struck that this cycle could continue throughout the night, causing repetitive disruptions for

Ditya and her entire family. Determined not to inconvenience them any further, I reached for my flashlight and delved into my daypack. I was desperately searching for my water bottle. It would become a makeshift solution for my bathroom needs for the remainder of the evening.

The struggle a woman faces when attempting to neatly relieve herself into a small bottle does not require elaboration, but I assure you, I tried to make the best of the challenging circumstances.

As morning broke, I discreetly concealed the water bottle containing its warm yellow contents within my pack, not wanting to leave any evidence of my unconventional solution. I expressed my heartfelt gratitude to Ditya and her family for their profound hospitality. And I made a solemn promise to myself to never again consume such copious amounts of liquid before bed. From that day forward, I carried with me a newfound appreciation for self-restraint and moderation.

12

THE GIFT OF ENOUGH

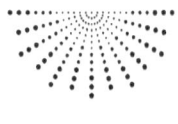

NEPAL

*L*iving in Kaskikot I connected most with my host mother, Dhriti. Her name translates to someone with patience and courage. With kind gray eyes that looked right into my soul, she soothed me. Dhitri became my Nepali mother. She took care of my every need, and patiently taught me the ins and outs of village life, from collecting water and farming in the fields to cooking by fire.

Dhitri's husband and the other men of the village spent a large portion of their time chain-smoking cigarettes and squatting under the shade of a tree chatting with friends. Meanwhile, the women of the village engaged in backbreaking labor, cutting grass for animals, harvesting food for dinner, and planting seeds for the future. This division of labor (or lack thereof) had been a tradition for generations, carried out unquestioned. It was even more noticeable during a festival period, when there were hundreds more tasks to attend to, and almost all tasks were left in the women's hands.

I was in the village for one festival where this was not the case: Teej. Many consider Teej to be one of the greatest celebrations for Hindu women. They dedicate it to Goddess Parvati because she achieved a union with Lord Shiva after her devotional prayer. Every woman desires and prays for a virtuous partner like Lord Shiva, don't they? That's what the significance of this festival was based on, a desire for women to attain a good husband in life and pray for his longevity and prosperity.

Both married and unmarried women fasted on this day, refraining from even a drop of water or a grain of rice. They explained that the fasting and rituals symbolized sacrifice and prayer for their family's, particularly for their husband's—or future husband's—health and well-being. I couldn't help but find it a bit ironic that the "greatest festival for Hindu women" was all about praying for men.

Nevertheless, Dhitri pulled me into the festivities with enthusiasm. Guiding me to a shaded corner of the courtyard, she motioned for me to sit on a wooden stool. Then, crouching before me, she balanced a small clay dish of henna paste on her knee.

"Blessing for you husband," she explained as she dipped a slender wooden stick into the paste.

With steady hands, she began to draw. Swirls and loops trailed across my palms like vines climbing a wall. Each curve and dot seemed purposeful, carrying a message I couldn't decipher.

The cool, earthy paste tickled my skin, but I sat mesmerized, watching the intricate art bloom across my hands.

When the henna was complete, Dhitri led me up a neighbor's narrow staircase to a rooftop, where a gathering of crimson and gold awaited. Every woman was a vision in red, draped in shimmering sarees that caught flecks of light from the dozens of golden bangles stacked along their wrists. Their hands were works of art: henna designs spiraling from fingers to forearms, still darkened from fresh application.

The scent of incense, a smoky blend of sandalwood and frankincense, lingered in the air. It curled upward, mingling with the bitter aroma of marigold garlands that hung from each woman's neck. My wrists, now wrapped in bangles, clinked and chimed softly each time I moved, echoing the collective, melodic rhythm of the circle we formed.

One by one, we clasped hands and swayed in time to the folk songs that poured from the women's throats. Dhitri's fingers were strong and warm in mine.

Around us, women laid out clay bowls of rice, Bijuli cigarettes, and small cups of local rice wine in reverence to the gods. "Seven gods, we make happy," Dhitri said, nodding at the offerings. "And now clean body and clean soul."

We each took turns covering our bodies with red mud. It squelched between our fingers as we smeared it across our skin. My hands dragged it over my arms and neck, spreading the thick clay until the crimson hue blended with my saree. Beside me, a woman pressed a rough tree branch of datiwan into my hands, her fingers firm but warm. I watched as she scrubbed the fibrous stem against her teeth. Mimicking her movements, I hesitantly lifted the branch to my mouth, the bitter taste of bark coating my tongue as I brushed.

Tears glistened in the eyes of the older women. Happiness and grief coexisted—accepted, understood, and honored.

I tugged on the edge of my saree, glancing around at these women who had become friends. "So...is there a festival where the men do this for the women?"

A split-second of silence followed before the women exploded into laughter. Their bangles clinked wildly as they clutched each other's shoulders. Dhitri doubled over, waving her hand in front of her face as if she'd just heard the most absurd thing in the world.

"Oh no, no! Men?" she managed through her laughter, pressing a hand to her side. "Men, no... no like this."

Another woman touched my arm, still chuckling. "Men...no festival. No fasting."

"No day to fast and pray for women?" I asked, raising my eyebrows in mock surprise.

They laughed again, shaking their heads.

Dhitri patted my shoulder, still grinning. "Only women. For husband, son, father. All...women do."

The idea of a day honoring women and women's health seemed like a ludicrous joke in their culture. However, despite the Teej festival being based around praying for the men of the village, according to my women friends and neighbors, the festival still empowered them. They were free to connect and enjoy the feminine. They were also thrilled to have a break from the usual work of laboring in the fields and tending to the household.

Throughout every aspect of Teej festival, Dhitri stayed by my side. Holding my hand tight, she led me through groups of women caravanning around the rooftop, reciting chants and prayers I could not decipher. With enthusiasm, she prayed not only for her own husband but also for me to find one. Burning candles and incense billowed up to the heavens, carrying our prayers within them. Precious moments like this with Dhitri only further invigorated the respect and appreciation I had for her.

Three weeks later, it was time for me to leave the village. I longed to leave Dhitri with a gift, something to reflect my love and gratitude, but as I sat in the dim, bare-walled dining space, I realized no object could ever truly suffice. Dhitri, who insisted I refer to her as Mama, had a small array of mismatched dishes, a few large pots burned on the outside, a chakla or belana, which is a wooden board used to roll dough and make chapattis, three wooden stools to sit on, and a small handmade wooden table to go with them. She had so very little, but simultaneously had everything she needed. Her beliefs, lifestyle, and culture had no need for the superfluous. Her genuine pride and joy was rooted deeply in simplicity and contentment.

On the foggy morning of my departure, my heart felt unbearably heavy. When Dhitri pulled me into her arms, tears spilled freely from us both. We had no shared language to fully express what we felt, but sometimes, there is no need for words. Her dark eyes, glistening with emotion, met mine, and in that moment, everything was understood.

I provided no physical gift to leave in my absence. What I left "Mama" with was love, respect, and genuine appreciation for all the experiences we shared. Mama had taught me something profound: the beauty of living simply, appreciating what we have, and resisting the constant pull of wanting more. As the village faded into the mist behind me, I held onto that lesson with the same strength I'd felt in her embrace—a gift I could never repay.

Still, the sting of knowing I'd likely never return settled deep in my chest. I was always chasing the next place, the next story, always moving, always leaving. And with every departure, I left little pieces of myself behind—scattered across landscapes and goodbyes. This life, this connection, had been real, even if it couldn't last. But maybe that was the point. Nothing ever does. *Somehow, that always hurts more than I expect.*

13

TREKKING TOWARD ADVENTURE

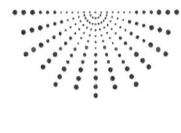

NEPAL

"𝒥magine having enough money coming in each month that you don't have to worry about finding work while you're traveling."

Xander's voice carried easily over the sound of our boots crunching against the rocky trail. We were deep in the Himalayas, where the air was thin and the views stretched farther than I thought possible.

After I wrapped up my stint teaching English, I knew I couldn't leave Nepal without hiking in these mountains. So I packed a bag, laced up my boots, and set off.

Then I met Xander.

We'd crossed paths at the start of my trek, one week prior. Since then, we'd been hiking together every day. Our connection was effort-less—easy conversation, shared snacks, and a steady rhythm side by side.

He walked just ahead of me now, moving with the practiced ease of someone who'd been on the road for months. His lean frame adjusted naturally to the slope, dark brown curls peeking out from beneath his woolen cap.

"I've been thinking a lot about passive income," he continued, adjusting his backpack straps. "I've been researching e-commerce. I want to start an online store selling travel gear—stuff that's really innovative and useful for backpackers like us."

"That sounds like a great idea," I said, pausing to take in the sweeping view of the valley below. Layers of lush, green terraced fields carved into the mountainside, stretching toward the horizon where peaks, dusted with snow, shimmered under the soft morning light. "But isn't it a lot of work to get something like that off the ground?"

"Sure. But that's the beauty of it. Once it's up and running, it can manage itself with just a bit of oversight. My girlfriend back home in Germany works in tech, so she can automate a lot of the processes."

"A girlfriend back home, hey? Why didn't she join you?"

"She's finishing her master's. I miss her like hell."

"That's sweet." I stepped over a gnarled tree root. "I broke up with my boyfriend awhile back. I needed some freedom, you know?"

"I get that. We're young. Enjoy it."

"You really have it all figured out, don't you?" I said.

He let out a hearty chuckle. "Not quite all, but I'm working on it. I've even been thinking about starting a travel blog to share my experiences and tips, too. With enough traffic, I could earn through ads and affiliate marketing."

"I admire your ambition, my friend." I responded with sincerity.

Xander's bushy brows framed brown eyes that sparkled with enthusiasm. "I think the key is to keep dreaming big and never stop learning. There's so much potential out there if you're willing to look for it."

We continued hiking; the path becoming steeper as we ascended. Crisp air filled my lungs with every breath. Xander pointed out a distant waterfall, its silvery thread cascading down the mountainside like a ribbon of light.

"See that?" he said, his voice filled with wonder. "That's what it's all about. Finding beauty in the world, chasing dreams, and making it all sustainable."

I nodded, feeling inspired by his vision and the incredible landscape around us. The Himalayas stretched out endlessly, evoking the vast possibilities that lay ahead. With friends like Xander, who dared to dream and act on their ambitions, anything seemed possible.

As we reached a flat plateau offering a panoramic view of the mountains, I asked, "What's your next stop after Nepal?"

Xander grinned. "India."

"No way, that's exactly where I'm headed next! I'm really excited." I let out a sigh. "But to be honest, I'm a bit nervous about going alone. Especially as a woman. It's…. Well, you hear stories, you know?"

Xander's face softened. "Maybe we could start off together? I mean, at least for the initial leg of the trip. We could check out Delhi and Varanasi. It'd be nice to have some company."

The idea of having a travel companion, even if only for part of the journey, made the prospect of India feel more like an adventure and less like a daunting challenge. "That would be amazing. I'd feel better knowing I'm not alone."

"Hell, me too! I've heard horror stories of bad bellies and illness from India. We can have each other's backs. You're planning to travel there by land, right?"

"Of course," I replied, biting my lip. "With these damn elections going on, though, I'm afraid my plan might get messed up." Heated elections were taking place in Nepal. Battling sides had resorted to violence, including the placement of explosives along the main roads. It was nearly impossible to safely navigate the country.

"Ya, it's been hectic! Things will clear up soon, though. Political situations like this usually calm down after a while. We might just need to sit tight for an extra week or so."

"You're right," I said. "I've just been too focused on moving forward. I always do that…."

Xander's eyes twinkled in the dimming light. "Don't beat yourself up. We're going to hang tight, enjoying Nepal. And when the government says the roads are safe to go to India, we'll head there together."

"All right," I said, lifting my canteen in a mock toast. "To new adventures with new friends."

"To new adventures," Xander echoed, clinking his imaginary glass against mine.

One week later, the government organized a relief bus from the lakeside town of Pokhara to embark on the five-hour drive to the Sunauli border crossing into India. The journey was marked by palpable tension. Police escorts flanked our bus for the entire trip. Two police cars trailed behind us, with another leading the way, their sirens blaring and their lights flashing in epileptic bursts.

Xander and I sat together, admiring the ever-changing scenery through the windows. Majestic mountains loomed in the distance, their snow-capped peaks crowned with wisps of clouds. Below, verdant valleys stretched out, dotted with terraced fields and quaint villages. The landscape was a tapestry of emerald greens and earthy browns, interspersed with splashes of colorful prayer flags fluttering in the breeze.

Despite the tense atmosphere, the bus buzzed with excitement as backpackers eagerly anticipated their onward journey to India. A warm sense of camaraderie permeated the space as everyone shared their treats. Samosas, savory pastries filled with spiced potatoes and peas, were my favorite. Their crispy edges and fragrant filling provided a delicious taste of local cuisine. Crunchy pakoras, deep-fried fritters made from chickpea flour and various vegetables, were also eagerly devoured.

"Has anyone been to Varanasi before?" a tall, bearded backpacker named Alex asked. "I'm planning to stay by the Ganges and explore the ghats."

A petite woman with curly hair nodded enthusiastically. "Varanasi is incredible! Make sure you catch the evening aarti ceremony—it's a fire ritual with chanting and music along the Ganges. It's magical. I'm heading to Rajasthan, to see the palaces and maybe do a camel safari."

Across the aisle, a group was deep in discussion about their plans for Goa. "The beaches there are supposed to be amazing," said Sam, a lanky guy with a surfboard strapped to his backpack. "I'm thinking of taking some yoga classes and just relaxing by the sea."

Next to him, a girl in a floral headband with a journal in her lap chimed in. "Don't forget to check out the flea markets. You can find some really unique stuff there."

The bus rocked gently as it navigated a bend, and the landscape outside shifted to colorful markets and roadside stalls. Vendors sold a myriad of items: vibrant textiles in every hue imaginable, detailed carved wooden statues, and an array of fresh produce. The scent of spices—cumin, turmeric, and coriander—mingled with the aroma of street food, creating an intoxicating blend that made my mouth water.

I caught sight of a woman expertly rolling out dough for momos, the beloved Nepalese dumplings. Beside her, a man fried crispy jalebis, their golden spirals sizzling in hot oil before being soaked in sugary syrup.

"Look at that!" someone exclaimed, pointing out a stall laden with brassware. "I need to get one of those traditional teapots for my collection."

Our bus continued its journey, and the conversations flowed as freely as the snacks being shared.

Xander leaned in and whispered, "This is going to be one hell of a trip, isn't it? I think we will never ever forget this otherworldly place."

"Absolutely."

As the sun set, casting a warm golden glow over the landscape, we knew that we had endless possibilities ahead on our journey. The road stretched out before us, and with it, the promise of new experiences and unforgettable memories.

14

A CURBSIDE GAMBLE

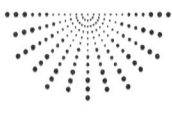

INDIA

*I*t was midnight when we finally arrived at the border. The scene was shrouded in darkness, illuminated only by the sporadic blinking of street lights that lined the dusty road. The immigration building, a dilapidated structure with peeling paint and weathered walls crying out for a touch-up, was closed. Steel bars at the windows cast ominous shadows in the moonlight, hinting at the formalities that awaited me in the morning.

Massive semi-trucks loomed on the sidewalk and along the road, a testament to the halted activity of the border crossing at this late hour. The drivers, a rugged assembly of men, congregated outside their vehicles, murmuring in the still night. The air was thick with the acrid scent of cigarettes as they chain-smoked, and tossed spent butts to the ground where they glowed like fireflies in the darkness.

It remains a mystery why the Nepalese government arranged for a bus packed with over twenty-five tourists to arrive at a closed border, devoid of any nearby accommodations, at two o'clock in the morning. Nevertheless, we were stranded at the curb with our dusty backpacks, commencing the tedious wait until the immigration office opened at 7:30.

A few travelers we'd met on the bus cracked jokes to kill time, and someone passed around a bag of weed—grown in the Himalayan hills, according to their proud announcement. It wasn't uncommon in Nepal; cannabis grew wild, thriving in the cool, nutrient-rich soil and temperate climate. It had long been a part of local culture, used in religious rituals and as a traditional remedy in many villages.

I politely declined, too nervous about the looming border crossing. Xander, on the other hand, didn't see the harm in partaking. "When in Nepal," he grinned, taking a drag and exhaling slowly into the quiet night.

As the hours crept by, the group gradually grew drowsy and scattered, some curling up beside their packs. I wandered aimlessly, watching the sky lighten shade by shade.

At 7:30, Xander let out a low whistle as we stood on the roadside, eyeing the small, crumpled bag in his hand. "Can you believe I'm ditching perfectly good weed?"

I glanced around, then nodded toward the curb next to a parked semi-truck. "Better to lose a few grams than end up in an Indian jail."

"Fair enough." He squatted and gently placed the bag down, like it was something sacred. "Rest in peace, little buddy," he said under his breath. "Hope someone finds and enjoys you."

A couple of travelers shuffled ahead of us, passports in hand, while immigration officers behind weathered wooden windows sipped chai and barely looked up.

"We good?" I asked.

Xander nodded, falling into step beside me. "Yeah. No contraband. No trouble. Just two responsible backpackers walking into India."

The immigration office was a simple setup, just a small room where we paid a fee, got our passports stamped, and were barely given a second glance by the officers. No security checks, no questions. And then we walked out the same doors we'd entered.

"That was...easy," I muttered as we walked toward the border.

"Yeah, that's the cruisiest immigration I've ever been through. I could have walked through with bricks of opium and no one would know," Xander replied. "And...it's still there."

"What?"

My eyes followed Xander's finger, pointing to the bag of weed he had ditched earlier.

Xander raised an eyebrow. "Should I...?"

I shrugged. "Your call. I'm not getting involved."

With a quick glance around, he scooped it back up and tucked it into his pack with the glee of a kid retrieving a lost toy.

"Piece of cake," he said, sauntering back over to me with a mischievous smile.

We continued walking, the weight of the heat pressing down on us. The sounds of honking horns, shouting vendors, and the distant hum of machinery filled the air as we stepped into the steamy, hot, and chaotic beast known as India.

15
STRENGTH IN STRANGERS

INDIA

*O*ur journey commenced in Varanasi, an ancient and revered city situated on the Ganges river in northern India. Over centuries, the river evolved into a spiritual nucleus where Hindus converge to embark on pilgrimages, partake in solemn mourning, and immerse themselves in intricate death ceremonies.

In Hindu culture, cremation is the preferred method of handling the deceased. Hindus believe that cremation releases the soul from the body and facilitates its journey to the afterlife.

Many Hindus believe that if a deceased person's ashes are laid to rest in the Ganges river in Varanasi, their soul will be transported to an enlightened state and escape the cycle of reincarnation. This belief makes Varanasi one of the most holy and sought-after cremation sites in India. People from all over the country come to pray, collect sacred water, bathe in the Ganges, and die.

Immersing ourselves in the vibrant chaos, Xander and I passed a haggard old man sitting in front of a brick wall covered in dark stains. He wore no shirt or shoes, and his pants appeared to have been half-eaten by vermin. His skin was a sickly gray, his eyes yellowed and clouded, signifying liver problems that no amount of begging could fix. He held out a tin soup can, brushing my knee with it. Xander dropped in a rupee, which clanked at the bottom with two others.

"He hasn't had much success today," Xander said with a frown. "It's crazy how many beggars there are in India."

"Yeah," I said, watching the man raise his eyes, a flicker of desperation behind them. "Seems like we're constantly passing pleas for money." My gaze drifted to the scene ahead of us, where the Ganges flowed sluggishly. "I guess an unfortunate reality of Varanasi is the hordes of boarding homes filled with old people."

"They all come here to die, but then they can't even afford it." Xander's shoulders slumped. "But how expensive can it be to burn a body?"

"Apparently, the wood used to make a pyre is expensive," I answered, my eyes fixed on the river.

We reached a bridge, and from there, we both stared down at the river's murky depths. My stomach twisted as I saw the bloated remains of a body drifting downstream. Half-burnt, the charred remnants clung to the water's surface like forgotten refuse.

"That explains the partially decomposed bodies floating downstream." Xander's eyes followed the body as it writhed in the current. "People can't afford a full cremation."

My eyes sunk to the floor. "That's so fucked up."

Xander nodded, swallowing hard. We watched for a moment longer. The body passed, taking with it a strange, disturbing silence. Then, the noise of life returned: children splashing in the water, people laughing and talking as they scrubbed their dishes, their hands submerged in the same river that carried the dead.

"They bathe in it," I said, my voice low, almost to myself. "Wash their clothes and dishes…. They even drink the water."

Xander shuddered. "We'd literally die."

Silence fell between us.

"Come on." Xander tugged gently at my sleeve, pulling me away. "Let's keep walking."

As we continued down the street, ancient temples with towering spires and finely detailed stone façades stood next to eroding old buildings with ornate balconies and latticed windows. Each structure showcased the craftsmanship and artistry of a bygone era, contrasting sharply with bustling markets and neon-lit shops where vendors hawked modern items like cellphones and data packages. Stalls overflowed with everything from colorful spices and exotic fruits to cheap electronics and imitation designer jewelry.

Lost in the maze of eleventh-century buildings, we stumbled upon lively shops beckoning us with exquisite carpets, silk weavings, and handmade crafts. Each shop was a treasure trove, a gateway to a world where craftsmanship and creativity danced hand-in-hand.

A man stood in the doorway of a sari shop, waving us in with exaggerated enthusiasm. "Come, come! Just look, no need to buy!"

A cascade of colors flooded the tiny space—magenta, peacock blue, shimmering gold. "This color, sir, perfect for your wife!" the man declared, gesturing toward me.

"We're not married," I said, but the man ignored me entirely.

"Very good price! You are my first customer. Always lucky! Special price for you, because you have such kind face."

Before we could respond, a teenage girl appeared at my elbow, her phone already outstretched. "Photo?" she asked shyly, eyes darting between me and her friends giggling behind her.

We posed, while the shopkeeper seized the opportunity to drape a crimson scarf across my shoulders.

"You look like Bollywood queen!" he declared.

"Oh sir, thank you. But I'm just looking for now. Maybe we will come back later!"

As we stepped outside of the shop, a boy no older than ten darted in front of us holding a tray of steaming clay cups.

"Chai for you! Best chai in all Varanasi!" he proclaimed with a pride that made it impossible to refuse.

We each took a cup, the warm, spicy liquid burning our fingers through the thin clay. The boy beamed as Xander handed him a few coins.

Calls of vendors mingled with the honking of auto-rickshaws—noisy, three-wheeled motor taxis commonly used across India. The smell of incense and marigolds from nearby shrines mixed with the scent of frying spices and sweet jalebis—a popular Indian dessert made of deep-fried batter soaked in sugar syrup. It all blended into sensory overload.

We passed a man selling live chickens next to another vendor offering glittering bangles. A snake charmer sat cross-legged on the ground, playing his flute to a cobra swaying in a wicker basket. A holy man wearing a loincloth blessed those who passed by in exchange for a few rupees.

Children ran through the crowd, laughing and chasing each other. An old woman squatted by a heap of fresh vegetables, carefully selecting the best ones for her evening meal. Next to her, a young man expertly folded freshly printed newspapers. He barely looked down as he snapped each sheet into place. His fingers worked from muscle memory as each finished bundle landed in a neat pile by his knee.

We paused at a stall, drawn to a vendor with a pot of molten sugar. His hands pulled and twisted the hot, amber threads into impossibly intricate shapes that looked like delicate glass sculptures.

"Good price, ma'am!" he said with a grin, holding up a sugar swan with a slender, curved neck.

Just a few steps away, a henna artist sat cross-legged on a woven mat. His head bowed in concentration as his fingers danced over a woman's hand. He dipped his twig into a dark brown paste between tracing floral patterns that bloomed across her skin, spreading like wildflowers reaching for sunlight. She sat perfectly still, her eyes fixed on the unfolding design.

As we moved out of the market area and deeper into the chaotic streets, we encountered Babas, holy men dressed in orange robes. People in India follow Babas for a variety of reasons, including spiritual guidance, seeking solutions to personal or societal issues, and the belief that the Baba possesses special powers or knowledge. The Babas we came across exuded an aura of mysticism. Their stoic demeanor and serene expressions stood out against the bustle of the city.

One Baba in particular caught our attention. He perched on a faded cushion, legs folded beneath him. Orange robes stood out against his tan skin lined with dirt from living on the streets. Mangy dreadlocks hung down his back, thick and matted—a deliberate choice, as the uncut and uncombed hair symbolized his renunciation of worldly vanity and devotion to spiritual enlightenment. His body was smothered in ash, a traditional practice symbolizing renunciation and purity. The fine powder clung to his skin, forming a ghostly mask that made his glassy eyes stand out. Beside him, a chillum packed with marijuana sat ready. For some babas, smoking weed was more than indulgence—it was a ritual, a way to connect with Shiva, the lord of destruction and transformation. Many believed this practice could help them transcend the physical world in pursuit of higher consciousness.

The Baba's clouded and distant eyes hinted at a life spent in a hazy reverie. His gaze drifted, lost in a realm only he could see. His lips moved constantly, mumbling chants and hymns to himself, the sound blending into the cacophony of the surrounding street. A small, chipped cup lay beside him, a simple vessel for alms from those who passed by. Despite his revered status, he didn't look so holy to me, appearing more like a figure worn down by the harshness of his chosen path.

As we stood there, a passerby dropped a few coins into the cup, the metallic clink breaking the Baba's trance for a moment. He glanced up, offered a half-smile, and blessed the donor with a soft murmur before resuming his chants. The poignant scene captured the intersection of faith and survival.

We continued our journey, the image of the Baba lingering in my mind. The streets of Varanasi were a theater of life; every corner revealed a new story.

The aroma of sizzling street food filled the air as we wandered through another market, a heady mix of earthy cumin and the sharp tang of tamarind chutney. We stopped in front of a roadside stall shaded by a blue tarp where a man with a white turban and potbelly served plates of fragrant biryani from wooden boxes. The rich smell of cardamom wafted up as he scooped steaming rice onto a banana leaf.

"That looks delicious," I said, my mouth watering at the sight of the golden rice studded with pieces of tender mutton and vegetables.

Xander glanced over, raising an eyebrow. "I'm more of a lamb korma kind of guy," he admitted, though his eyes betrayed a flicker of interest.

"Just try it," I urged, nudging him playfully. "You must be hungry. We've been walking for hours."

The Indian purveyor caught our exchange. "You will love my biryani. I have a secret ingredient that no one else uses!"

"What is it?" Xander asked.

The vendor chuckled, shaking his head. "I cannot say, but you will like it, I tell you."

I handed over a few rupees, and the vendor scooped generous portions of biryani onto two plates. The first bite was a revelation. The rice was perfectly cooked, each grain infused with spices. A hint of sweetness mingled with the savory notes, something floral and magical.

"Oh wow," I murmured. "This is incredible."

As we ate, the sounds of the market buzzed around us—voices of locals bargaining, and the occasional ring of bicycle bells weaving through the crowd.

"This place is something else," Xander said, looking around with a mixture of awe and amusement.

"Yeah, it's overwhelming, but in the best way."

We finished our plates, handing them back to the vendor. "Thank you," I said. "That was truly special."

The vendor bowed slightly, his smile widening. "Come back anytime. There is always more to discover in Varanasi."

Xander and I continued our exploration of the ancient city, our footsteps accompanied by the soft rustle of temple flags and the occasional thud of monkey paws landing on corrugated tin roofs. Rhesus macaques—ubiquitous in Varanasi—leapt gracefully between rooftops and electric wires like trapeze artists in a dusty circus. Their pink, expressive faces peeked from temple columns, eyes gleaming with mischief.

One darted toward a fruit vendor, tore a mango from the pyramid-shaped pile, then scurried up a lamppost, triumphant. Juice dribbled from its chin as it gnawed through the flesh with satisfaction, ignoring the curses hurled up at it.

Another, an older-looking macaque with scruffy white fur and a missing toe, planted itself atop a mountain of refuse, looking every bit the ruler of disarray. It rummaged through plastic bags with impatient flicks of its long fingers, flinging peels and foil packets over its shoulder. It paused only to glare at a passing dog, baring yellowed teeth in a silent warning.

Sacred cows meandered freely through the streets. I gently patted one on its rough, warm flank, marveling at its serene indifference. Around it, metal pots clattered from a nearby chai stand, the calls of street vendors singing out their daily specials and the occasional squawk of a chicken darting between scooter wheels. The cow's massive, unblinking eyes gazed past me, flicking its ears as a fly buzzed near its face.

As we continued to wander, the distant crackle of fire reached my ears. On my left, a man lay sprawled across a bed of nails, his chest rising and falling as if he were reclining on silk. His assistant, barefoot and sweat-slicked, stoked a row of glowing embers with a long iron rod, sending sparks into the air. A crowd around them murmured, anticipation rising like the heat from the coals.

Without a word, the performer rose from his bed of nails, his face a mask of concentration. With slow, deliberate steps, he strode across the burning coals, his feet leaving only the faintest wisps of smoke in their wake. I caught a glimpse of his calloused soles—cracked and blackened, worn from years of practice. Each of his steps was an act of defiance against the physical world.

A chill ran through me—something both awe-inspiring and unsettling about the human capacity to endure such pain. I marveled at the mind's ability to push the body beyond its limits. There was so much more strength in us than I'd ever thought possible. The human spirit, when sharpened by belief, could conquer just about anything.

Amidst the beauty and wonder of Varanasi, we also encountered the harsh realities of daily life. The pungent scent of urine mingled with the sweet aroma of incense, while the smoke from funeral pyres settled like a hazy shroud over the riverbank. I held my breath as we navigated narrow alleys, the overpowering stench of rotting garbage and sewage wafted in the humid air.

Varanasi was a city of contrasts, presenting itself in raw, unfiltered layers. As we ducked beneath strings of laundry flapping between weathered rooftops, a sudden rustling caught my attention.

Before I could react, a rat as big as a forearm launched from a barrel we passed, landing inches from my feet. Its slick body disappeared between piles of refuse. Xander let out a startled laugh, as I stumbled back.

Above us, electrical wires hung precariously at every conceivable angle, a tangled mess that resembled an unkempt bird's nest. The cables swung dangerously low, sparking occasionally. It seemed a miracle they didn't ignite the ramshackle buildings that lined the streets. These structures, with their crumbling exteriors and peeling paint, looked as though they might collapse at any moment. Their windows, often just empty holes, stared vacantly like the eyes of forgotten souls.

I was careful to avoid stepping into murky puddles that dotted the street. Children played barefoot in the muck as though immune to the filth, their joy untainted by the decay that surrounded them. Stray dogs with matted fur and visible ribs roamed the streets, their eyes reflecting a mix of hunger and resignation as they scavenged for scraps.

Yes, the streets were filthy and overcrowded, but what was lacking in hygiene was made up for in character.

In one poignant moment, we stood by the river at dusk. The steps leading down to the river, known as ghats, were illuminated by hundreds of flickering candles set afloat by devotees. The soft glow of the earthen lamps—small clay vessels filled with oil and a cotton wick —shimmered across the water, their reflections rippling and shifting with the current. The chants of priests and the occasional splash of water from a ritualistic dip in the Ganges wove together into a melody uniquely Varanasi, a city where life and death coexisted in an eternal embrace.

A procession appeared at the edge of the ghat, emerging from the narrow lanes above. Solemn-faced men carried a bamboo stretcher with a body resting atop it. The body had already been washed, the skin glistening with the last droplets of water from the sacred river. Bright floral garlands lay across the chest—a parting gift.

In the face of this somber spectacle, Xander and I stood transfixed, the clangs of bells vibrating inside our chests. The procession moved with a reverent purpose. The mourners' voices rose in soft, melodic chants as they descended the steps. At the water's edge, the family paused, gently lowering the stretcher to the ground. A final touch to the forehead, a whispered prayer, a moment of stillness—and then they began to build the pyre. Wood was stacked carefully, the body placed tenderly atop it, before the flames were kindled.

The flames quickly grew into a furnace-like heat radiating into the air. It made me take a step back. Sobs came from a hunched old woman standing too close to the flames. I wanted to reach out and pull her back from the orange embers.

Xander whispered in my ear, "Not how I want to go."

For a moment, I considered the idea of my own body being consumed by fire. Maybe I wouldn't mind, I thought. Why not return to the earth, like everything else? Let the flames take what's left behind and transform it into something new. It seemed almost fitting, in a strange, unsettling way.

Chants continued, mingling with the crackle of wood and the soft lapping of the river against the steps. The flames consumed flesh and most of the bone, but not all of it—some dense pieces would remain: a fragment of pelvis, a shard of spine. They would be sifted out later, gathered alongside the ash and scattered into the Ganges.

There was no curtain between life and death, no polite separation. The sacred and the ordinary flowed together, just as the living and the dead shared the same steps, the same river, the same breath of smoky air.

Remarkably, as days wore on, the extraordinary became ordinary, and our awe faded. The frequency of these solemn processions of bodies carried through the streets became commonplace.

Pondering about death was not the focus of our visit to Varanasi, though. Diwali was.

"Can you believe it's finally here?" I said, my voice full of excitement. "Diwali in Varanasi! I'm so stoked we managed to get here for this."

Diwali, also referred to as Deepavali, is one of the major celebrations for Hindus, Jains, and Sikhs. It is recognized as the festival of lights, and during this five-day event, Varanasi becomes a radiant spectacle. The Ganges ghats shimmer under the glow of more than a million earthen lamps. This arrangement of lights not only serves as a visual delight, but carries symbolism of the triumph of light over darkness, good over evil, and knowledge over ignorance. According to mythological tales, it is believed on this auspicious holiday, the gods themselves descended to Earth, drawn by the sacred waters of the Ganges, to partake in a divine bathing ritual, infusing the atmosphere with a transcendent aura of spiritual significance.

"I know!" Xander responded. "We get to be in one of India's holiest cities during one of the holiest festivals of the year."

"The atmosphere is insane, hey? Very festive."

Xander broke into an impromptu Bollywood-style dance, moving his hands fluidly and swaying his hips with exaggerated flair. "The concerts will be the best, I think," he said, still dancing. "I've seen them setting up loads of different stages. Bands and musicians are getting geared up, too."

I laughed, clapping along to his performance. "You've got the moves, Xander! You're ready for Bollywood."

He struck a final pose, grinning. "Just getting into the spirit of things. Tonight's going to be unforgettable."

I smiled, feeling a deep sense of connection to the city and to Xander. "I'm really glad we're here together for this."

After a quiet dinner at our hotel, I threw on my ankle-length skirt and long-sleeved top. In this culture, modesty wasn't just a matter of respect, but a layer of protection. Revealing clothes could attract unwanted attention or even unwelcome advances. Dressing conservatively was my way of trying to blend in.

"OK. Ready to go!" I hollered. And we set off into the crowds.

India is a country of over 1.3 billion people, and it felt as though there were millions of them in Varanasi that night. A surge of collective joy pulsed through the dense gathering. A tangible excitement enveloped me as thousands gallivanted through the streets, sending prayers to the heavens. Large stages with story-high sound systems sent vibrations of music and bells reverberating out to the streets.

Xander and I hooked arms as we pushed our way through the dense crowds. With each step, the crowd grew more tightly packed. I squeezed my insides in an effort to shrink enough to casually slip past bodies colliding with mine.

A hand palmed my backside, but I ignored it. Maybe it was a mistake in the closely packed crowd? Then another hand grabbed my ass. We continued to push through the crowd. An unfortunate truth of this world is that we women have become so used to sexual harassment that we have developed a sickeningly uncanny way to ignore it and go about our business.

Then another hand on my butt.

A hand now grabbed for my breast.

By this point, I was forced to accept that none of these uninvited touches and grabs were mistakes. For a brief moment, I attempted to characterize them as minor annoyances. I swatted the hands away as best I could as we continued to maneuver through the thickening crowd.

Until it became unbearable.

Dozens of hands ferociously grabbed my body in such rapid succession that it was impossible to shoo them away. The moment I grabbed one hand off my breast, there were immediately six more. I wrenched hand after hand from my ass only to find four more.

On each side.

Xander realized the assault taking place and joined in my desperate attempts to remove the hungry hands grasping every inch of me.

The long sleeves of my shirt were ripped off. Within seconds, the rest tore away too, leaving me clutching what little fabric remained to cover myself. To my horror, my arm became unraveled from Xander's. I was snatched and yanked backwards and away from him, engulfed into a crowd of hungry, sexualizing monsters. Xander was dragged and pulled in the opposite direction.

I had heard about these moments in the news.

And now it was happening to me.

It was my turn to be raped in India.

By a crowd of people in a public gathering.

Within minutes, the pleasant men in ironed, buttoned-up shirts I had walked past had quickly turned into a monstrous creature with many hands. How could a crowd of seemingly normal individuals turn to such heavy abuse?

The thick press of bodies closed in, tearing at me like I was nothing more than an object to be claimed. Fingers dug into my skin —my ass, my breasts—rough, insistent, faceless in the chaos. My heart thudded wildly, each frantic beat a hammer pounding against my ribs.

Just moments ago, Varanasi had been a dream—the holy city, a place of devotion, of rituals older than time itself. Now, the city had turned on me, swallowing me whole.

I screamed Xander's name, but the crowd devoured my voice. I shoved, twisted, fought against the hands pulling me deeper, but there were too many. A terror I had never known wrapped around my throat.

And then a miracle.

A local teenage boy emerged from the crowd. He threw clenched fists, aggressively screaming and hauling bodies off me.

"Get away from her!" his voice echoed with a primal intensity as he flung bodies aside. "Leave her alone!"

The heroic actions of the young boy snapped the pack of men out of their lustful trance. One by one, they retreated from my vulnerable body.

Emancipated from the clutches of my aggressors, the boy wrapped a secure arm around me, offering both physical and emotional support. He not only held up the ragged remnants of my shirt but also shouldered the weight of my shattered spirit.

Together, we forged a path through the teeming crowd, ascending the stairs of the ghat. Each step brought us closer to a secluded corner where the chaos was muted, leaving only the two of us gazing down at the mass of humanity below.

I stood in a hollow state of terrified shock.

Feeling as exposed as a raw wound, I awkwardly held up the frayed remnants of my shirt to cover my chest. I felt more naked than I was.

The boy burst into tears.

"I am so ashamed of my people. I am so sorry you had to experience this. You have traveled across the world to come and visit my country, and this is how we treat you!" The tears continued to flow. "I'm disgusted by how they treated you."

I placed a shaky hand on his shoulder, still reeling, trying to piece together what had just happened to me. "Hey, it's...it's not your fault."

"But my people—my country—this is how we treat you," he gasped. "I am so sorry. It makes me sick inside."

I appreciated his heartfelt apology. I admired this young man, an absolute hero in my eyes. A human brave enough to push back when everyone else followed blindly, to literally fight for what was right. But the world was spinning. I hadn't fully come back to myself. "That wasn't you... You didn't do that. You stopped it."

It felt strange, this sudden reversal, where I was the one trying to comfort him, when I could barely hold myself together. "Because of you, I was saved. That's what matters."

His chest heaved as an apology spilled from his lips again. I could feel my heart breaking for him, but it was still heavy with my own trauma. I didn't know how to help him. I could barely process my own emotions.

I rubbed my face with my hands, trying to get a grip. "Thank you," I whispered, barely hearing my own voice. "Thank you for saving me."

For a moment, we just stood there, both of us broken in our own ways. I saw the flicker of something in his eyes—maybe relief, maybe guilt, maybe a mix of both. "May I walk you home safely, please? Help you find your friend? I know the back roads we can take."

The only route I knew back to my hotel was through the same crowds where I almost lost my body and soul moments ago. I couldn't fathom facing that once more. And so, attempting to gather my dignity like a tattered shawl, I followed him away from the ghats and back into the winding maze of Varanasi. Neither of us spoke as we hurried through the narrow streets, my legs trembling beneath me. When we reached the hotel, he stopped just short of the entrance, scanning the road behind us, making sure we hadn't been followed.

I turned to him, my voice unsteady. "Thank you. I don't...I don't even know your name."

"Vikram." His eyes lingered on me. "I wish I could say it was nice to meet you tonight...I wish I could undo this." Then, without another word, he melted into the night.

As I stepped into the hotel lobby, I spotted Xander pacing back and forth, his face pale. When he saw me, his eyes widened with relief, and he rushed over.

"Thank God, you're OK!" Xander wrapped me in a deep embrace, his heart pounding against my chest.

"I was so scared," I admitted. "If it weren't for that boy..."

Xander pulled back slightly, his hands resting on my shoulders as he looked me over. "I tried to stay with you, but the crowd was insane. They pushed and pulled until I lost sight of you. I searched everywhere, but it was impossible to move against the tide of people."

He ran a hand through his hair, frustration etched on his face. "I went to the police station, hoping they could help. But they were indifferent, said they'd write a report and sent me on my way. I felt so helpless."

Xander did not need to explain to me what it felt like to be helpless in a moment.

Tears welled in my eyes, but I blinked them away. Xander pulled me into another tight hug, his voice choked with emotion. "I didn't know what to do. I just kept hoping I'd find you here."

Time seemed to pause as we held on to one another, letting the silence say what words couldn't. Finally, I pulled back, offering him a tired smile.

My body still ached from the struggle. My mind still swam in the anxiety of what had happened. But beneath the terror, something else stirred—gratitude. Gratitude for Vikram, who had appeared out of nowhere to save me. Gratitude that, even in a world capable of such darkness, there were people like him.

"I won't let this be the only thing I remember about Varanasi," I said softly. "There's still beauty here. There are still good people."

Xander searched my face, then nodded, exhaling heavily. "Yeah. Yeah, there are."

Outside, the city pulsed on—bells ringing, voices rising, the Ganges reflecting the glow of endless flickering flames. Life doesn't stop for tragedy. It never does. It just keeps moving, sweeping you along with it, for better or worse. And maybe that was the lesson. You take the beauty. You take the horror. You survive. And you keep going.

16

THE RIFT

*M*y mother and father lived separate lives under the same roof. Taking on the traditional breadwinner role, my father put on his suit and left for work every day, where he managed a furniture sales company. After some successful years managing her own business, my mom, the mother bear, focused all her attention on raising my sister and me. She was involved with every aspect of our lives: carpooling to school, carting us off to gymnastics and Taekwondo classes, packing lunches, cleaning house, doing the shopping, managing our homework, coordinating social visits with friends, attending field-trips, and volunteering for yard duty at school.

My dad rarely took part in challenging parenting tasks such as disciplining, assisting in the rigmarole of school, or contributing to those hard conversations that every parent of a teenager is forced to face—but he had his own way of showing love. He was the one who filled our lives with extravagant family trips, spontaneous dinners out, and tasty barbecues hanging by the pool on the weekend. Even if he avoided the hard parts, I never doubted that he adored me.

My saint of a mother, wanting her daughters to be blessed with a male role model in their lives, tried her best to avoid any "daddy issues" for her two little girls. She hid a lot of my father's dark truths and personality flaws from us. I never knew about the cheating, DUIs, or hundreds of thousands of dollars of debt. I never knew how the man opted to take a holiday in France while my mother battled alone with breast cancer, while simultaneously trying to take care of two small children. No, I only knew "the fun dad."

My father enjoyed rafting trips down the Fulafoo in Chile, smoking weed in our hot tub, renting cars to drive through the Irish countryside, and sipping beers while listening to live music. My mother enjoyed documentaries, plain Western dinners out with friends, and playing cards with family. I imagine they once had something in common, but those days were behind them.

With the naïve view I had of my father, I could not for the life of me understand how someone so carefree and adventurous could be with someone so uptight and on edge as my mother. The poor woman became the brunt of all our teen angst as she was the one to single-handedly face the harsh moments of raising two experimental and moody teenage daughters.

During our teenage years, my sister and I remained in a chaotic dance of curiosity and rebellion. We dabbled with alcohol, sneaking sips from bottles hidden behind kitchen cabinets and pretending not to flinch at the burn. And boys—oh, the lure of something forbidden and thrilling, where we tiptoed the line between innocent flirtation and something that could have led us down a road we barely understood.

My mother was the one who caught us every time, whether red-handed or red-eyed. She'd confront us alone, with the frustration of a thousand battles fought over barely there skirts, curfews gone awry, and eye rolls. My father always escaped the fallout. And so, my mother became the lightning rod for all our frustrations and endless demands to be left alone. Her voice trailed after us with warnings. "I just worry where all this so-called harmless experimenting is going to lead!"

The differences and resentments between my mother and father hung heavy in our household. Intense discussions between them didn't erupt, they sank in.

From the hallway, I heard their voices rising and falling.

"I can't keep doing this alone, Michael," my mom pleaded, her voice shaking. "Just once, I'd like you to help me discipline them, instead of shrugging it off."

"Discipline?" my dad scoffed, a dry, bitter laugh. "They're just being kids, Bobbie! Not everything has to be some grand crisis."

I could picture my mother, clutching her arms to her chest, her eyebrows knitted in frustration, eyes pleading as they searched his. "It's like you don't even care!"

"Those kids are my everything! You're just being uptight. I don't have it in me to play bad cop after a long day at work. Do *your* job!"

"*My job?* It's *our* job, Michael."

"Damn it, Bobbie!" My father's tone made me flinch. "We have roles. I bring in the money, I keep this roof over our heads—that should be enough. This conversation is finished."

"Fine," my mother whispered, barely more than a breath. "I'll take care of it, *like I always do.*"

She turned and walked out of the room, her footsteps soft yet weighted with a sadness that echoed louder than any words. Wounds left open, scars forming in the silences that stretched too long and the words that never came.

Crouched behind the armoire in the hallway, I held my breath as a lump rose in my throat. As a teenager, I usually sided with my dad. I was a daddy's girl, drawn to the adventures he shared with us. He brought a sense of freedom and fun that I craved, especially compared to my mom's strict rules and constant worrying. Back then, I almost felt sorry for him, like she was picking on him for simply wanting to enjoy life.

It took me years to understand that she wasn't nagging—she was carrying the weight of a marriage without a true partner. Yes, he got up every day and worked hard to give us an incredible life in an over-priced corner of California. But providing financially wasn't the same as showing up for her.

The differences between my parents filled every corner of the house, like dust that refused to settle. They lived together, danced through the motions of a suburban married life, but only in an uneasy truce, held together by a thin, fraying thread of obligation.

I often found myself wondering why my parents bothered to stay together. I engaged in many conversations with each of them, almost soliciting them to divorce. I assumed they'd be happier without each other, and I thought I would be too. But, as the years carried on, my parents remained together through to my adulthood, their relationship increasingly marked by unspoken grievances and a widening emotional divide.

Over the years, my father's sanity and ability to function began to slip. One evening, he forgot to turn off the stove, causing a small fire in our kitchen. He proved himself unable to do his own laundry, shop, cook, or clean up after himself. He voraciously overspent beyond his means, racking up over $200,000 of debt. He re-mortgaged our house twice, without informing my mother of this detrimental loss to their retirement plan.

At sixty, which is far too late in the game for a career change, my father realized he hated his job. Since the majority of a man's waking existence consists of working hours, the fact that my father hated his job with a passion, in effect, meant that he hated his life. I suppose this explains why his habits of drinking and smoking increased. Substance abuse is an excellent means of avoiding reality.

After thirty-six years of marriage, my parents' lives and finances were so intertwined with one another that it seemed near impossible to unravel that intricate web. Since the two had perfected their act of living under the same roof and remained married by societal standards, what would be the point of going through the hassles of a divorce now? But one Thursday in November, my mother finally had enough.

My father showed up late to a Thanksgiving dinner with my mother's conservative right-wing family, wasted and slurring his words. He had driven over two hours to get there with coffee mugs full of wine by his side. It was at this point that my mother realized my father's continuous poor decisions were putting her life and future at risk. What if my father had gotten in a drunk-driving accident, murdering someone on his way to that Thanksgiving meal? They both would have lost everything. And so, my mother finally divorced my father. I found out in December 2014, through an email she sent while I was in the middle of my trip, backpacking around India.

Given all I knew about my parents' relationship, it wasn't a shock to learn of their divorce. The surprising part was my father's impulsive decision to retire in Thailand in three weeks.

As I sat on a lumpy, stained mattress in my cheap backpacker accommodation in India, my mother's face filled my laptop screen. Her face was pixelated, but unmistakably weary. Her shoulders slumped forward, eyes downcast as if the weight of the world sat squarely on her chest. "Shannon, I don't know who else to ask. Your father...you know he can't do this alone. He has no clue what he's doing, and honestly, he won't even admit it."

I shifted uncomfortably, propping my chin in my hand as I slumped back on a pillow. "Mom, I have plans. I'm supposed to be in Sri Lanka next week. I've been looking forward to it for months."

"I know, sweetheart, I know." She looked away from the screen, her mouth tightening as if the words she was about to say pained her. "But...he's your father."

"I know." Something in me yielded. "He's the one who taught me to drive, took me to plays in San Francisco, camping in Lake Tahoe, and on hikes in the forest behind our house. He showed me the world was big and worth seeing. I love him, Mom. But that's why I don't want to watch him throw himself into something he's not ready for."

She shook her head. "But I think this could be so good for him, Shannon. Imagine—golf every day, swimming in the ocean, being part of a big expat community where he can make friends and socialize. Thailand could be exactly what he needs."

"I don't think this is a good idea, Mom. He's not functioning well. There's something wrong with him. And carting him off to Thailand? He's never even been to Asia!"

"Thailand is perfect for him. Warm weather year round, affordable cost of living, good healthcare, a retirement visa he can actually get. You know he doesn't have much left financially after..." She trailed off, her eyes shifting as she grappled with the reality of his dwindling funds. "After his poor financial decisions."

"Yeah, Mom, I know. He's full of bad decisions these days. He's such an easy target for someone to take advantage of him," I said, biting back. "Thailand can be a haven for expats, but a lot of them get into bad situations. The place is a hotbed of drunken debauchery and prostitution. So many retired expats flock there with stories of substance abuse or escaping issues back home. Sound familiar?"

My mother's eyes stayed rooted down.

"Mom, you do everything for him. He will be absolutely lost without you! He'll be such an easy target for someone to take advantage of."

"Who's going to take advantage of him, Shannon? Jeez, I thought I was the dramatic one."

"Mom, there are countless stories of men just like him getting entangled with some evil Thai woman." My voice was sharp. "Some of these women prey on men like Dad. They skillfully pick these vulnerable men out of the crowds and become a beautiful armpiece for them."

My mom opened her mouth to speak but stopped herself.

"Foolish idiots just like Dad are thrilled that a younger, attractive woman wants to be with them," I pressed on. "And then...poof! Blinded by sex and the desire for companionship, these guys suddenly find themselves ensnared in cliché abusive relationships with a woman who takes every penny they have."

My mother's expression shifted, guilt and helplessness in her eyes. "Shannon...you know your father would never get into a scene like that."

"I don't want to be a part of this plan, Mom." Heat rose in my belly. "I think it's a bad idea."

"Please don't make this harder than it is," she continued. "He's decided. You know how stubborn he is. This is happening. He's lost right now, and he needs you. He is your father."

I looked down, jaw clenched. Her words filled me with a sense of reluctant obligation. With a defeated sigh, I looked back up, meeting her eyes through the screen. "Fine. I'll do it. Just let me know what date I need to buy a ticket to meet him in Bangkok."

Relief softened her features. Her eyes glistened as she exhaled deeply. "Thank you, Shannon! I know this isn't fair, but...you're such an amazing daughter. You're doing the right thing."

As I ended the call and the screen faded to black, a hollow unease settled in my chest. I told myself my mom was right, that I was doing what needed to be done—helping my father, stepping up when he needed me. But something felt off. I couldn't shake the strong sense that my father's impulsive decision would lead to disaster. I felt as though I was walking straight into a storm.

17

CAUGHT IN THE CURRENT

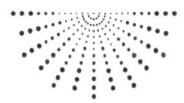

THAILAND

*T*he arrivals terminal buzzed with noise—families reuniting in tearful embraces, backpackers reeking of sweat, tour groups shuffling behind guides holding up laminated signs. I spotted him near the baggage carousel.

"You came all the way to Thailand with...this?" I gestured to the duffel bag and golf clubs at my father's feet. "A couple of shorts and T-shirts with zero information about what you want to do with your life? Dad, seriously? Did you even buy travel insurance?"

My dad shrugged, looking down sheepishly, scratching his head. "I forgot. Maybe you can help me buy some now? Things happened quickly, you know. I figured I'd just...figure it out when I got here... that you could help me."

"Unbelievable." I folded my arms across my chest. "Any idea where you want to live? Do you know anything about retirement visas? Banking?"

He fiddled with the hem of his T-shirt.

I sighed, rubbing my temples. "Got it."

This was the moment our parental roles reversed.

First, I needed to decide where he would settle down. Since my dad was a beach lover like me, I chose Hua Hin, a seaside resort town two hours south of Bangkok. We hopped on a bus to start his new life.

I didn't realize that Hua Hin had been a fashionable escape for Bangkok residents since the 1920s, when the Thai royal family built summer palaces there. I was on a strict backpacker budget, on a long-winded travel affair with no end in sight, and it was a struggle to find affordable accommodation as we (I) figured out the next step. After hours of trolling up and down the streets, I found a modest, barebones room, complete with screens barely clinging to the window frames, threatening to fall at the slightest breeze. The guesthouse was aptly named Dam Wrong Hotel. If that hotel name wasn't an omen, I don't know what was.

A few days later, my older sister, Tara, flew in to help. She'd taken a week off from her busy work schedule to tag in for the messy emotional unknowns I'd been wading through alone. We were close, even if we lived different lives: she, the responsible one, with a husband, a career, and matching luggage; me, the barefoot vagabond with a hole in my backpack.

Still, there was no one I'd rather be navigating this with.

Our hotel room smelled stale. Afternoon light slanted through the gauzy curtains, casting soft stripes across the carpet and the edge of the unmade beds. Our suitcases lay gaping open, contents strewn like a crime scene of indecision.

My dad sat on the edge of a floral-print armchair, shoulders hunched forward, eyes rooted to the floor. "Thank you for being here, girls."

"I know it's scary being single for the first time in thirty-six years," Tara said, wrapping an arm around his shoulder and giving it a tight squeeze. "But we're going to help you get settled into your new life, Dad."

I crossed to the window and pulled the curtain back to glimpse the glimmer of turquoise between palm trees. "Let's head to the beach today, relax our jet lag away. We'll hit the ground running with logistics tomorrow."

The fierce sun made the sand beneath our feet scorching hot.

Humid mist clung to our sweaty skin like a second layer. The smell of sunblock drifted from tourists lazing on towels, their bronzed bodies glistening. Some stretched out, letting the sun bake their skin, while others sat at beachside cafes, the cold condensation of beers dripping onto the plastic tables. The scent of grilled seafood and fried snacks wafted by, mixing with the salty ocean air. In the background, the swish of waves, the low hum of chatter, and the occasional burst of laughter carried by the wind.

"I'm going to have a swim," Tara exclaimed. "The water looks far too inviting to ignore!"

"Go enjoy with Dad. I'm going to chill out and read for a bit," I responded. "And Tara, thank you so much for taking time off work to help. I was freaking out that I'd have to do all this by myself."

"I'm sorry it's just for a week," she replied with a wink. Grabbing my dad's arm, she tugged him towards the water.

After reading a chapter in *The Power of Now*, I glanced up. Where were Dad and Tara? The bright blue sea extended to the horizon unbroken by any figures.

I shot to my feet and rushed to the edge of the waterfront. The bath-warm water lapped around my ankles, as a flicker of motion to the left caught my eye. I pivoted, and everything inside me clenched.

My father's body flopped like a rag doll, limp and uncontrolled. Ferocious white-wash threw him against razor-sharp rocks jutting out of the sea. He disappeared beneath the crashing waves. Seconds later, he exploded back to the surface, gulping in desperate breaths, only to be dragged down once more.

My sister was forty feet offshore, perched on top of a rock, clutching her knee, which spurted blood with the force of a fire hydrant. Her agonized screams echoed across the water. Tears streamed down her face.

My legs moved before my mind. Tara was closer, bleeding, vulnerable—and I had to get to her. Fear slammed through me, but beneath it was something fiercer: survival mode kicking in.

I waded out and pulled her into my arms, hauling her back to shore. Her body was limp as I laid her down gently. Cuts marred her pale skin, blood staining the length of her slender legs.

"Shan...the current..." she stammered. "It dragged me down the beach. It kept pulling me under...I couldn't breathe."

"You're safe now." My voice sounded too calm, like it belonged to someone else. "We need to make a tourniquet for your knee, though. You're losing a lot of blood."

"OK. Yes, thank you." She winced as I tightened my beach towel around her knee. Her hands gripped the sand like the ground might slip away beneath her.

"Wait, where's Dad?" Her wild eyes darted around as if searching. "Is he...is he OK?"

I shot a quick look at the water. "I'm going to get him."

Her pale hand grabbed my arm, eyes pleading. "Be careful."

I nodded and then raced back to the waterfront.

My father frantically paddled his arms, attempting to swim toward shore. Water splashed around him as he clawed at the surface. Panic contorted his face.

My chest tightened. I didn't know if I could save him—but I knew I had to try.

I raced into the water to help him. At first, it was deceptively calm, but as I pushed past my waist, the current grabbed hold of me—sudden, invisible, and mighty. Each step forward became harder, the pull dragging me sideways toward the jagged rocks where waves exploded in white spray. I froze. My mind screamed at me to move, but a cold hand of fear gripped my legs. If I continued, I could be swept straight into the rocks and might not make it back.

I locked eyes with him. With the determination of a rhino, stroke by stroke, he was making slow, deliberate progress toward shore. Holding his gaze, I took two deep, exaggerated inhales and exhales, letting my arms rise up as I filled my lungs with air, and theatrically pushing them down upon my exhale.

My dad got the message.

After over twenty years of whitewater rafting trips with his mates, my dad had battled his share of ferociously raging rivers. More than once, he'd been tossed from the raft and swept downstream, dodging craggy rocks that jutted up from the riverbed. Those experiences had taught him how to stay calm in water emergencies. As he struggled toward shore with slow, labored strokes, he matched my deep, grounding breaths—offering silent reassurance with every inhale.

But this wasn't a river, and his instincts betrayed him. Instead of swimming sideways to escape the rip current, he battled against it, trying to push straight for the shore. He kicked furiously, but his movements grew more erratic, his strokes sloppy. He was tiring, his desperate efforts losing to the rip's relentless pull. It was obvious he'd never make it on his own.

Two young men stood on the beach close by, one kicking at the sand, the other with hands casually in his pockets while a cigarette dangled from his mouth. Their eyes drifted lazily over to my father battling for his life in the water.

I waved at them and screamed, "PLEASE HELP ME! HELP MY DAD! HE'S DROWNING OUT THERE!!"

The two men sighed, looking at each other with detached disregard.

"Bloody oath." The accent gave them away—Australians.

"That's your dad...?" the bleach-blond one asked, dusting a bit of sand off his boardshorts.

I was hoping his conscience would get the best of him. "YES, PLEASE! HELP HIM!! PLEASE! HE'S DROWNING!!" I sobbed.

The reluctance of this inconvenient favor hung heavy. Finally, they nodded and threw off their shirts before wading in.

I believed these men could bring my father back to shore safely, so I raced off to call an ambulance. I thought having the beach lined with one fancy resort after another would make it easy to find help. Without hesitation, I bolted into the nearest one.

Compared to the reality I faced on the beach, there was an eerie sense of serenity inside the resort. Traditional Thai music floated from speakers scattered throughout the sprawling courtyard. Vibrant tropical blooms and towering palm trees bordered the space, while the scent of coconut oil mingled with the sweet aroma of flowers.

I raced into the pool area. A few sunburned tourists lounged around the expansive pool. I sprinted past them and straight to the attendant at the bar.

"Sir! Please help! I need an ambulance! My dad and sister are severely injured on the beach just outside the hotel!"

Before the bartender could respond, another staff member appeared at my side. "Ma'am, I need to ask you to leave immediately. You are not allowed to be here unless you are staying at the hotel."

"Did you hear me? I need an ambulance NOW. People's lives are at risk! My family is bleeding out in the sand right in front of this hotel! Please help and I will leave!"

"Did you hear me? You need to leave NOW. We cannot help you."

"I will leave when you call an ambulance. PLEASE!"

Having had enough of our back-and-forth battle, the staff member grabbed my arm and yanked me toward the stairs that led back down to the beach.

As they hustled me off the hotel premises, the bartender snuck up behind me and handed me a wet, warm hand towel. It was a peace offering, but I was stunned by its uselessness. I let it slip from my fingers and drop to the ground as I rushed back to the beach.

My sister was sitting where I had left her, clinging to the towel tourniquet. Crimson blood pooled beneath her, coagulating on the sand. She drew in slow, purposeful breaths, in a deliberate effort to stay calm.

My father lay sprawled next to her, soaked and trembling. Large amounts of blood smeared across his skin. The uncertainty of where it was coming from or how serious his injuries were had pushed him into a panic. His chest heaved in ragged bursts, each breath rapid and shallow. He clenched and unclenched his hands, as if searching for something solid to hold onto to subside the overwhelming storm of emotions.

I dropped to my knees and wrapped my arms around his shaking frame. "It's OK, Dad. You're OK." But were those words true? There was so much blood. I ran my hands over his body, pressing against his skin, desperate to find the source before it was too late.

A crowd had formed a circle around us. Every person had their phone out recording, as if we were part of their vacation's entertainment.

Passersby continuously observed the horde of people circling around some sort of spectacle. They joined the crowd, like curious fish swarming a dangling hook. Twenty, forty, then fifty people gathered.

"HELP!" I screamed out in a frenzied rage, "Somebody! PLEASE CALL AN AMBULANCE!"

No one moved. Everyone continued to film. My panic seemed to feed their intrigue.

My heart raced. I had to think fast. My father and sister needed to get to the roadside, so we could flag down a vehicle to take us to the hospital. But with her knee busted wide like a piñata on Cinco de Mayo, there was zero chance my sister could walk.

Fear gripped me as I turned back to the men who pulled my father from the water. My lips quivered as I spoke. "Please, *please* help carry my sister to the road."

The men shifted awkwardly, their gazes glued to the ground. One scuffed his feet against the sand, rocking back and forth on his heels. "Mate...she's covered in blood." He rubbed the back of his neck, glancing at his friend before dropping his eyes again.

"Yeah, we, uh...we'd love to help, but...you know," the other added, fidgeting with his hands. "It's just...you never know, right? Blood and all. Could be HIV. Could be anything..."

From the ground, my sister—despite the pain, now eerily calm—spoke up. "Listen, I get it. I really do. But I promise you, I don't have any blood-borne diseases. No HIV, no hepatitis, nothing like that. I'm clean."

The two men exchanged glances, still hesitating. "Yeah, right, it's just...you know, we can't be too sure."

I took a step closer, my voice firm. "Please...we're desperate. Just to the road, that's all. We'll handle the rest."

My sister nodded, her eyes locking onto theirs. "I swear, you're safe. I just need to get to the hospital. *Please.*"

The taller one scratched his head, letting out a slow sigh. "All right, mate. We'll help ya."

The second one nodded. "Yeah, all right. Let's get her up then."

Together, they bent down, their movements cautious. I could see the apprehension in their eyes, but also a quiet resolve. One slipped his arms beneath her back, the other supported her legs. Her arms hung limp as they rose in unison, careful not to jostle her injured knee.

My father and I wrapped our arms around one another so I could help him to the road. Channeling every ounce of my inner fortitude, I bore the weight of his six-foot frame. The muscles in my arms and back tensed as I accessed a hidden reserve of power, fueling a burst of energy.

The crowd followed, filming and recording. My glare was sharp enough to shatter diamonds.

At the road, I was relieved to find a police car waiting. When they saw my blood-soaked dad and sister, they insisted on lining the backseats of the police car with newspaper. As we worked out the geometry of fitting them both in the car, a man with a phone hovered over us, filming "money shots" of the mayhem. One of the police officers snatched the phone from the man's hands and flung it to the ground. I was so thankful I could have kissed him. And we were off, racing to Bangkok Hospital.

Upon arrival, nurses quickly positioned my father and sister in beds and began attending to their wounds. They realized the majority of my sister's cuts and bruises were not serious, except for her knee. For that, she would need surgery immediately.

My father was more difficult to handle. His entire being unraveled, overwhelmed by fear and trauma.

I watched helplessly as he thrashed when put in a wheelchair. The nurse's gentle touch as she tried to assess his wounds sent him further into a fit. His guttural screams tore through the sterile hospital.

When they wheeled him into a shower, I felt sorry for him—in a way that made my chest ache. My dad had always been the adventurer and light-spirited one in the family. But now, he was reduced to this—screaming in terror as if the water hitting his skin were burning acid.

Hands trembled at my sides as I stood. I peeled tiny bits of skin off my lips with distracted bites. I'd done everything I could to get him out of the ocean, to bring him to safety, but it wasn't enough. Now I had to stand back as the nurses tried to help. I was powerless to do anything except witness his torment. Time stretched and warped, seconds crawled like eternity.

Eventually, we learned that none of my father's cuts were too serious. The nurses sedated him, cleaned, and bandaged his wounds. They informed me he would be sent to our hotel that evening.

He was severely shaken and mentally unstable after the events of the day. He couldn't be on his own. That put me in a serious bind—I had no intention of stepping away from the hospital while my sister was in surgery, but I also needed to get my weakened father back to our hotel. Near breaking point, I did what every worn-down human in this world does....

I called my mommy.

Over the years, my mother earned the nickname "The Queen of Doom," because she commonly looked at the worst-case scenario *of every situation.* As a teenager, if I told my mom I was going to the mall, she'd ask what I would do if I ran into a bad man who would likely attack me there. If I told her I was going on a hike, she'd ask what I would do when I inevitably fell, broke my ankle, and got lost in the wilderness alone. Every time I called my mother, the first words out of her mouth were, "ARE YOU OK?" Her worst fear when she saw my phone number pop up on the caller-ID was that I was calling with an emergency.

When I called my mother from the hospital that evening, she started the call no differently than she ever did. "Are you OK?"

"Yes, Mom, we're all going to be OK. Just sit down and take a deep breath." I waited a beat, then continued. "Dad and Tara had a swimming accident. Dad's fine, just some cuts. Tara cut the tendons in her knee, though. She is on her way to surgery now. But she's in a good, clean hospital and will be fine. I just wanted you to know."

There was a pause. Then her voice softened in a way that surprised me. "Well...what about you? Are *you* OK?"

I hadn't realized how much I needed that question until she asked. "I'm hanging in there." My shoulders loosened as I exhaled. "It was...a lot, Mom. It was terrifying. I thought Dad was drowning, and then Tara's knee...and people's responses, Mom! It was so shocking!"

"What do you mean?"

"No one gave a shit. A few people were interested in the drama unfolding and just stood around watching, like we were a reality TV show or something." My eyes filled with tears. "How could they just stand there? Just to observe us in our lowest and most vulnerable moment?" The dam burst. My tears flowed freely.

"That's horrible, Shany." The hurt in her voice matched my own. "I'm so sorry. In a lot of ways, people really have become desensitized from what we see on our screens every day, I suppose."

"It's frightening," I wiped my tears. "Supposedly more connected than ever, yet also completely disconnected from one another."

My mom let out a long breath. "I know, sweetheart. But you need to take care of you right now. Your father and sister are so lucky you could be there for them today. You always have been there for both of them."

Tears welled once more. "Yeah...I guess I have."

"You've always been a rock in the family, Shany, holding things together. I know sometimes it breaks you inside. This must have been very traumatic for you. It's OK to feel that way."

Hearing her acknowledge this—acknowledge *me*—brought an unexpected wave of relief. The tension in my brow loosened. My jaw, clenched for hours, eased. "Thanks, Mom. That means a lot," I whispered, swallowing back the lump in my throat.

"I'm proud of you, you know that?"

For the first time all day, a sense of calm settled over me. "I think I needed to hear that." A soft warmth filled me. "I need to go, though. I'm taking Dad back to the hotel now."

"OK, sweetheart. Please keep me posted on everything. I love you."

"Love you too, Mama." I pressed the red button to end the call. The lingering comfort of her words stayed after the line went dead. Just me and the dim glow of the screen.

The staff kept my sister in the hospital for several days after surgery, monitoring for infection. My father, battered and unable to walk, remained at the hotel, his hands wrapped like a mummy. He needed me to spoon-feed him every meal. I spent those days ping-ponging between the hospital and the hotel, caring for them both.

It wasn't the trip any of us imagined. My sister came to help our dad rebuild a life in Thailand, and instead, I found myself piecing both of them back together. But maybe that's the reality no one warns you about: sometimes you're the one who has to hold it all together—not because you're ready, but because there's no other choice.

Plans fall apart. They always do. And you learn to gather up the broken pieces.

The roles between my father and I flipped so fast I never had time to brace for impact. There was no manual for this kind of shift—when you became the caretaker, the protector, the one holding the spoon.

But maybe that's what growing up really is: realizing that the people who once seemed unshakable are just human after all.

"Yes, not everything went as planned. It all fell apart terribly, spectacularly. No problem, the pieces are all still there. I can put them back together in a new way. That's the power of hope." -Topher Kerby

18

WHISPERS OF THE MEKONG

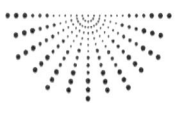

LAOS

*H*elping my father build a new life in Thailand was supposed to be a short detour. But six weeks passed in a blur of bank accounts, insurance forms, and apartment viewings. Every day felt like a tug-of-war between duty and freedom. The weight of responsibility pressed down on me. By the time I got him settled in his new home, I was exhausted. I longed for the kind of solace only solo travel could offer. I didn't know what I was looking for exactly—only that I needed to recharge. So I left.

I found my escape in Si Phan Don, Laos—the 4,000 Islands. It was a place so quiet it felt like time had forgotten it.

The islands were located in the Mekong Delta of Laos, a land-locked country between Thailand and Vietnam. The Mekong River is one of the world's longest rivers, flowing nearly 5,000 kilometers from its source on the Tibetan Plateau in China, through Myanmar, Thailand, Lao PDR, Cambodia, and Vietnam. It's more than just a geographical feature—it's a lifeline for the 4000 Islands. In this sleepy pocket of the delta, the river nourishes the land, powers local boats, and sustains the fishing and farming that many families depend on.

I based myself on the small island of Don Det. Life moved at an unhurried pace, framed by thick clusters of banana trees and dense bamboo thickets. My rustic backpacker's lodging was a little hut, constructed from local wood and reeds. Grooves were worn deep in the floorboards from countless footsteps. The hut murmured with age, each step stirring a tired groan from the wood.

Inside, there was nothing more than a lumpy twin bed with a hole-ridden mosquito net surrounding it. The air, thick with humidity, clung to my skin. A hammock swayed lazily on the balcony. Its gentle, creaking movement brought a welcome breath of relief from the oppressive tropical heat.

As a backpacker, I had the luxury of time. I enjoyed meandering on a rented bicycle down riverside pathways and idyllic lanes flanked by palm trees. One of my favorite stretches was the old French railway bridge—a rusting steel relic that spanned the gap between the islands of Don Khon and Don Det. Its beams were streaked orange from years of sun and rain. Built during France's colonial rule over Laos from 1893 to 1939, the bridge once carried trains meant to bypass the fierce rapids of the Mekong. Now, it carried only the occasional tourist or local cyclist, passing over a dream the French had long abandoned.

In a nearby village, old colonial villas stood with their paint peeling, now repurposed into guesthouses or underfunded municipal offices. Market stalls offered warm baguettes beside baskets of sticky rice. The past hadn't disappeared—it had just faded, absorbed into the present like an old watermark on paper.

As I guided my bike over the bridge's rough, uneven surface, each bump of the wooden slats echoed under my tires. The weathered planks sagged beneath the weight of decades of tropical heat and countless footsteps.

With the Mekong River glistening below, the view stretched out on either side—a vast, slow-moving current flanked by untamed greenery, dotted with small fishing boats idly drifting. The air was filled with the scent of river mud and blooming water hyacinths. A warm breeze ruffled through my hair as I pedaled forward, crossing a piece of living history in a place where time lingered.

Crossing brought me to the island of Don Khong, home to the

mesmerizing Khone Phapheng Falls—the largest waterfall in Southeast Asia. The approach was lush and wild, with dense foliage lining the path and towering trees sprinkling dappled sunlight across the forest floor. As I neared the waterfall, the air grew cooler and mistier, carrying a rich, earthy scent of wet soil and moss. The fragrance grounded me, connecting me to the natural world.

I settled onto a smooth rock. The continuous roar of the falls enveloped me, a sound so powerful it vibrated through my bones. From my perch, I watched the water tumble and twist. Each drop sparkled under the sunlight like scattered crystal beads. The water's white foam churned as it plunged into the swirling, frothy pool below.

The trees surrounding the waterfall rose tall and proud. One, slightly apart from the others, loomed with its branches stretching out like open arms—a mirror to my own solitary journey, embraced by the world yet content in its solitude.

A single leaf, vibrant and green, drifted on the surface of the water, its path uncertain yet serene, like my own journey. It danced atop the ripples, carried by the currents. I considered it a symbol, to trust the flow of life, letting it take me where I needed to go without resistance.

The simplicity of the moment, the sheer joy of being present, filled me with quiet satisfaction. I found strength. I could navigate the world on my own terms, savor my own company, and find beauty in the stillness. This profound appreciation for solitude marked a shift in my life, where I understood the power and beauty of being alone, yet never lonely.

19

A DESPERATE ESCAPE

CAMBODIA

*A*fter ten days, the tranquility of Don Det had worked its magic, but a restlessness stirred within me. I had my fill of hammock hangs and calm riverside strolls. I yearned for a change of scenery, a more active adventure. That's how I ended up in the Ratanakiri Province of Cambodia, a region that shares a border with Vietnam and Laos.

I ventured to Ban Lung, a remote town in the country's northeastern corner, to take part in a jungle trek. I heard it was possible to spend time cooling off in waterfalls, build a bamboo raft to ride downriver, and indulge in a jungle soup prepared by guides. How enchanting it would be to sit cross-legged on the forest floor, flickering firelight casting a shadow among the trees, while I enjoyed a soup made from freshly harvested young banana flowers, green mango, wild-caught fish, bamboo shoots, and forest-gathered mushrooms. I had to try.

The evening before I was meant to leave on my trek, I booked a stay in a local guesthouse. Inside the cramped room, the air hung heavy with the odor of mildew. A tired, rusting fan sat wobbling in the corner, slicing the air with a clank at every rotation. The grating gnawed at my nerves. Its futile attempt to fend off mosquitoes only added to my frustration. Outside, motorbikes zipped by like fleeting shadows in the moonlight.

I lay back, trying to relax, letting my thoughts drift with the sound of the night insects singing their mating chorus. But slowly, an unfamiliar tension crept in. A dull ache gathered at the back of my neck, working its way into a throb, then down my spine. My skin became hyper-aware, alive with a faint itch that prickled along my arms and shoulders, then turned into a steady, uncomfortable heat. I shifted, feeling the sheets grow damp beneath me as beads of sweat formed tiny rivers that flowed from my naked body into them.

At first, I thought it was just the warmth of the room. But the heat continued to build. My skin burned. My pulse pounded, echoing in my ears. I wiped my forehead, but the sweat returned instantly, pouring out of me like water from an open faucet.

I sat up, feeling the room lurch as a wave of dizziness hit me, sharp and fierce. I closed my eyes, willing the nausea to pass, but it only intensified, twisting my stomach in tight knots. A sour taste rose in my throat, and I stumbled toward the bathroom, clutching the walls for balance.

After each trip back to the bed, delirium tightened its grip. I couldn't tell how much time had passed. Was it minutes? Hours? My body ached. My head pounded, and in the growing haze of exhaustion, my vision blurred. Shapes in the room began to shift. The shadows in the corners deepened, expanding outward, taking on a strange solidity. I blinked hard. But the darkness was no longer just darkness—it felt alive, creeping, watching. A pair of yellow eyes glared back at me from the foot of my bed, glinting in the half-light.

A guttural growl echoed in the silence. A mangy orange cat, its fur tangled and matted, had somehow slunk its way not only into my room but under the mosquito net. I could feel its claws pricking my skin, drawing blood. I flailed, desperate to shove it away. It hissed, arching its back, scratching my arm as I wrestled it. My hands shook as I caught hold of it. I tossed the creature across the room, where it disappeared into the shadows.

I collapsed back onto the bed, sweat trickling down my temples.

My heart raced as I looked around, scanning the empty room, searching for any sign of the creature. But there was nothing. Only silence, broken by the fan's relentless drone.

The realization struck with a jolt.

There had never been a cat. I was slipping, spiraling into a fevered dreamscape where reality bled into fantasy.

Continuing to shiver as if I was standing bootless in snow, I found myself lying in my ex-boyfriend's bed. He had a habit of sleeping with an industrial power fan blowing directly at us, which always irked me. Sleeping on the edge of the bed I shook and froze through the night.

My fevered mind jumped to my mother's soft, comfy couch, wrapped in a homey blanket waiting for her to serve me with comforting love in my moment of sickness.

Return to reality.

I was sick. Alone. In a third-world country. My body was getting weaker each minute. My lips had chapped and cracked. Dehydration tormented me. My throat had shrunk. My joints ached. My muscles buckled like wet paper towels, unable to bear any weight. Fever had taken control of my mind, warping reality to an abstract, hazy mirage. **I needed help.** I needed a hospital.

I tossed and turned, in and out of consciousness, until sun-rays from an early morning daybreak burst through the windows. When that first touch of morning light illuminated the sky, I grabbed my backpack and headed for the street. With my mind fogged, I was in no state to create or initiate a well-thought-out plan to support myself. My steps were uncertain, feet dragging. My eyes squinted as they struggled to adjust to the glaring light.

I wandered the roadside in a haze, drifting aimlessly, like a bobber on a fisherman's line. The distorted street stretched ahead, with dirty, cracked asphalt and narrow, uneven sidewalks. I stumbled over a pothole, catching my big toe on the jagged edge, bending my foot backward with a jarring pain. I bit my lip to stifle a scream.

Motorbikes zipped past, honking their horns. Everything felt distant, like I was moving through a dream. My body swayed, every step more laborious than the last. One hand clutched my stomach, while the other pressed against my burning forehead.

I waved down each passing vehicle, hoping desperately for someone to stop. My arms felt like lead, heavy with exhaustion. My legs trembled beneath me, a mix of fear and fatigue threatening to buckle them entirely. A dust-caked Toyota Corolla rattled past without slowing. The driver glanced my way before speeding off, leaving me coughing in a cloud of dust.

At last, a battered gray minivan slowed to a halt. Its engine rattled. A small plume of smoke billowed from the exhaust. I rushed to the window, my breath coming in ragged gasps. "Hospital," I croaked, gripping the window frame for support. "Phnom Penh hospital." I thrust a crumpled wad of cash toward him with shaking hands.

The local driver eyed the money before his gaze softened. With an enthusiastic nod, he waved me into the car. The door shuddered open with a grating sound, and I collapsed onto the backseat.

I came to consciousness five hours later, as we entered the capital city of Phnom Penh. The chaotic rhythm of the city pulsed through the crowded thoroughfares, where rickshaws weaved through traffic with nimble agility. Families on motorbikes passed by, their children squeezed helmetless between parents. Some mothers nursed their infants while perched on the backs of motorbikes, their arms cradling their babies with tender care amidst the noisy streets. As we continued driving, pockets of urban decay emerged, with pieces of trash littering the sidewalks and alleys. Beggars sat at street corners, their weathered faces reflecting years of hardship as they extended their hands in silent pleas to passersby.

I caught the driver's reflection in the rearview mirror, his brows knitted together in a subtle frown, and the corners of his mouth drawn tight, portraying a silent concern as he glanced back to ask, "What hospital?"

I hesitated, the answer to that question slipping through my mind like water through a sieve. It was a detail I'd never thought to consider. My voice wavered. "Uh…just the nearest hospital. Please."

"OK. Soon there."

As I staggered into the emergency room, the smell hit me first—a thick blend of disinfectant barely masking the odors of sweat, damp clothing, and stale air. The walls, once painted white, had yellowed with age and grime, peeling in places to reveal patches of concrete beneath. Dim, flickering fluorescent lights cast a sickly hue over the cracked linoleum floors, the battered benches, and the hunched bodies waiting in silence. The floors, scuffed and stained, felt sticky underfoot. Crowded benches lined the room, where Cambodians of all ages sat slumped with exhaustion or doubled over in pain. The weariness of long waits and uncertain outcomes etched on their faces.

A wave of shock rippled through the small group of staff as they spotted me—a foreigner stepping into a world rarely seen by tourists. Their eyes darted between each other, hesitant movements revealing their uncertainty.

The nurse who approached me was visibly tense. "Ma'am. This public hospital."

I didn't register her words as a warning. "That's OK. I'm very sick. I just need help immediately please. I have severe fever and nausea. Every muscle and bone in my body feels broken. I'm dehydrated. Please help me!"

"We check for dengue and malaria, ma'am. Blood test. They pass through bite of infected mosquito."

I glanced down at my ankles and legs, covered in festering mosquito bites. They were clustered like tiny landmines on my skin, their edges raised and inflamed.

Of course, mosquitoes have always been drawn to my seemingly sweet blood. I'm a walking buffet for these tiny disease-ridden insects.

A nurse pricked my finger in a side room the size of a broom closet. The fan above stirred the air just enough to move the smell of antiseptic and sweat around the room. I hesitated before sitting, eyeing the chair's stained cushion and the roll of gauze that looked like it had been used many times.

The nurse dabbed my blood onto a narrow strip, then placed it beside a row of others on a cluttered counter—no labels, no refrigeration—just a scattered lineup of test strips, all waiting their turn like nervous lottery tickets.

She gave a curt nod toward the door, her eyes flicking toward the plastic chairs lined up in the waiting room. "Wait der."

I stood, still pressing a cotton ball to my finger, and followed her command, unsure whether I was more afraid of the results or the place itself.

Within an hour, the same nurse shuffled over to me, her steps slow and hesitant. "Ma'am. Dengue fever. You must stay for help."

CDC statistics, stating that dengue kills 400,000 people worldwide each year, raced through my anxious mind. My palms became slick with sweat. My heart pounded, each beat reverberating like a drum. The walls of the room closed in around me.

"How long do I need to stay? I thought there's no cure for dengue?"

Her voice was soft, almost apologetic. "Yes, ma'am. No cure. Viral infection." She fidgeted with the hem of her white skirt, nervously creasing the fabric between her fingers. "We manage symptoms till you OK. Maybe two days. Maybe seven. When you healthy sickness is gone forever. You come wit me."

She ushered me out of the waiting room into the grimy emergency room. The space teemed with people, each showing signs of their mortality.

A man lay sprawled on a bed, his body covered in scabs and stitches. A large gash ran across his forehead, the edges of the wound pulled together with thick, black thread. His face was swollen and bruised, one eye nearly swollen shut, the other staring blankly at the ceiling.

Across the room, a small child lay in a bed that seemed far too large for her withered frame. Ribs jutted out sharply, her cheekbones overly pronounced, her eyes sunk deep into the hollows of her skull. Pale skin clung tightly to her bones, as if all vitality had been drained away. Whether from malnutrition, a parasite, or some other cruel affliction, her condition seemed dire.

The entire room was thick with the acrid odor of sweat and illness, a suffocating congestion hanging in the air.

Crammed to capacity, the hospital beds stood positioned merely six inches apart from one another. This proximity only amplified the overwhelming sense of claustrophobia and desperation.

As I settled onto my assigned bed, a wave of revulsion washed over me. The sheets, once presumably white, were marred with the telltale stains of blood and bodily fluids. The walls also showed signs of unspeakable suffering, their surfaces marked with blood, and feces, the residue of past battles fought against illness.

Despite the wall splashed with feces and vomit, I considered myself lucky to be shoved into a corner, with only one neighbor pressed up against my other side. A local man, probably in his late twenties or early thirties, sat beside me. He was hooked up to every machine the hospital seemed to have, including a ventilator reaching deep into his throat. The man's elderly mother sat at his side, contributing to his care twenty-four hours a day.

Every patient in the emergency room had friends or family by their side. It didn't take long to realize that, unlike hospitals back home, this severely understaffed facility relied on loved ones to do much of the basic care. Bathing, dressing, assisting with bladder functions, changing linens, and bringing food and water—all of it fell to the patient's family and friends.

The hospital staff repeatedly requested I call my friends and family to come support me. I did not have that luxury. There was no one to reach out to for reinforcement. This meant that in the throes of my illness, when I vomited on myself, I was left to sit in it. I was left without food for days, and the only water I received was pumped into my system through an IV.

Throughout the days, I moaned in agony, begging for relief from the fevers and severe muscle aches. Every muscle felt as though it had been relentlessly pounded, leaving me with an intense, throbbing pain that made even the slightest movement excruciating.

Between fractured sleep I barely noticed a doctor approach. I caught the gleam of a needle in his gloved hand. "No!" I lifted a trembling hand, blocking him from moving closer.

"Pain and fever medicine, ma'am."

"I need you to open a fresh box of needles. In front of me." The words came out in a demanding tone, more forceful than I intended.

The doctor's eyes narrowed. His lips pressed into a thin line and his jaw tightened as he paused for a moment, his gaze flickering between me and the needle in his hand.

I sat up straighter, my arms crossed tightly over my chest. "I'm not sure if the needle you're holding is sterile, sir. You need to open a new pack before you inject me with one, *please.*"

I could feel the weight of his judgment as he reached for a new box of needles. High-maintenance. A nuisance. I didn't care. My mother's voice echoed in my head. *Always advocate for yourself in the hospital, Shannon. No one who works there will do it for you.*

The doctor turned and placed the box on the edge of my bed, making sure I saw the subtle roll of his eyes as he did so. He didn't speak, but the stiffening of his posture, the way he straightened his back as if bracing for a battle, told me I was becoming more trouble than I was worth.

In the early-morning hours of my third day at the hospital, the man beside me began to convulse uncontrollably. The machines he was hooked up to beeped like an angry American with road rage. As if possessed by an evil spirit, his entire body was lifted up off the bed and then forcefully thrown back down. His cot, inches from mine, repeatedly bashed into mine. Blood burst out of his throat, clogging the ventilator. The piercing screams of that man's mother were a curse I've never forgotten.

Within minutes, nurses and doctors noticed the precarious fight for survival unfolding. They converged upon the struggling man, their white coats billowing behind them as they moved with purpose. In their hands, a defibrillator emerged as a beacon of hope. With practiced precision, they connected the device to the man's fragile form.

The defibrillator crackled to life, delivering a surge of electric energy that jolted through his body, a desperate attempt to reignite the dwindling embers of his failing heart. The heart monitor commenced its frenetic rhythm, a rapid staccato of *beep beep beep beep beep.* It cried out at an urgent and fast pace, resonating through the tension. Yet, fate seemed cruel as the sound abruptly halted. The heart monitor's monotonous beeping morphed into a haunting flat-line, an unyielding *beeeeeeeeeeeep*, heralding an unwelcome finale. The doctor's face dropped as the man's once animated body went limp, as though it were a marionette whose strings had been severed.

In the midst of the unfolding tragedy the mother's anguished cry tore through the air like a wounded animal's howl. Her body crumpled with the weight of unbearable grief, collapsing over her son's motionless form. In this heart-wrenching scene, the world halted, frozen, as if time had stopped to bear witness to the sorrow and disbelief.

I couldn't handle it.

I had seen enough.

With adrenaline coursing through my veins, I leaped out of my hospital bed, reaching for the IV bag tethered to my arm. I snatched my backpack, stored haphazardly under my bed, and beelined for the hospital exit.

"Ma'am! Ma'am!!" A worried nurse leapt in front of the exit before I could leave. "Where you go?!"

"I'm leaving!" I responded in a panicked rush. "I have to get out of here! I don't belong here! I need to go!"

"I need to remove IV first, ma'am."

Of course. Where was I possibly heading with an IV still inserted into my arm?

I reached my arm out for the nurse to remove the needle. "I need to pay also. How much do I owe please?"

"You no worry. Just go," the nurse responded, fully aware of my agitation and intense need for escape.

I raced out of that hospital door, staggering to the curb to wave down a taxi. I hopped in and headed straight to the airport to buy the first flight back to my home, California.

As I sat in the taxi en route to the airport, the bustle and grime of Phnom Penh passing me by, I felt thankful to be American. I firmly believed our healthcare system is corrupt, ripe with greed, and in absolute shambles, but it sure appeared to be a hell of a lot better than the Cambodian healthcare I had witnessed and received. I felt most thankful for my mother though, the rock I knew and know I can always turn to when faced with hardship. That's right, twenty-five years old, a full-fledged adult in the eyes of most people worldwide, *but you bet your ass I was running back to my mommy.*

The fifteen-hour journey from Cambodia to San Francisco was grueling but unexpectedly bearable. Miraculously, my symptoms were milder than I had anticipated. However, as I sat uncomfortably wedged in the middle seat between two strangers, I frequently succumbed to waves of nausea. I was mortified as I struggled to discreetly manage my bouts of vomiting. Each time I leaned over to use the tiny, flimsy bag provided by the flight attendants, I felt the eyes of my seatmates on me, their expressions a mix of sympathy and disgust. There was a silver lining though. The relentless fever that had plagued me began to subside, providing a glimmer of hope that I was nearing the end of my illness.

When I finally arrived at San Francisco International Airport, a surge of solace enveloped me the moment I laid eyes on my mother. With a heart brimming with love and anticipation, she propelled herself towards me. In an instant, her embrace enfolded me like a colossal cozy blanket, a haven of warmth that seemed to erase the sickness and fatigue etched into my body. Nuzzled within the tender haven of my mother's arms, I felt as if she possessed a magical touch that could heal the wounds of a thousand battles. Regardless of the challenges encountered, or the distances journeyed, her love would forever be a steadfast source of comfort and resilience. In that fleeting moment, time stood still, and the world outside dissolved into insignificance, for in her arms, I found the true essence of home.

"A mother's love liberates." Maya Angelou

20
TANGLED IN THE TIDES OF KOH RONG

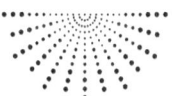

CAMBODIA

*H*aving recovered from dengue fever, I was left with an overwhelming desire to return to Southeast Asia. With savings left over from my year of living and working in Australia, I had both the means and determination to explore all I'd missed.

Cambodia had been the setting of a mission I hadn't finished, and something in me refused to be conquered by it. I didn't just want to return—I *needed* to. To reclaim the story. To prove to myself that I could finish what I'd started. And so, I returned in the fall of 2014. This trip would be my redemption and what better way to seek that than on a tropical island?

Koh Rong, the second-largest island in Cambodia, was an idyllic paradise in the Gulf of Thailand. The first touch of sand underfoot slowed my thoughts, as if the island itself had pressed a cool palm against my racing mind. The beaches were its crown jewels, stretching for miles, framed by a backdrop of swaying palm trees. I couldn't resist the call of the ocean, and soon found myself floating on my back in the warm waters, weightless as a buoy, gazing at the endless expanse of blue sky above. White fluffy clouds morphed and danced, fueling my imagination with their ever-changing shapes. A pair of wings stretched wide before dissolving, and a moment later, two figures leaned toward each other before melting into a blur. The images flickered and vanished one after another, leaving a faint sense of restlessness in their wake.

When I tired of floating, I wandered along the beach, my toes sinking into the sand as I scoured the shore for seashells. These treasures, carefully selected and tucked away in my backpack, were my souvenirs, each a reminder of the magic of Koh Rong.

The sun dipped lower in the sky, casting a golden hue over the island, when I heard the faint sound of music in the distance. Intrigued, I followed the melody, until I stumbled upon a lively, touristy market.

The market was a blend of food and knick-knack stalls. Everywhere I looked, I saw colorful trinkets—handcrafted jewelry, woven baskets, and fragrant herbs offering a taste of the island's culture.

My eyes were drawn to a stage where a handsome musician played, his fingers gliding over the strings of a guitar. I froze, transfixed. Stupified, I couldn't stop staring. He was handsome in a way that didn't seem entirely fair—a chiseled jawline, prominent cheekbones, and an impeccably groomed beard. With his wavy blond hair and broad shoulders, he looked like he'd just stepped out of a Viking legend, a modern-day Thor serenading the crowd.

He started singing a slow, honey-smooth version of "Sexual Healing." A group of backpackers sitting in front of the stage clapped along, some swaying as they belted the chorus out of tune.

As he sang, he scanned the crowd with a twinkle in his eye.

And then—his eyes locked on mine.

For a beat, it was just the two of us.

He winked. I felt my stomach flip, cheeks burning, stunned by the unexpected attention.

When his set ended, the crowd erupted into applause, some calling out for "one more!" He stood, setting his instrument carefully to the side, and with the same casual confidence he'd had on stage, he made his way through the throng—not to the fans reaching out to congratulate him, but straight toward me.

And when he opened his mouth to introduce himself, a charming crisp English accent spilled out.

"Hey, I'm Blake. I saw you listening to the music. Couldn't help but notice you."

I blinked, still processing the fact that this effortlessly cool guy was standing in front of me. "Uh, hey...I'm Shannon."

His smile was easy, his gaze steady, as if only the two of us existed in that moment. The distant chatter, the clinking of glasses, the low hum of conversation—all of it faded, leaving only the quiet weight of his attention. "Nice to meet you, Shannon. Hope you enjoyed my music."

"Yeah, it was amazing," I managed, my heart racing. "You've got, uh...great stage presence." *Why would someone who looked as if he belonged in a Viking epic have a desire to talk to me?*

"Been doing it for years."

"Oh yeah? You in a band or something?"

"Nope," he said, flashing a grin that could melt glaciers. "I'm a one-man show! I usually make my money in Lagos, Portugal. I go there every summer and busk on the streets or play in bars and restaurants."

"Interesting." I crossed my arms over my chest, then immediately dropped them to my sides, unable to figure out what to do with them.

"Yup." He leaned back slightly, rolling his shoulders like a man without a care in the world. "Work for four months playing music and then travel the rest of the year. It's the good life for sure."

I wanted to be a part of that; his confidence, his freedom. Everything about him felt magnetic, intoxicating.

"That's crazy you could make money for the year after only four months of work."

"Portugal is affordable. And I travel to cheap places, too, of course. You'd be surprised how good musician money can be. Crowds love me. I can make an easy four thousand euro a month, no taxes."

"More money than I've ever made." I laughed nervously as I tucked hair behind my ear. "Lucky."

"Well, I'd feel even luckier if I could use some of that money to buy you a drink. What do you think?"

An unexpected sense of significance washed over me. The way he looked at me made everything more alive, like it was a privilege to be a part of his world. "Yes, please!"

Spending time with Blake over the next few weeks was stepping onto the edge of something exhilarating and raw. He was as wild as he was confident, with an ease about him that made it seem like I could be, or already was, more adventurous.

One afternoon we kayaked through a quiet stretch of mangroves on the island's eastern side, gliding through narrow channels where twisted roots reached down like fingers into glassy water. Later that night, Blake convinced me to swim out past the boats and into the open bay. The moon was a faint smudge behind the clouds, and the shoreline was just a silhouette behind us.

"You've never done this before?" he asked, grinning as he peeled off his clothes and waded in, bare and unapologetic.

"Swim into total blackness? Not on purpose."

"Trust me. You won't regret it."

I hesitated, then slipped off my own clothes and followed him into the warm, inky water. As soon as I moved, the ocean lit up—glowing tendrils trailing from my fingertips, sparks dancing off my arms like underwater fireflies.

"It's bioluminescence!" Blake said. Microscopic organisms stirred to life by motion, like stars shaken loose from the seafloor.

Every stroke, every splash set off another burst of electric blue light. We spun and kicked through it, wide-eyed and whooping loudly. Our bodies shimmered with each motion, glowing at the edges as if outlined in moonlight. It felt unreal, like drifting inside a dream.

That was Blake—pulling me past hesitation and into the wild heart of adventure, whether I was ready or not. The same untamed spirit that made him magnetic also made him intense. He had a sharp tongue and unapologetic attitude, which often turned our conversations into heated exchanges. Unlike Noah, Blake didn't shrink from a challenge or hold back to keep the peace. There was something unsettling and irresistibly compelling about that.

One night we sat side by side on the sand, backs pressed against a rocky outcrop. The air carried the scent of salt and faint smoke from a distant bonfire. The gentle sound of waves lapping against the shore created a calming backdrop as we gazed up at a canopy of stars scattered across the deep indigo sky.

I rummaged in my backpack and pulled out a beer. It hissed as I popped it open, breaking the silence.

"You Americans are a funny breed," Blake began, his tone casual but the words loaded. "Everything's so individual. Each person for themselves." He paused, eyeing me as if sizing me up. "Like how you just got yourself that beer. Didn't even think to ask if I might want one."

I stiffened, beer halfway to my mouth. "I'm not sure what you're getting at. If I want a drink, I get it. You're very capable of doing the same for yourself. We can be independent, right?"

He raised an eyebrow. "Sure, independence is a thing, but it's as if Americans forget other people even exist. Sometimes I wonder if you ever think about the person sitting beside you."

My grip tightened on the cold, damp bottle in my hand. "That's not fair, Blake. You know I'm always thinking of you. But yeah, I'm independent. Can you handle it?"

He shrugged casually, unflinching. "Independent, huh? Or selfishness in a pretty package?"

His words landed like small punches, intentional and too close to home.

"So, what? You want me to start catering to your every whim, sire?"

He tilted his head, eyes glinting. "Just a little acknowledgment and thoughtfulness is all I'm asking for. I'm not worried though. I can kick the American out of you with time. You'll be the dream woman." He reached over, his hand resting on my knee. "You already are."

I glanced down at his hand, my pulse quickening. The edge of irritation I'd felt dissolved into something softer, leaving only the warmth of his hand on my knee, the way his thumb brushed my skin in slow, lazy circles. The sharpness of his words faded as I melted into the sweetness of that moment. Blake was fire and ice, harshness and warmth; cold one moment, then suddenly, disarmingly tender the next. He pulled me in and swept me along like a stray leaf in a current, carried forward even knowing there might be rocks ahead.

"Come on. Let's get off the sand and into a party. I heard there's a cool DJ on tonight." Blake stood up, hand outstretched in my direction. "It'll be a privilege to show up with the most beautiful woman there."

I took his hand, as a warm flush crept across my face.

We started toward the distant lights of the party, his hand clutching mine, as if he were afraid I might slip away. With Blake, I never knew exactly what to expect, and somehow that uncertainty only made me want to hold on tighter.

Blake stepped into the bar like he owned the place. All eyes gravitated to him. The flicker in his stare made it clear he was about to stir things up. "Another round for everyone!" he shouted, his voice carrying over the thumping music. The backpackers cheered as the bartender filled glasses.

Blake raised his glass. "To the madness!" he shouted, and the rest of the bar echoed him, our voices melding into a chorus of wild abandon.

I slammed my shot down, the burn shooting through me like wildfire.

Blake, never one to sit idle, jumped right into a conversation with the guys next to him, as if they'd been friends for years. "So, you just arrived, huh? Where're you from?" His fingers drummed on the bar, keeping time with the beat of the music.

The backpackers shared stories. One lanky Aussie laughed and slapped Blake on the back, his words slurred as he talked about a wild night in Vietnam. "Mate, swear to God—we're in a little village, right? Me and this Irish bloke, Danny. We're eight beers deep, thinkin' we're invincible. Danny bets me I can't ride a water buffalo. I'm like, 'Watch me.' So we find one—middle of the night, just grazing by the river. I climb on, all proud of myself—until the damn thing bolts. Took off like a bloody motorbike, me hangin' on for dear life, screaming my head off." He took a gulp of his beer. "Woke up next morning covered in mud, no shoes, one sandal tied to my wrist like a trophy. Best night of my life."

Blake threw his head back laughing, completely in his element. "Sounds like my kind of night. But let me tell you about this one…. Picture this, me and my mate Brek end up at this hole-in-the-wall strip joint in Phnom Penh, the kind that smells like stale beer and regret."

The crowd around us leaned in, hanging on every sentence. I smiled to myself. Blake had a knack for making connections, pulling people into his orbit.

He leaned forward, eyes gleaming with mischief. "We grab a table, and this lady comes up to us. She's in this tiny dress, fake smile plastered on her face, and she goes, 'You want girl?' And I'm like, 'Nah, we're good.' But she's persistent, right? She sits down next to Brek, who's already eyeballing the stage like a kid in a candy store."

Blake paused for effect, a sly grin creeping up on his face.

"So, she starts talking to Brek, asking him all sorts of questions—where he's from, why he's in Cambodia, all that crap. Brek, being Brek, gets all chatty, and she's feeding him the usual line. 'You want special show?' Brek's had a few too many, looks at me and goes, 'Why not? Let's see what a special show's like.'"

The group erupted in laughter.

"The next thing I know, they pull the curtains back and it's not a stripper, mate. It's a guy. And not just any guy. I'm talking a full-on, bald-headed, tattoo-covered, bodybuilder-looking dude who starts doing this, like, aerobic dance routine to a Backstreet Boys song. I'm sitting there, trying not to spit my beer out, but Brek? He's loving it. Guy's twirling, doing flips, and Brek's cheering him on. At one point, the guy lifts him up like he's some kind of ragdoll and spins him around!"

The group was howling with laughter now. Blake kept going.

"I didn't know whether to be concerned or impressed. After the 'show,' the guy comes up to us and says, 'That'll be 50 bucks.'" Blake leaned back, shaking his head. "And that, my friends, is why you never,

ever trust a place that advertises 'special shows.'" He grinned. "You never know what you're getting yourself into."

The night rolled on, the crowd growing louder, looser, as the drinks kept flowing. Top 40 hits blared from the speakers, shaking the very foundations of the makeshift bamboo dance floor, where sweaty backpackers crowded together. Scantily clad bodies in bikinis and Daisy Duke shorts gyrated with unrestrained joy. Groups of guys in board shorts and tank tops cheered, clinked bottles, and jumped along to the beat. Arms draped over shoulders, bodies swayed in unison, and laughter blended with the undercurrent of flirtation and possibility.

Blake threw his arm around me and pulled me into the chaos like it was the most natural thing in the world. The disco ball above spun, scattering kaleidoscopic patterns across the room, its flashing lights pulsing with the music. Bodies were everywhere, close enough that the heat of their skin seeped into mine, yet nothing mattered but the music, the laughter, and the moment we were in.

As the sun rose, we dragged our weary feet through the warm sand back to Blake's hotel, crashing into his bed.

As I lay there, the night's energy still spinning in my head, my thoughts drifted to Blake. I was falling fast, totally smitten, captivated by every detail—his piercing blue eyes, long blonde hair that fell in perfect disarray, reminiscent of a golden wheat field, his strong, well-built frame, and the way he commanded attention wherever he went. At that moment, Blake was all mine, and I intended to soak up every ounce of attention I could get from him as we took in the beautiful island of Koh Rong.

21
BETWEEN TWO WORLDS

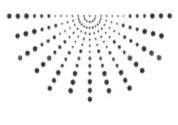

CAMBODIA

When I woke the next morning, Blake lay there, staring at the ceiling as if he were trying to meditate the pain away. "That was a wild one," he muttered, his voice hoarse.

"Oh man, I really didn't need that last tequila shot," I groaned, massaging my temples. "My head feels like an overused kick drum."

"Yeah. The end of the night feels cloudy... Did we even pay the tab?"

I laughed weakly. "You paid the tab for us and the entire table of backpackers we were partying with."

"Right... Bacon cheeseburgers? Only grease can save me now."

"Let's do it."

We dragged ourselves to a beachside café and collapsed at a table, with our heads hung in a fog. Our feet dug into the soft sand, while our shaky hands attempted to lift coffee mugs to our parched lips. Around us, a dozen other tourists were in the same state—slouched, eyes half-closed, and nursing their own mugs, while the café's pack of dogs wandered between tables, gently nuzzling for attention.

Among them, a scruffy brown dog with one floppy ear meandered from lap to lap. His wiry coat glinted in the sunlight, and whenever he received a pat, his tail wagged like a little flag. The dogs of this restaurant, rescued as strays from the streets, were well-known by back-packers in Koh Rong. Every traveler who visited the restaurant was greeted with a friendly sniff.

As I watched the tourists dote on the dogs, the scruffy brown pup wandered from person to person, eagerly soaking up attention. I couldn't help but feel the stark contrast between these cherished pets and the harsh reality faced by so many other dogs in Cambodia. For many locals, dogs are not seen as companions but as unwanted outcasts, roaming the streets unneutered, unprotected, and often mistreated. Limited resources and access to animal care meant that stray dogs were frequently viewed as nuisances, sometimes even captured for the meat trade. The consumption of dog meat is rooted in a long-standing tradition in some parts of Cambodian culture, where it is believed to bring strength, vitality, and good fortune.

I was still digesting these thoughts when a local man stormed up to the oceanfront restaurant. Each step threw up small sprays of sand as he moved with purpose. Fire burned in his eyes. He held a thick wooden club in one hand and an empty rice sack in the other. His lean, muscular frame moved with an intensity that drew the attention of everyone nearby.

The restaurant's dogs barked wildly at the man as he paced rest-lessly. One large, shaggy black dog stood next to the bar, hackles raised and body tense. His low rumbled growl contrasted with the frantic yips of the smaller dogs clustering around him, tails tucked.

The shrill burst of barking pulled me from my daze just in time to witness the man smash his wooden club down on the spine of a yapping white bichon frise. I was stunned as the dog dropped dead immediately, its yipping cut off mid-breath. It seemed far too easy for life to end in a sudden blink.

The man casually picked up the dog's body and threw it inside his rice sack, then continued on his warpath, swinging and striking another barking dog on the spine. This slightly larger dog did not die immediately; instead, it let out a sharp, high-pitched yelp before collapsing onto its side, its hind legs limp and useless. Trembling, it whimpered and clawed weakly at the ground, dragging itself inch by inch toward the nearest shelter—a table where a group of stunned tourists sat, paralyzed in shock.

As the dog reached their feet, one woman dropped to her knees. Her hands shook as she stroked its matted fur. Another cradled its head through choked sobs. Meanwhile, the man continued his rampage, his stick swinging mercilessly at any dog within reach.

The expat staff, heartbroken at the sight of their pets being massacred in front of their eyes, begged and screamed for the man to stop. The young waitress, a bronzed backpacker with bleach-blonde hair, cried out, "Please! You're hurting them!" Tears streamed down her cheeks. "Somebody do something!"

A cook, covered in tattoos, burst from the kitchen. His mouth hung open for half a second, as if struggling to process the scene before him, then twisted into a grimace. "What are you doing? They're just dogs! Stop it!"

"Enough!" a bartender yelled, his bloodshot eyes wide. "These are pets! They're part of our family!"

But the swings continued.

Blake, confident in his ability to lead and influence others, took it upon himself to play the hero. He stood tall, chin high, eye contact steady and slowly approached with a puffed up chest. He crossed into the man's line of sight. In a deliberate gesture, he dramatically raised his arms up and down, modeling deep inhales and exhales.

But the man's gaze was vacant. He stared right through Blake. There was no human inside those bulging, fuming eyes. The man had entered that unreachable state human beings transform into when they morph into a killer. The man's chest rose and fell with the rapid pace of his overworked breathing. He waved his arms at Blake, a crude warning that he needed to get out of the way or risk becoming a target of the wooden club.

Blake took his cue and backed down. His gaze remained fixed on the ground, avoiding any confrontation. His shoulders relaxed slightly, and his arms fell back to his sides.

No one else stood brave enough to confront the seething and infuriated man. He swung and killed two more dogs, heartlessly picking up the limp bodies to toss in his burlap sack.

My pulse raced in my ears, breath caught somewhere between my throat and lungs. I felt a sick, hollow ache in my stomach. But I couldn't look away.

Thankfully, the man was soon done. He turned on his heel and marched out of the restaurant, his rice sack slung over his shoulder like a bag of groceries. A heavy silence clung to the air in his wake, broken only by the hiccupping sobs of a young woman clutching a napkin to her face. At a nearby table, a man sat hunched over, hands gripping his head. His untouched meal remained pushed aside. Behind the counter, the owner stood frozen, his lips slightly parted, as if he might speak, but no words came. The staff exchanged glances, eyes glassy with disbelief.

The police arrived soon after. From their meeting with the staff and owners we learned that one of the restaurant's pet dogs had recently ventured into the local village and bit a small child. The restaurant staff, who owned the dogs, apologized for the pup's wrongdoing and offered to pay for any medical care the child might need, but the village refused this offer. In their culture, if a dog bites a person, the dog is immediately killed, no questions asked. Rules like these had been set in place because there are so many rampant stray dogs there, dogs that can sometimes prove to be violent and dangerous, or even spread dangerous diseases such as rabies. The men of the village had demanded that the offending dog be handed over to be killed.

The restaurant owners, heartbroken at the thought of losing one of their beloved dogs, refused to give the animal up. By rejecting the cultural norms of the village, they unwittingly escalated the situation. The villagers, angered by what they saw as disrespect and disregard for their rules, took matters into their own hands. The resulting violence led not only to the death of the dog that had bitten the child but also to the loss of three other innocent dogs.

I struggled to process what I had witnessed. The man's actions had been brutal and heartbreaking, but they were not entirely senseless.

His rage and determination weren't born solely of malice, but were deeply rooted in his community's understanding of safety and justice. In his eyes—and perhaps in the eyes of many in his village—the refusal to surrender the dog was a dangerous disregard for their way of life.

As I reflected on the events, it became clear how easy it is to judge another culture through the lens of our own values.

Culture isn't just food, language, and tradition—it's the beliefs and practices that have evolved to help communities navigate their unique challenges and realities. What might seem cruel or extreme to me can feel logical and necessary to someone else.

At the same time, there are moments when our moral compass pushes back against cultural norms, leaving us in a gray area where empathy and outrage coexist. These are the moments that challenge us most as travelers—not because they provide simple answers, but because they force us to confront the limits of our understanding.

The lesson, I realized, is about approaching cultural differences with humility. Sometimes, respecting a culture means stepping back and acknowledging that our perspective is just one of many. Other times, it means recognizing that our values may conflict with local norms and making peace with the discomfort that follows. Above all, I learned the importance of treading carefully—striving to learn from what I don't understand and honoring the complexity of the world I'm so fortunate to explore.

"Let us not take ourselves too seriously. None of us have a monopoly of wisdom, and we must always be ready to listen to and respect other's point of view." Queen Elizabeth II

22
TWO WHEELS, MANY SMILES

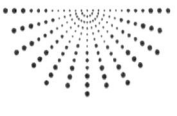

VIETNAM

$\mathcal{W}$e travelers have itchy feet, which almost takes the form of restlessness, wherever we happen to be. No matter how enjoyable a location is, the questions always loom, *What else is out there? What else is there to experience, learn, and engage with? Roads are surely meant to be traveled, right...?* And so, with the spirit of a traveler within us, Blake and I left Cambodia, traveled through Thailand, and made our way to Vietnam, starting in the northern city of Hanoi.

Navigating the labyrinthine streets in the Old Quarter, also known as Hoàn Kiếm District, I immersed myself in the choreographed chaos of daily life. A never-ending stream of scooters whirred past, their engines buzzing like angry hornets, layered with the constant bleating of horns. Street vendors called out over the roar, chatting with customers seated on low plastic stools or yelling greetings to friends zipping by. Meanwhile, pedestrians—mothers clutching the hands of barefoot children, delivery men balancing crates on shoulder poles, old women with baskets of fruit—threaded deftly through the sea of motorbikes, like schools of fish maneuvering through a reef. Crossing the street in Hanoi felt like playing a game of frogger, a high-stakes dance, a delicate balance between timing and courage.

Nearby, a blacksmith in a burnt frock swung a heavy hammer onto glowing metal, his veiny forearms straining with each strike. Sparks leapt with every impact, sending jolts through the air that reverberated off the alley walls. It was as if the streets were an open-air museum, showcasing the traditions of Vietnam's skilled artisans.

Craftsmen shaped lacquerware, their hands steady as they carefully brushed layers of glossy black and crimson onto wooden boxes. I slowed our pace, drawn in by the quiet intensity of their work. One man with deep-set eyes wore a simple conical hat that cast a shadow over his brow. His cheeks were pitted, giving his otherwise calm expression a rough, weathered texture. His movements were slow and deliberate, as if each brushstroke was a meditation. I found myself holding my breath, afraid even that small sound might disrupt his focus.

Another craftsman in a faded green shirt and frayed brown trousers sat hunched over a piece of sandalwood, chipping away with a small chisel. He paused to stretch his neck as he caught me staring.

"Take long to get right!" he said, the words slightly slurred through the gaps where a few front teeth were missing. Then he turned back to work.

My thoughts lingered on his words. It struck me how much time and care went into each object—how different this was from the fast, forgettable pace of home.

We ventured into the depths of a vibrant market, pausing by an old woman in a headscarf with a cigar hanging from her lips. She lifted a long, bone-handled knife and sliced cleanly through an eel. Its gray and pink innards slid onto the table with a squelch. A tabby cat crouched below, its eyes fixed on the scraps, tail twitching. The woman looked up briefly, registering my presence with a thin smile, then flicked the scraps toward the cat, which pounced without hesitation.

"Ponchos." Blake nodded toward a stall strung with colorful rain gear—a must for our upcoming motorbike trip.

A wiry vendor greeted us. "You buy? Very good for rain!"

"How much for two?" Blake asked, fingering the plastic material.

"Two hundred thousand dong." The vendor didn't miss a beat.

I knew better than to accept the first price—haggling here wasn't just common; it was expected. "That's too much." I shook my head. "One hundred."

"Ah, no, no!" The vendor placed a hand over his chest, as though wounded. "Special friend price for you, one-seventy."

Blake countered, "One-twenty."

The vendor squinted, lips pursed in exaggerated contemplation. Then he tapped his fingers over his heart. "One-sixty? Good price for you!"

I shook my head, ready to play the final trick in the book when haggling—feign disinterest and begin to walk away. "No, thank you. We'll look somewhere else."

"Wait, wait!" The vendor reached out, mouth tightening in a flicker of panic. "OK, one-forty. Final price."

"One-thirty." Blake crossed his arms.

The vendor sighed, shaking his head. "You...hard customer." He tapped his fingers on the table, then waved a dismissive hand. "OK, OK! One-thirty."

We handed over the cash, I stuffed the ponchos into Blake's backpack. "Think we got a deal?"

Blake grinned. "No idea, but at least we won't get soaked."

As we meandered down the street, traditional medicine shops, their shelves lined with exotic herbs and remedies, emitted a heady blend of cinnamon, star anise, and clove that mingled with the smoky aroma of incense from nearby temples.

A streetside doctor performing surgery on a peasant's foot. It looked like he was cutting out some kind of growth or embedded shard. The patient winced but remained silent, gripping the edge of a wooden stool with white-knuckled fingers.

Just a few steps away, we ducked into a small shop to pick up a few basic medical supplies for our trip—just in case. Bandaids, paracetamol, a bottle of Betadine. Behind the counter, an old man scrubbed syringes with a grimy brush. His tools sat in a cracked porcelain basin, the water gray and murky.

I froze, taking in the scene. The contrast to the sterile clinics I'd always known was jarring. Back home, the thought of reused syringes or open-air surgery would have sparked outrage. Here, it was simply reality. My stomach twisted with a mix of unease and gratitude—gratitude for the healthcare I'd always taken for granted.

Disquiet lingered as we stepped back into the street. Scars of the past were woven into the fabric of the city. Not far from the shop, I stumbled upon a crumbling structure, its walls pockmarked from shrapnel. Vines crept over the surface like nature was trying to reclaim it. It stood as a haunting reminder of the relentless bombings during what the Vietnamese call the American War. Americans know it as the Vietnam War.

Men outside the building sat on low plastic stools, sipping tea and playing chess. Some bore the unmistakable marks of war: a missing arm, a leg replaced by a wooden prosthetic, or the hollow stare of someone who had witnessed too much. These weren't just random injuries—they were living reminders of a conflict that had scarred an entire generation.

Later, we visited a small war museum tucked away near the Old Quarter. The rusted remnants of conflict—fragments of bombs, twisted bicycles used to carry supplies, and grainy photographs of soldiers deep in the jungle—told stories of hardship and survival. Outside, a man sold tiny keychains made from repurposed shell casings. His gait was uneven, each step a quiet triumph over his injuries. In every corner of the city, the resilience of its people shone bright, reflecting their unyielding spirit in the face of unimaginable hardship.

Hanoi had its charm, but after a few days, the constant motion wore thin. Blake and I weren't built for cities. We were itching for something quieter, something green. It was time to get out.

Public transport, where hordes of people squeeze into small spaces and then bump along dusty, pot-holed roads, was not an option. We'd been on one bus in Vietnam, when we first entered the country, and that was enough for us.

Buses commonly became menageries, housing not only people, but also farm animals. I sat next to a woman who smelled like moldy potatoes and had a baby goat in her arms. There were no seats with back support, so I leaned against burlap sacks of rice. Every pothole elicited a bleat from the goat. It wouldn't have been so bad had the temperature and humidity been under ninety-five. Sweat dripped from my brow and trickled from my waist down my legs.

After that arduous journey, Blake and I decided to explore Vietnam on our own terms. We had a mission to purchase a motorbike to tour the country. At the time we were in Vietnam, this was a popular means of travel for many backpackers.

With our own transportation, we would have the freedom to go wherever we pleased, leave whenever we wanted, and stop along the way to stretch, eat, or take photos. It also allowed us to venture off the beaten track, reaching more remote or less-visited destinations.

We found a used motorbike shop—a corrugated metal shack that appeared ready to collapse during the next stiff breeze. Motorcycle parts were scattered across the floor like discarded puzzle pieces—old tires slumped against walls, chains coiled like snakes, and engine parts stacked on sagging wooden shelves.

Two men, their faces and hands smeared with blackened oil, crouched by a bike with its guts exposed. Faded T-shirts clung to their wiry frames, soaked through with sweat, and stains streaked their trousers. One of them wiped his hands on a cloth that had seen better days. He stood as we approached, eyeing us curiously.

"Excuse me," Blake cleared his throat, "we're looking to buy a motorbike."

The man squinted, tilting his head. After a brief exchange with his colleague in Vietnamese, he turned back and motioned for us to follow him deeper into the shop.

"We have," he said, gesturing to a row of used bikes propped against the wall.

Blake crouched to inspect a Yamaha Nuovo with faded black paint and scratches across the bodywork. It wasn't pretty, but it looked solid. The seat was long enough to carry two people, and a rear rack could be welded on easily enough—just a metal frame bolted to the back to hold our bags.

"Mind if I test it?" he asked.

The seller gave a nod.

Blake fired up the engine, which coughed to life in a puff of smoke. He revved it a few times, listening, then rolled it toward the alley for a short spin. I watched him zigzag to the corner and back, weaving around potholes with a grin tugging at his face.

"She'll do," he said, killing the engine with a tap of his thumb. "How much?"

The man scratched his head, muttered something to his colleague, and then held up three fingers. "Three-fifty U.S. dolla," he said.

Blake raised an eyebrow and shook his head. "Too much. Two hundred is a good price for this."

What followed was a rapid-fire exchange in Vietnamese between the two men, peppered with animated gestures toward the bike and us. One of them pointed to the tires as if justifying the price, while the other shrugged and waved a dismissive hand.

"Two-fifty," the man finally countered.

Blake leaned in. "We can give two-fifty. *If* you include two helmets. It's a good deal."

The man muttered to his friend again before sighing heavily. "OK," he said, holding up two fingers. "Two-fifty. Two helmets."

Blake grinned, shaking his hand. "Deal."

Before we handed over the cash, Blake gave the bike one last inspection—checking the brakes, headlights, tires, and oil. Licenses, registration, and paperwork? Not needed. The men waved off such questions with a laugh. In Vietnam, such formalities were distant, irrelevant concepts. In less than an hour, the bike was officially ours.

The motorbike hummed beneath us as Blake and I drove away from the repair shop. I wrapped my arms around his waist. The wind tangled my hair as it whipped past. Freedom buzzed in the air.

"OK," I raised my voice over the growl of the engine, "she needs a name. Something strong, something adventurous."

Blake chuckled. "How about Black Lightning?"

I wrinkled my nose. "Too cheesy. She's not a lame superhero, she's a warrior."

"A warrior, huh? What about Xena? Like the warrior princess from that TV show."

"Yes! Xena. She's tough, independent, and takes on the world. It's perfect."

"Xena it is, then. Let's see what she can do." Blake revved the engine, and the bike surged forward. Xena, our warrior princess, was carrying us into the unknown, and I couldn't wait to see where she would take us.

Before leaving Hanoi we needed to minimize the weight on our new ride. Blake insisted we get rid of anything that wasn't essential to our cross-country trip. Tears welled as I was forced to leave behind all of the cherished knick-knacks I had gathered during my travels through Cambodia, and Thailand.

"We haven't got all day, Shan. These little souvenirs won't mean much if we end up stranded 'cause we're hauling too much junk."

"They're not junk, Blake. They're memories. They mean something to me."

He let out a sharp breath, running a hand through his hair. "Look, we're about to cross an entire country on one motorbike. We can't have too much weight. All our stuff needs to be consolidated into one bag."

"Well, why are we lugging around your damned guitar then?"

"You know it's my baby." He crossed his arms as he tapped his foot impatiently. "I've had it for over a decade. Hell, it's how I make money in the summer season! This isn't negotiable."

My fingers tightened around my pack. "Fine." Biting back a wave of frustration and sadness, I sorted through my treasures, each one feeling heavier than the last as I prepared to let it go.

I held my prized Tibetan singing bowl one final time, its smooth surface cool against my skin. As I struck it gently, its melodic resonance filled the air. Its rich tone sent one last calming vibration through my body. The sound lingered in the room, carrying with it memories of peaceful moments spent in meditation.

I gently ran my fingers across the woven basket from Cambodia. Crafted with remarkable dexterity, it showcased the skill and artistry of the local woman who had painstakingly harvested and woven the reeds to create this masterpiece. I marveled at the hours of labor that went into its creation.

It was hardest to give up my books, all seven of them. Each page, well-worn from reading, held a world I wasn't ready to let go of.

Blake shifted his weight, clearly restless, as I picked up a tattered copy of *Shantaram*, its spine cracked from countless readings. "You're so ridiculous carrying a library on your back."

"These were my companions while traveling solo!" I shot back.

"Sure. But you're not solo traveling anymore, are ya? Time to be practical. Haven't you read this one already?" Blake held up *The Alchemist*. "It's being tossed with the others."

I let out a shaky breath.

After we'd lightened our load and hired a welder to attach a metal rack to the bike for our gear, we were prepared to embrace the open road. The souvenirs of my past travels might have been gone, but the memories they held stayed with me. What I carried now wasn't tangible. The beauty of the world would become my most treasured possession.

Armed with our motorbike, no phones, and a measly tourist map that only showed the main highway, we took off to the north. With no particular destination in mind, we could never be lost. Our plan was to wander aimlessly, take in the culture, small villages, and nature along the way. If we were intrigued with a location we would stay, and if not, we would keep driving on through.

Each morning we stuffed our faces with bánh mì, a Vietnamese sandwich, or a big bowl of phở, the quintessential staple of Vietnamese cuisine. The sandwich features a crispy baguette—thanks to French colonial influence—filled with marinated pork, pickled carrots, daikon, cilantro, and a bit of chili sauce. It's a perfect mix of crunchy, spicy, and savory, packed into each bite.

After we finished, we set out on the road. Lucky for me, Blake always drove. This left me with the privilege to snuggle up behind him, hold his waist for support, and daydream as I marveled at the passing sights. Misty green mountains rolled into the horizon. Clusters of stilt houses nestled among banana trees. Water buffalo plodded along narrow dirt paths, as villagers in conical hats tended their crops.

As we moved through remote villages in the far north, local people stared at us with a mixture of shock and curiosity. I got the impression they had not seen a foreigner in decades. It was quite possible that the last time a white foreigner had been seen was during the Vietnam War, when American soldiers pummeled those villages.

In one tiny village, our arrival sparked an instant frenzy. Swarms of people rushed out from small shack houses, crowding the dirt road. Children darted ahead, their faces lit with exhilaration. They leapt over rocks and patches of broken earth, waving their arms as they shouted, "Hello! Hello!"

A few children chased after us, running barefoot on the uneven path, hands outstretched to reach us as if we were mythical creatures come to life. "Where you from?" they called in unison.

"America!" I replied warmly. "Nice to meet you!"

The children giggled, their smiles never fading as they waved us on with more shouts of "Welcome to Vietnam!"

I blinked in surprise. Even here, tucked deep in the countryside, stray words of English surfaced like driftwood. Maybe they'd picked it up from dubbed movies playing on old TVs inside those crooked houses. It was a surreal reminder of how far certain words can travel, even when so little else does.

I snapped out of my reverie when an older man with a wide, toothless grin clapped his hands and shouted, "Hello, hello!" The enthusiasm in his voice cracked as he cupped his hands around his mouth to amplify his greeting.

I wondered, *Is this what it feels like to be a celebrity? Your mere presence met with awe wherever you go? The pressure to be a polite representative of kindness even when you're tired or lost in thought?*

I reflected on the privilege and challenge of being in the spotlight. What had begun as a journey of exploration had transformed into something deeper—an opportunity for human connection. It taught us that with open hearts and genuine intentions, we could leave a trail of smiles in our wake.

However, traveling through a foreign country also provided many opportunities for confusion while interacting with locals.

One afternoon, Blake and I rode through a valley tucked deep in the remote northern mountains. Towering peaks loomed all around us. There wasn't a single sign of human life. Every so often, a hawk glided overhead, casting a fleeting shadow on the winding dirt road. We felt like insignificant specks in the vast expanse of nature.

The roar of the engine echoed off the mountainsides, almost swallowed by the vastness of the valley. The bike vibrated beneath us. After hours on the road, the hard seat had become unbearable, every bump jolting up my spine. I shifted on my seat, my thighs and lower back aching, but there was something grounding about the discomfort—a reminder of the effort it took to reach this untouched corner of the world.

As we drove further along the rugged terrain we passed sparse fields, carved meticulously by hand, their rows tilting gently down slopes toward small, thatched-roof shacks. The fragrance of freshly tilled soil filled the air, like the damp scent of a forest floor after a summer rain.

As we continued further into the mountains, the air grew cooler, a welcome change from the hot, sticky embrace of Vietnam's lowlands. At first, we reveled in the fresh, crisp breeze, but soon a torrential storm rolled in like a beast waking from slumber.

Lightning bolts ripped across the sky, illuminating the landscape in eerie flashes of electric blue. Thunder shook us with mighty roars echoing through the mountains. Blankets of rain pelted down with unrelenting force.

We slid around a sharp curve. Waves of water cascaded down the muddy road, rushing toward us like a river reclaiming its path. The bike skidded slightly as Blake gripped the handlebars tighter, his voice rising above the storm, "Hold tighter!"

The road, once a winding trail of adventure, had transformed into a treacherous path, nearly invisible beneath the flood of rain. In a desperate attempt to protect ourselves, we quickly pulled off the road at the first simple wooden hut we could find. Soaked clothes clung to my skin as water dripped down my face in rivulets. I wiped it away with one hand as we hurried toward the door of the one-room wooden structure, our shoes squelching in the mud.

Behind me, Blake muttered, "Brilliant idea to pack the ponchos at the bottom of the bag. Honestly, Shan, top-tier logic."

I shot him a glare, but said nothing, too cold and wet to argue.

An old man with crinkled eyebrows, dark brown eyes, and a slightly stooped back answered the door. Based on his dirt-clad clothes and the plethora of tools stacked against the walls of his home, I assumed he was a farmer. We could not directly ask him because we spoke very little Vietnamese.

I gestured wildly to the sky, my hands mimicking the falling rain, hoping he would understand our predicament.

Blake stood beside me, arms crossed against the chill, his shoulders hunched as he shivered. He edged closer to the farmer, his voice raised to be heard over the rain. "Can we...shelter?"

The farmer furrowed his brow, glancing between us and the darkening sky, but a faint smile broke through as he nodded, inviting us into his home, gesturing for us to sit down on the floor with him.

As we sat awkwardly cross-legged in silence, I scanned the modest home. A framed photograph of the man in military regalia hung on the wall. A single twin bed with no sheets lay in a corner on the floor. Nails pegged into the walls held the man's meager collection of dusty clothes. A row of sharpened machetes leaned against the wall by the door, along with a shotgun.

The farmer initiated conversation, using body language. With a sparkle of curiosity in his eyes, the man pointed to me, then to Blake, then to his crotch.

"Excuse me?" Blake responded in bewilderment.

The man again pointed to me, and then outstretched his arms in front of his stomach, encircling them near the womb, creating a symbol for pregnancy.

With this gesture Blake immediately went into a protective mode of panic. "Shan, I think he's talking about having a baby with you?

Like having sex or something. Did you notice the shotgun in the corner? I want to get out of here immediately."

Presumably not understanding a word Blake just said, the man began to nod in agreement, pointing to me, Blake, and his crotch once more. This time he wiggled his hips a bit before he pretended to hold a baby nestled in his arms.

"What the fuck!" I responded in a whispered scream. "Yes, please! I don't feel comfortable. This guy is creepy."

The man jumped to his feet and walked towards a cabinet that sat next to the bed. Blake followed his movements. My heart-beat ran a million miles a minute as the man pulled open a drawer. I feared he was grabbing for a weapon, in an attempt to sexually harass me.

But he was grabbing a family photo album.

He opened it to the first page, which had a picture of him holding a baby. He then pointed at Blake and me once more, and then made a questioning gesture with his arms.

Blake and I burst into laughter.

"He's asking if we have a baby! Not if I will have sex with him!"

With a grin, I pointed to Blake, then back to myself, rocking an imaginary baby in my arms with a lighthearted sway. Then I waved my hands in front of me, brushing the idea aside.

"No baby!" Blake managed to say through chuckles. He shook his head emphatically, then crossed his arms in a big X over his chest, hoping to convey a firm *no*.

I joined in, pointing between us, shaking my head with an exaggerated motion, adding a final cross of my arms in front of me, mimicking a big, playful *no way!*

The farmer gave a cheerful nod, as if to say, "*Ah, got it!*" He clapped Blake on the shoulder, then shot me a thumbs-up, his toothy grin saying it all—lost in translation, but found in laughter.

Within minutes, the heavy storm vanished as quickly as it had come. Blake and I exchanged a quick, knowing glance—it was time to move on.

Blake stepped forward, placing a hand on his chest in a gesture of gratitude, bowing his head slightly. "Thank you, thank you," he said.

I joined in, pressing my palms together and giving a slight bow, then pointing to the door of his small home. "Cảm ơn, cảm ơn," I attempted, using the one phrase of Vietnamese I knew for gratitude. The farmer's grin widened, his head bobbing with understanding. He waved his hand in a dismissive yet warm way, as if to say it was no trouble at all.

With one last wave, Blake started our motorbike. The engine sputtered to life as we backed onto the muddy path. The farmer watched us go, standing in the doorway of his small wooden home.

As we rode off, I turned back for one last look, catching him still waving, his silhouette gradually fading into the mountain fog. We were back on our journey, destination unknown, as always.

23

SHAMANIC BLESSINGS

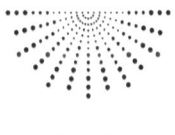

VIETNAM

*B*lake and I eventually found ourselves in the mountainous town of Sapa, located near the Chinese border. Sapa sits at the head of an expansive valley of magnificent rice terraces plunging down from cliffs that are cultivated the same way they have been for centuries.

Generations of farmers have carefully maintained the terraces, following ancient methods to channel water from the mountains and ensure the rice paddies remain fertile through the seasons. The terraces curved around the mountainsides in a series of delicate steps, their edges lined with bright green shoots in the wet season and golden stalks before the harvest. Narrow footpaths wound between the tiers, and thin streams of water trickled down from higher elevations, filling the paddies with a glassy sheen that reflected the shifting sky. From a distance, the terraces resembled giant, layered ribbons of green and gold, cascading down the valley in undulating patterns that mirrored the contours of the land.

Not much is known about the first people to inhabit Sapa. Experts believe that a number of worn-down petroglyphs, dating back to the fifteenth century, are all that remain of the area's original inhabitants.

The first groups to move into the area after these earlier inhabitants were the Hmong and Dao peoples, who developed rich agricultural practices and preserved distinct cultural traditions that remain visible in Sapa today.

The history of the Hmong people is difficult to trace, passed down only through oral records, through legends and ritual ceremonies from one generation to another, as well as through Hmong textile art or story cloths, sewn by women.

Genetic and linguistic studies suggest that the Hmong people originally came from the Yangtze River basin in southern China, where they practiced rotational farming on forested hillsides, moving every few decades when soil fertility waned. Their mobile lifestyle, however, conflicted with the centralized Chinese dynasties, who viewed their shifting settlements as difficult to control. This led to the Hmong being targets of forced labor, taxation, and cultural suppression, driving many to seek refuge in the rugged highlands along the borders of Laos, Myanmar, Thailand, and Vietnam, where they continued their traditions in relative isolation, under the constant threat of political domination. Over time, the Hmong became an ethnic group now native to several countries. In Vietnam, they are one of the largest ethnic groups, with nearly one million people living there today.

Rooted in a strong cultural identity, the Hmong have long clashed with the Vietnamese government, often facing cultural ostracism and persecution. One example of that occurred in the twentieth century, when the Hmong were forced to switch to permanent cultivation on a single plot of land. The Vietnamese government claimed this as a necessity because they believed there wasn't enough uninhabited land remaining for the Hmong people's traditional type of agriculture.

Despite the many challenges faced over time, the Hmong have continued to adapt to the world around them. This has included shifting a large part of their economy from agriculture to tourism. In places like Sapa, a colorful array of handicrafts, jewelry, and garments can be purchased from Hmong people. It is also possible for tourists to take part in homestay experiences, to get an inside peek into these intriguing communities. This was our goal while visiting the Sapa region.

As we roamed through the streets, we stumbled upon a local bar. Its walls were a patchwork of stone and weathered wood, giving it an old-world charm. Natural daylight poured in through tall windows, casting a warm glow over the room. Inside, long wooden tables stretched across the room, inviting strangers to sit shoulder to shoulder. The setup created a communal atmosphere where people naturally leaned in, exchanged smiles, and fell into easy conversation.

We were drawn to the bar because it was overflowing with hill tribe Hmong women. We were able to identify them by their traditional Hmong clothing. Their jackets, wrapped tightly around them, were embroidered with cobalt blue and deep green threads, forming tiny geometric patterns that rippled in waves across the fabric. Delicate motifs of spirals, stars, and cross-stitch diamond shapes traced the cuffs and hems. Bright pink and red sashes cinched their waists, offsetting the navy blues of the cloth. Thick, hand-stitched skirts billowed out in pleated layers, striped with contrasting colors of maroon, yellow, and turquoise. The meticulous craftsmanship was unmistakable, with every line and border sewn with a precision that spoke of both tradition and a skilled hand—an artistry passed down through generations.

I scanned the bar, hoping to spot an open seat among the lively crowd. A young local woman with dark hair spilling loosely over her shoulders waved and caught my attention. She gestured for me and Blake to join her.

"I'm Shannon, and this is Blake," I said as we sat down.

"I'm Lan," she said, then gestured to the friend beside her. "This My. She not speak English, but she understand little bit."

My smiled, her face framed by long, straight hair, with a slight shadow of freckles across her cheeks. The lightbulbs hanging from the ceiling in recycled plastic bottles cast a warm, diffused glow on her amber skin. She was petite, almost delicate, but her grip on the drink in front of her showed strength in her hands.

Lan tilted her head, studying me and Blake with curious eyes. "You drink beer?"

"We sure do," Blake responded. "Two please."

Lan yelled an order to the nearby bartender.

As the waiter plopped our beers down on the table, an older woman approached, her energy filling the room. She wore traditional Hmong clothing, an indigo jacket lined with silver coins that jingled softly as she moved. A wide, toothy smile made her eyes nearly disappear beneath laugh lines. She reached out a small, strong hand. Her voice rang out cheerfully. "Hello, I am Mama T! You are new friends, yes?"

"We'd love to be! I'm Shannon, and this is Blake," I replied, matching her enthusiasm.

"Ah, I like you! You both look strong, ready for trekking, yes?" She winked at Blake, who grinned back, clearly charmed.

"Are you a guide?" he asked.

"Oh yes! Many years," she said, nodding proudly. "I take people through mountains, rivers, all the way to my village. We walk, we laugh, we see so many beautiful things. Always best way to know Sapa."

Moving a little closer, Lan whispered, "You should go with Mama T. Tourists always have good time with her."

Mama T flashed Lan a grin. "Yes, yes, Lan know! We don't just walk. I show you flowers, herbs, teach you Hmong stories. We cook together at night. Is good, simple way."

"That sounds amazing," I said.

Mama T gave a delighted laugh. "I share good life. Hmong people, we know how to be happy with simple things. I wake up, see the mountain, eat rice, talk to family, meet new people—what more I need?"

Blake and I exchanged a look, feeling the pull of her infectious spirit.

"And how much is it?" I asked.

She waved her hand as if brushing the question from the air. "Only fifteen dolla per day. Food, homestay, walk with me, stories. You don't spend more than that."

Before we could respond Mama T clapped her hands together, nodding as if the decision had already been made. "Good, good! We meet tomorrow morning. I show you my village, my home," and then with another wink, "and I have surprise for you tomorrow. Very special you will see."

"OK, Mama T. Sounds great. Meet you here in the morning then? What time?"

"7 a.m. early bird gets worm as you say!" Mama T playfully nudged my shoulders. "I go collect supplies now! Thank you, my new friends." She put a hand to her heart and then turned to leave as quickly as she came.

Upon our meet-up the next morning, Mama T shared with us the significance of the day. "Morning, my friends! I tell you I have surprise today! Special day! The local shaman coming to bless our home and drive away evil spirits."

Blake leaned forward. "Really? What does the ceremony involve?"

Mama T smiled warmly, her eyes crinkling at the corners. "Well, it's tradition that happens once a year. The shaman make rituals and prayers to protect us and our home."

I nodded, intrigued by this glimpse into their culture. "That sounds fascinating. How long does the ceremony last?"

Mama T chuckled, shaking her head. "Oh, it can go whole day. But it's worth it for peace of mind."

"It's amazing how your family still holds onto these beliefs," Blake remarked.

Mama T's expression turned serious as she nodded. "Yes, important to us. Especially after missionaries came in nineteenth century. They try to convert everyone to Christian. We held our faith, animism. It is our culture. We must preserve."

I could sense the pride in Mama T's voice as she spoke of her family's resilience. "That's really admirable," I said. "I've never met a shaman before. I don't really know anything about them."

Mama T's eyes sparkled. "Shaman, or 'master of spirits,' is heart of our Hmong culture!"

"What exactly does a shaman do?" Blake asked.

"Well, shaman act as mediator between human and spirit world. They perform rituals, talk with spirits, and heal sick."

"But what does that have to do with animism?" I asked. "I must admit I don't know a thing about animism either..."

Mama T nodded understandingly. "Many indigenous people around world have animism belief. It's good to understand!" She continued patiently, "Animism is belief that all objects, places, and creatures have a spirit. In our culture, everything is alive with spirit."

Blake's eyes widened. "So, it's about seeing the interconnectedness of all living things?"

Mama T nodded, her expression radiant with pride. "Exactly! Animism teach us to respect and honor all. We see the sacredness of life. You will learn more. Let's head out!"

As we started walking, her words stayed with me. There was something about the idea of animism that felt right. Everything *does* carry energy. Maybe this belief was just a more intuitive way of acknowledging and honoring that. I liked the idea of humans seeing themselves as part of nature rather than separate from it—or worse, in charge of it.

That thought lingered as we moved through the landscape. Mama T led us along a narrow, rugged trail that twisted through dense bamboo groves and wild, green expanses. The morning mist clung to the valleys, parting here and there to reveal glimpses of terraced rice fields carved into the steep hillsides. The earthy scent of damp leaves and rich soil filled the air, mingling with the delicate perfume of wild orchids and bright yellow marigolds that lined our path.

As we hiked, birds sang around us. Scarlet minivets darted through branches, their brilliant red feathers flashing against the green foliage. Coos of black-breasted thrushes echoed from deeper in the forest. Every now and then, we caught sight of a crested serpent eagle soaring above, its wings stretched wide as it glided over the valley, searching the land below for prey with sharp, watchful eyes.

Mama T moved gracefully along the rocky path, pausing occasionally to point out wild tea plants and lush ferns covering the forest floor. "This flower—moon orchid," she said, bending to brush her hand across a delicate white blossom. "Hmong people use for medicine, for tea. Good for calming spirit."

We continued on, our steps softened by patches of thick moss and the crunch of fallen pine needles. Mama T paused beside a bush with small, delicate pink blossoms. "This one," she said, pressing a finger to a leaf and giving it a gentle rub, "called 'gao ben.' Good for headache, for body aches."

A few steps later, she gestured toward a cluster of tall, thin stems topped with pale blue flowers. "This is 'cao gai leo'—snake fern." She broke off a piece and held it out for us to smell. The scent was faintly spicy. "We boil this, make a drink for cough or fever."

As the forest grew denser, Mama T knelt beside a tiny, bushy plant with yellow flowers and plucked a few sprigs. "This is 'ngo gai,' or sawleaf." She placed the leaves into her basket. "Hmong people use for stomach pain. Sometimes we add to soup. Good for cooking, give strong taste. We use for dinner tonight."

With each step, I grew more connected to the natural world around us, marveling at the beauty and tranquility of the untamed landscape.

After four hours of hiking, we entered Mama T's village. It looked like something from another century—wooden stilt houses with tin or thatched roofs, chickens weaving between laundry lines, and woven baskets stacked high with corn husks and firewood. A few elders watched us from shaded doorways, their hands busy threading. The distant clang of metal hinted at someone sharpening a blade or hammering a tool.

Vegetable gardens spilled out from the edges of each home—patches of leafy greens, herbs, and chili plants bordered by crooked bamboo fencing. Pigs snuffled in the dirt beside piles of foraged roots and stripped corn cobs. Plastic bowls, cracked buckets, and worn sandals were

were scattered across the hard-packed earth, as if dropped mid-task and forgotten.

Hordes of barefoot children welcomed us, their blissful shrieks echoing through the air. Small, calloused hands reached eagerly for our arms, their fingers sticky with the remnants of fruit. Their chatter was an untranslatable yet universal language, a melody of joy and wonder that needed no subtitles.

The children's clothes, mismatched garments worn thin by use, bore the earthy tones of the village—dusty browns, faded greens, sun-bleached yellows. Some went without shirts entirely, their bellies poking out as they laughed. Their bare feet, toughened by years of navigating rocky paths and muddy trails, kicked up tiny clouds of dust as they danced around us.

Close behind the children, a couple of mangy village dogs trotted, their ribs visible through patchy coats. They paused to snap at fleas or scratch vigorously, their nails raking their sides. Occasionally, one let out a high-pitched yelp as another nipped at its heels in a burst of playfulness.

One girl had a face that radiated a pure, unguarded warmth. Traces of dirt on her cheeks told the story of the day's adventures running around outside, untouched by the constraints of technology. She clutched a treasure born of resourcefulness: a bicycle tire, long deflated, which she rolled along with a stick. Her giggles rose each time it wobbled dangerously close to falling.

The children's presence reminded me of the precious innocence that often gets lost in the whirlwind of our fast-paced lives. It was a reminder of the simple jubilation found in running through fields, climbing trees, and chasing dreams. I was filled with gratitude for the chance to visit this place, a location still largely untouched by modern life, where nature ruled and the passage of time appeared irrelevant.

Mama T led us further into the village. Black water buffalos sat with legs folded beneath them while chewing long grass. Flights of grasshoppers exploded from beneath our feet. Pillars of dung smoke rose from the village homes, carrying a pungent, earthy aroma that mingled with the humid air. We were immersed in an undeniably Asian landscape.

The home we arrived at was nothing more than a ramshackle, two-room plain building. Its walls and frame were crafted from weathered wood cut from the surrounding forest. The house was low and windowless, to protect it from the climatic conditions of the mountains.

Inside, life had been stripped down to its bare essentials. There was no furniture, other than a few low-to-the-ground wooden stools, their surfaces polished smooth by years of use. A single double mattress lay directly on the dirt floor, its stuffing of hemp and straw poking through a patched covering. Two lightbulbs hung haphazardly from the ceiling. The second room of the house, used as the kitchen, consisted of nothing more than a firepit placed in the middle of the floor.

Mama T seemed to notice the way we lingered at the threshold, quietly absorbing the simplicity of her world. "We not have much. But it's enough. All we need."

Her words hung in the air, a soft reminder of a truth often over-looked. This home, with its dirt floors and smoky walls, was enough to hold a family, their laughter and their tears.

The shaman arrived soon after. The lines on her face held the weight of wisdom, carved deep by a lifetime devoted to her spiritual path. High, sharp cheekbones framed a face the color of sun-warmed clay. Silver-streaked hair, pulled tightly into a low knot, exposed a broad forehead and deep-set eyes that looked straight through me. She moved slowly but deliberately, with the authority of someone used to being listened to. Even in silence, she emanated presence—rooted, watchful, and at ease in the world around her.

In many societies, women are often relegated to subordinate roles, confined to domestic duties and child-rearing. Witnessing a woman occupy such a revered position in her community was a welcome revelation.

Mama T stood beside us. "You like her clothes? Traditional."

"Yes, very much," I answered, admiring the rich mix of colors in the shaman's clothing, along with her headdress adorned with feathers and intricate beadwork.

"These fabrics, we make from plants. The colors—they come from roots, leaves, bark. Each one has a story."

"This from the *lacquer tree*," Mama T explained, gesturing to the dark reddish-brown hue that ran through her blouse in wide, bold swaths. "We crush bark, boil it for many days, then it gives this color." Her fingers traced the fabric gently, as though feeling the years of tradition embedded within each thread.

"And these," she continued, her hand moving to the collar, "every stitch tell story. The designs—they stories of our people. The *spirals* here," she pointed to a swirl of stitches, "they tell the cycles of life, the seasons. The *diamond shapes* are protection—keep us safe from evil spirits. And you see long straight line?" She traced her finger along a row of sharp, clean lines. "They show path of ancestors. Each piece sewn with meaning."

She pointed to the shaman's headdress, a work of art. The colorful beads shimmered, and the feathers, long and soft, swayed gently with her movements. "The feathers are from birds of mountains. They bring wisdom of sky. They connect our world and spirits. They help guide the shaman, remind her spirits are with her."

Following brief introductions and respectful greetings with the family, the shaman promptly initiated her ceremony. Her aim was to bless the household and expel any lingering, unwanted spirits.

I assumed the ceremony would be solemn. I thought the entire family would be expected to pay utmost respect and attention. Instead, they carried on with business as normal; the kids played loudly, the women chatted in the kitchen, and the men chain-smoked from tobacco bongs outside. In Northern Vietnam, tobacco bongs, or điếu cày, can be found everywhere. These bongs, typically made from wood or bamboo, are tall and narrow, with a curved neck that leads to a small, rounded mouthpiece at the top. Men and sometimes women enjoy using these bongs to smoke thuốc lào, which is a potent variety of tobacco. A strong head high and slight dizziness are guaranteed when smoking a bong load of thuốc lào. In Vietnam, people smoke it after a meal on a full stomach. It's an old custom they believe aids digestion.

Though everyone in the family seemed uninterested, the shaman's presence fascinated Blake and me. We stood at the back of the house for five hours, silent and intrigued by her procedures. Members of the family occasionally came by to check in and then dispersed to continue their business.

The shaman's ritual had many stages. Each included some sort of prayer, but more interestingly, distinct conversations with invisible ghosts or spirits in the room.

She gripped a handful of buffalo horn tips and shook them in her calloused hands with quick, sharp movements. Their hollow rattle cut through the air before she smashed them to the ground. The tips scattered in jagged patterns across the dirt floor, and she stared at them, eyes narrowing, face tightening. There was an apparent meaning behind the ways the horn tips fell to the ground. Whatever she saw didn't please her.

This sent her into a frenzied debate with the invisible spirits. Her voice rose, as she spoke quickly in her Hmong dialect, as though the spirits argued back. She gestured wildly, her hands slicing the air, as she engaged in enthusiastic back-and-forth conversations with no one but the sky.

Then she gathered the horns again, shaking them with more urgency before letting them fall. Over and over, she repeated the process—shake, throw, read, react. Each time, she grew louder, her frustration spilling into frantic movements and sharp tones. Between rounds, she downed shots of rice whiskey, one after the other. Her motions became more erratic as the whiskey worked its magic, loosening her body and pulling her deeper into a trance.

Mama T slipped into the room and crouched beside us. She whispered, low enough not to disturb the ritual. "The mask she wear, it help her block out this world, so she can focus on spirit world. It also hide her from evil spirits. They cannot recognize her face this way. More safe."

The explanation added weight to the scene. It wasn't just a piece of cloth—it was her shield, her bridge between the worlds she navigated.

By the time the shaman finished with the buffalo horns, the majority of the family had entered the house. They stood at a respectful distance and watched silently. In a gesture of reverence, the man of the family presented the shaman with a live chicken. She viciously grabbed it, restricting its movement by holding its legs and neck. She then began a spirited dance, vigorously shaking the chicken above her head, toward the earth and around her body. She continuously chanted and sang throughout.

In a flash, she grabbed a sharp knife and slit the chicken's throat. I sucked in a sharp breath, startled by the suddenness of the kill. Crimson blood spilled into a metal bowl as the chanting continued.

I was astonished to notice young children, aged three to nine, standing by. They did not wince or flinch at the sight of the slaughter. They did not stand disgusted or worried by the sight of blood pouring from the chicken's throat, but rather beheld the spectacle with a mixture of wonderment and curiosity.

I wish I could say the same for myself as a pig was led into the center of the house.

Have you ever heard the sounds of a pig being killed? Their shocked and scared squeals resemble a human screaming in distress. Animal rights activists argue that pigs are at least as cognitively aware as monkeys, and they are often considered the fifth most intelligent animal in the world by researchers and animal behaviorists. They have been shown to have the capacity to experience emotions similar to humans: happiness, excitement, fear, and anxiety. Given their intelligence, I couldn't help but think this pig was aware of what was happening, understanding it was being prepped for slaughter.

Unlike the primed and ready children, I had to fight the urge to look away.

Mama T gripped the pig firmly, holding him down on the table. Its body trembled beneath her, breath quickening in desperate gasps.

As the shaman drew her knife across the animal's throat, the sound was sharp—a sickening, wet *slice*—and then the pig screamed.

"Eeeeyaahhh. Eeeeyahhh," the cries erupted, raw and guttural. Each yelp ripped at my insides. I pressed my palm against my mouth, but the taste of bile still rose.

The pig's blood flowed in a steady stream, splashing into a metal bowl beneath it. My eyes flicked to the pig's face, glassy pupils dilated, its expression frozen in fear—staring at its executioner.

I clenched my jaw. Blake's hand found mine, his fingers wrapping in a tight grip. He didn't say anything, but the warmth of his touch was grounding.

Still, I couldn't escape the *feeling* of it—the presence of the animal's soul leaving its body, the finality of it hanging heavy in the air. The guilt of watching this death would haunt my dreams for days to come.

And just like that, the shaman's ceremony was complete.

In keeping with Hmong tradition, the end of the ritual signaled the beginning of something more familiar: a communal feast. Ceremonies like the one I had just witnessed typically concluded with a shared meal, where everyone who attended was invited to eat the sacrificial animals.

I was impressed by the collaborative spirit that went into the preparation of this meal. Each person knew their role—some set up three long tables, others arranged chairs for the twenty-plus family and community members who would join the ceremonial meal.

What surprised me most was how "civil" the meal felt. Despite being in a sparse hut, everyone sat in chairs with a full set of dishes and cutlery before them. No one touched the food until the man of the house raised his glass and launched into a long-winded toast, his words punctuated by hearty laughter and the occasional cheer.

When the plates were passed around, conversations overlapped, hands reached eagerly for food, and conversations bubbled up from every corner. The spread was a feast: steaming bowls of white rice, chicken seasoned with mint and ginger, tender pork glistening in a soy sauce glaze, and an assortment of vegetables straight from the local farms, their flavors intensified with cilantro and lemongrass. Small piles of fiery hot peppers anchored the spread.

Among the dishes, the centerpiece was the large bowl of pig's blood, thickened into a jelly-like mass, with chunks of fat and flecks of herbs floating in the dark crimson mixture. The aroma had an iron tang that clung to the back of my throat. I was not interested in chowing down on spoonfuls of pig's blood. My stomach churned at the thought even before I took a bite.

Unfortunately, based on everyone's excitement over the blood, I gathered that it would be rude not to try.

With a forced smile, I scooped up a spoonful. The texture was both foreign and unsettling, a gelatinous substance that melted and broke apart in my mouth. Soft yet lumpy, cold and slimy. The taste was overpowering—rich and gamey, coating my tongue.

Eager eyes darted toward me, waiting to see how I would react.

I wanted to recoil, but I kept my face steady, determined not to offend. My fingers tightened around my glass of rice whiskey, and I chased the spoonful down with a fiery gulp. It took another gulp to burn away the aftertaste.

The room erupted in cheers, with hands clapping and faces beaming approval at my effort. Mama T refilled my glass with a knowing smile. Blake and I were considered honored guests at the dinner, and therefore person after person continuously offered us ceremonial glasses to raise a toast and drink immediately out of respect.

Usually, I promote feminist values of equality. However, I let go of my cries for this when it came to rice whiskey being poured at the table. Women were not expected to drink the powerful liquor as is. I considered this to be a godsend as I found the homemade booze resembled the taste of rubbing alcohol. Women were given a watered down, sugary version of the rice whiskey. *I was beyond grateful.*

The table wobbled beneath me as the evening wore on. My jokes, once mediocre, were suddenly hilarious. Despite my weakened rice whiskey, both Blake and I were pleasantly inebriated by the end of the evening.

Mama T escorted us down the dirt path to her brother's home, where we would sleep that night. As we stepped into the modest dwelling, a mattress was already laid out on the floor, simple but welcoming.

Mama T wasted no time in setting a pot on the firepit. "I get water boiling for you," she said. "I don't want our water give you bad belly. For me, OK, but tourists get sick if they drink."

Blake chuckled, swaying slightly from the effects of rice whiskey. "You're too kind, Mama T. We're lucky to have you looking out for us."

Mama T waved off his thanks with a laugh. "No problem, my friends! My heart is so happy to share special day with you!"

We sat together joyfully, buzzing from the day's adventures. For a moment, I lost myself in a quiet reverie. My gaze wandered, drawn to the peg on the wall where Mama T's pleated skirt hung, its turquoise fabric faded at the edges, softened by years of wear. The hem was lined with hand-stitched patterns, resembling tiny waves and peaks— a homage to the mountains and rivers that surrounded the village.

Mama T and the women of her village had a relationship with hemp. They grew it, harvested it, and painstakingly spun it by hand into fine strands that formed the foundation of their art. The love they poured into their textiles was evident in every stitch.

As I admired Mama T's needlework, a lightbulb lit up in her eyes. She suddenly jumped up from her seat and hustled outside to a nearby shed. She came back with an armful of marijuana. "My friend, I hear that tourists like to smoke this flower from our hemp plants. Is that true?"

Blake and I burst out laughing.

Between our giggles Blake was able to squeeze out, "Yes, Mama T, tourists LOVE to smoke the hemp plant flower."

Satisfaction swept over her face as she shuffled across her brother's dirt floor to grab his bamboo bong. She cradled it like a teapot at a dinner party. "Maybe I try with next guests," she mused, turning the bong over in her hands. "Or offer as a welcome gift?"

"I think..." I bit my lip, struggling not to snort. "That might be a hit!"

Mama T nodded, pleased with herself. "Tourists love this flower," she repeated, tucking a few buds into a small clay jar for safekeeping.

She placed the bong gently back on the shelf, then returned to her spot beside us, settling in with a satisfied sigh. The conversation drifted.

As the night wore on, I found myself stifling a grin at the image in my head: future guests arriving at her homestay, greeted not just with hot tea and a freshly cooked meal, but a cheeky little herbal side offering—her own unofficial version of a welcome tray.

24
LAGOS BECKONS

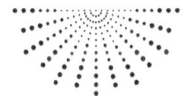

"Shan, the time has finally come." Blake's deep blue eyes searched mine. "I need to get some work and stack up cash in my account."

"Me too... I can't believe the money I saved in Oz lasted this long. But I'm almost out..." The weight of our predicament settled heavily upon me. After four months traveling together, enjoying some of the most extraordinary adventures of my life, our trip had come to an end.

"We can find work somewhere together."

"It's almost impossible for Americans to get work visas anywhere. I don't think it's going to happen, Blake." My nerves prickled.

He leaned in, a furrow creasing his brow. "What about Lagos, Portugal? You know I've spent years going there playing music for tourists in the summer."

"And what about me, Blake? I can't get a work visa in Europe."

"I have lots of connections in Lagos. You could go on a tourist visa and we could find you some under the table work in a bar or something."

"Seriously? You really think you could find me work there?"

"Definitely."

I hesitated, my apprehension bubbling. "But Blake, I feel vulnerable following you across the planet. Lagos is your place…"

Blake reached for my hand, his gaze softening. "Trust me, you'll love it. The beaches are stunning. We can find an apartment downtown for one hundred euros a month. I got a crew of friends there. And I promise, you'll have work in a flash."

With a tendency to follow the throes of love wherever they led me, I nodded, a mix of nervousness and excitement swirling in my mind. "OK. Let's do it."

25
MY AWAKENING

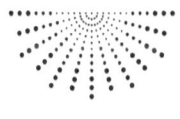

PORTUGAL

"*S*ometimes the flame can be mistaken for warmth." -Darius Foroux in his book, *Think Straight*

Four days after our arrival in Lagos, Blake paraded me into town for a job search. We stopped at every bar on the main strip. I was greeted by a dimly lit interior as I stepped inside a well-known dive named Edie's. Vintage posters showcasing legendary rock bands like The Doors and The Who adorned the peeling walls. Flickering lights cast a moody glow on mismatched tables and worn-out barstools. The air smelled of cigarette smoke and spilled beer. Raucous laughter and animated conversations reverberated through a smoky haze. I immediately fell for the down-to-earth vibe of the place. It reminded me of the local watering hole I spent many a Saturday in my university years.

A man with loose clothes on a skinny frame chain-smoked as he poured beers into thick glass mugs. I found out later the man was Edie himself, an irascible Englishman who claimed he'd partied harder than Keith Richards in his youth. The deep lines carved into his face made it easy to believe.

"Hey there," he greeted me with a gravelly voice, a cigarette dangling from the corner of his mouth. "You must be the new face in town."

"Yeah, that's me. I heard you were looking for some help?"

Edie leaned against the bar, his eyes appraising me with a mixture of curiosity and amusement. "Aye, that's right. I need someone to stand outside the bar from 9 p.m. to 2 a.m., six days a week. You'll be trying to lure passersby inside for a drink. Five euros an hour. Twenty-five euros a night."

I hesitated, not entirely thrilled about the prospect of working late hours for such a measly wage. "Five euros an hour?"

Edie shrugged, taking a long drag from his cigarette. "It's the going rate, lass. Your accent tells me you're Yank. Not able to legally work, right? You're lucky to be getting anything at all. This is all under the table."

I frowned, feeling a pang of frustration at the reminder of my legal limitations. "But isn't there any room for negotiation? I'm a university graduate, after all."

Edie shook his head, his expression unyielding. "Sorry, love. Your degree ain't doing shit in this bar. Take it or leave it. Minimum wage here is two euros and fifty cents an hour. You're lucky to be getting double that."

I chewed on my bottom lip, weighing my options. The truth was I needed the money. With a sigh of resignation, I nodded. "Fine, I'll take the job."

Edie grinned, stubbing out his cigarette on the edge of the bar. "That's the spirit. Welcome to the team, lass. This means you drink for free every day. Go on then, drink this shot of whisky with me to celebrate."

"To new beginnings," he declared, clinking our glasses together before we both downed the fiery liquid.

Blake and I threw ourselves into the local party scene to live out a wild and reckless summer. Edie encouraged me to drink on the job daily, and so I did. When the bar closed at 2 a.m., I'd stumble out the back door, alcohol coursing through my veins. The night was far from over.

Blake and I joined the other summer season workers in a friend's cramped apartment nearby, where the atmosphere thickened with the pungent smell of marijuana. Lines of cocaine were snorted off a scratched coffee table and bottles of liquor passed around like lifelines. I stayed clear of the drugs, but the way they were passed from hand to hand like candy made it clear—I was in a world where rules had long since dissolved.

"Oi, another round!" Blake bellowed, his voice barely audible over the thumping music. He raised his glass, sloshing some of his drink onto the sticky carpet.

"To a good night!" I nodded, feeling the room spinning ever so slightly.

The line between night and day blurred like ink bleeding through paper. The first light of dawn crept through thin curtains, but it went unnoticed. Bodies sprawled on mismatched furniture, eyes glassy and movements sluggish.

Hours later, the sun high in the sky, the party showed no signs of slowing. Blake sat slumped in a corner, laughing maniacally at something nobody else found funny.

"Blake, mate, what are you on about?" slurred Dave, another bartender, as he stumbled over to us.

"Just livin' the dream, aren't we?" Blake replied, his eyes unfocused as he gazed around the room. "We need more gear." He attempted to stand but collapsed back onto the sofa. "Can't let the party die, can we?"

"Blake, it's getting late," I mumbled, struggling to keep up with his pace. "I mean, the sun's out! Let's go home."

"Don't be daft, bitch," he snapped, waving me off. "We're just havin' a bit of fun. Come on, you're boring me. Let's go out."

The word *bitch* landed like a slap. The urge to snap back flared up, but I swallowed it down. Arguing would just blow up into a huge fight, and I was too drunk to care. I let out a half-hearted laugh instead, a brittle attempt to smooth it over, and let the moment pass.

We roamed the streets in the afternoons, perpetually hazy. Our bloodshot eyes and drawn faces made us look more like zombies than the carefree partygoers we believed ourselves to be. Each day blended seamlessly into the next, an unending loop of intoxication and debauchery. The destructive pattern gradually consumed me, leaving me blind to the chaotic mess my life had become.

The mornings were filled with the groans of hangovers. Our living room was a battlefield of empty bottles and crumpled cigarette packs. Blake lay sprawled on the couch, a barely conscious heap. He clutched his head, struggling to sit up.

"Bloody hell, what a night."

My eyes fluttered open, bloodshot and unfocused. "You called me a bitch again for no reason. Said I was boring."

"First thing in the morning? Nagging? Seriously, lay off it."

I rubbed my temples, too drained to feel much more than a dull irritation. Arguing was pointless— we were both hungover, barely functioning. I rolled my eyes and sank back onto the couch, letting silence swallow the moment.

Later that day, Blake sat at the kitchen table, popping a Valium and washing it down with a swig of whiskey. His hands shook as he lit a cigarette, taking a long drag before exhaling with a sigh of temporary relief.

I leaned against the counter, watching him with a mix of concern and frustration. "I think we should slow down a bit. It's getting to be a bit much, don't you think?"

He glanced up, a bitter smile on his lips. "The boring bitch strikes again. You don't get it, do you? It's the only way I can sleep."

"And how do you always wake yourself back up for the night of partying and playing music then?"

"Pills, baby. Stop talking shit. It's the only way I keep up with the fun."

Time lost its structure. Days dissolved into nights, and mornings arrived without warning. Blake and I drifted through the madness— where music never stopped, sleep was optional, and boundaries slipped quietly out the back door.

Another bleary-eyed morning crept in. Blake stumbled through the door, his unsteady gait echoing the chaos of another night out. His shirt hung untucked and wrinkled, his breath thick with the stench of whiskey and cigarettes. I followed a few steps behind, my heart pounding in anticipation of what was coming.

"You embarrassed me tonight, Shan," he spat, his voice slurred but laced with venom. "Clinging to me like some lost puppy. Jesus, can't you just let me breathe?"

"Clingy?" I stammered, stunned by the accusation. "Are you serious? Last week you were mad because I wasn't giving you enough attention at a party. I can't keep up, Blake! One minute, you want me to stay close; the next, you're pushing me away. What do you even want from me?"

He flung his jacket onto the couch, missing it entirely, then turned to glare at me. "What I want? What *I* want?" He took a menacing step closer, towering over me, his breath hot against my skin. "How about a girlfriend who doesn't make everything about her? The selfish American. I can't breathe. You're suffocating me."

"That's not fair, Blake! You—"

"Fair?" he interrupted, his voice rising into a shout. "I'm out here trying to have a good time, and you're dragging me down. You think that's fair? You're pathetic."

His words hit me like a punch. I flinched as if he'd actually struck me. "I've been trying so hard to make you happy, Blake. It's like nothing I do is ever good enough for you."

He threw his hands up, letting out a bitter laugh. "Maybe because it's not. Maybe you're just not good enough."

The air left my lungs in a painful rush. I stared at him, speechless.

"I don't have to deal with this. I'm going back out. Plenty of people out there who appreciate me," he said.

Before I could muster a response, the door slammed shut behind him.

The silence engulfed me. Then, as if my body could no longer support itself, I crumpled to the floor. Curled into the fetal position, I wrapped my arms tightly around my knees as sobs wracked my body.

Tears came fast and unrelenting. His words echoed in my mind, sharp and cruel: *You're pathetic. You're not good enough.*

The next morning, as I turned over in bed, Blake's peaceful face greeted me. He looked so harmless in his sleep, his features soft and untroubled, like the chaos of last night didn't exist in his world.

For a fleeting moment, I let myself believe it too.

Then his eyes fluttered open, those piercing blue irises locking onto me. "Morning, Shan," he said with a calm, oblivious tone as if nothing were amiss.

"Good morning? Like last night never happened? Like the countless nights that were the same never happened?"

"Shan, please," his voice was still rough with sleep, "I'm hungover and can't handle this right now." His voice softened as he cradled my face in his hands, his touch warm, but heavy with manipulation. "You know I love you. I just get carried away when we drink sometimes. I'm working on my temper. You know that. I'm sorry."

I pulled the blanket closer to my chest, as if it could shield me from the hurt. How many times had I heard this same apology, with the same pleading tone, only to have it shattered by the next outburst?

The words felt hollowed by overuse.

And yet, his eyes searched mine with what looked like genuine affection. *He loves me. He's trying. We all have our flaws, don't we? Love is up and down. That's what relationships are.*

I let out a shaky breath. "We need to slow down, Blake."

Blake groaned and rubbed his temples, "Oh my God, woman." He reached for a stale beer on the bedside table. "Don't be a killjoy. We're just having fun. You don't want me to have fun with other women, do you?"

As he said it, I could see the exhaustion in his eyes, the toll of the constant highs and lows etched into his features.

The old saying goes, "Sticks and stones can break my bones but words can never hurt me." That phrase couldn't have felt further than the truth. Blake's words possessed an insidious power capable of inflicting as much harm as any physical blow. They embedded themselves deep within my mind, haunting and taunting me long after they had been uttered. The repetition of his hurtful words eroded the foundations of my spirit.

"Whatever, Blake. I can't talk to you when you're like this." I pushed the blanket aside and slipped out of bed. With each step, something in me gave out—strength unraveling, like a rope worn thin by too much strain.

Day by day Blake's temper intensified within the context of our partying lifestyle. Regular eruptions of violent arguments plagued our daily existence.

One overcast Sunday morning, I stumbled into the kitchen, head throbbing. Shadows clung to the corners, and dim light made everything feel colder.

Blake was slumped at the table with a cup of black coffee. Empty bottles and scattered remnants of the night before littered the counters.

A punishing wave of nausea surged, like my body wanted to purge more than just the alcohol. I took a deep breath, trying to muster some semblance of normalcy.

"Morning, Blake. About last night...you accused me of looking at some guy in a sexy way *again*. I swear, I didn't. Why do you always get so jealous?"

Blake looked up, his eyes narrowing as he processed my words. He sighed heavily, running a hand through his disheveled hair. "Look, I might've been out of line, but you've got this...sex vibe you give off. I'm not OK with it. I mean look at you, that shirt shows cleavage and your ass is almost spilling out of those shorts. What do you expect me to think?"

What the hell? His statement felt completely unfounded. But then my mind began to spin. *Did I act too flirtatious without realizing it?* I wasn't trying to do anything, but maybe I had given off the wrong impression. *Did I make him feel this way?* I shook my head slightly, feeling a mix of confusion and anger. "Blake, I'm just...me. You gotta stop making me suffer for it. You're half-apologizing and blaming me in the same breath. It's not fair."

He pushed his chair back with a screech and stood. "Just...let it go," he muttered, brushing past me as he headed to our bedroom.

Moments later, his angry voice echoed through the apartment. "Are you a fucking idiot? How the hell I put up with your shit is a goddamn miracle. Make our fucking bed when you get out of it!"

I clenched my fists. "Blake, I know you're hungover and tired, but the way you speak to me has got to stop. It's the morning; how about a hello and a kiss to start the day?"

He reappeared in the doorway, his expression twisted with irritation. "You're the one who came waltzing into the kitchen accusing me of shit."

"I was just telling you the facts, Blake. How you treated me like shit last night, like you do most nights these days."

"Don't you see I'm tired?" Blake fired back. "Leave me the fuck alone."

I stared at him. A tear slipped down my cheek. "Blake, this isn't how we should be living. We're destroying ourselves, our relationship."

Blake's eyes flickered with a moment of something softer, but it quickly vanished. He turned away, retreating back to the bedroom with a dismissive wave of his hand. "Just...give me some space."

As he disappeared, a void settled in my chest, an aching emptiness. The morning light seemed cruel now, pouring in through the window and spotlighting the disarray of our lives—ashtrays overflowing, plates crusted with food we never finished. Sticky rings from spilled drinks marked the table, ghostly reminders of nights gone wrong. I stood there, the kitchen silent except for the faint sounds of the outside world, realizing how far we had fallen into this cycle of anger and addiction.

A week later, I was in the bathroom, prepping for a much-needed date night with Blake. The dark bags under my eyes were becoming a permanent fixture, deepening with each passing day. I slathered on mountains of foundation, desperately trying to mask the hollowness that had settled into my face. My skin, pale from nights of excess, needed copious amounts of rouge to inject some semblance of color back into my cheeks. As I leaned closer to the mirror, I clung to the fragile hope that tonight might be different—that maybe, somehow, we could start piecing things back together.

Blake paced the living room. His footsteps and the occasional muttered curse bothered me as I finished applying my makeup. I'd hoped to look nice for our evening together, but it seemed that Blake was in no mood for patience.

When I finally emerged, feeling somewhat satisfied with my look, Blake's eyes widened with visible disgust. He scoffed, glaring at me.

"Jesus Christ, you look like a fucking clown."

I flinched at his words. A wave of shame washed over me. "What's wrong? My makeup?"

"You've got way too much on. It's like you're auditioning for a circus. And those clothes? They make you look cheap."

My heart sank as he spoke, each word cutting deeper than the last. It appeared as though he derived a perverse satisfaction from piling heaps of shame and guilt on me, scrutinizing and berating every aspect of my appearance, clothing choices, and behavior. I lowered my eyes, not daring to look at him. I tried to remain calm, pressing my nails into the soft flesh of my palm, hoping it would pass. No intense reaction, I told myself. Don't give him more to feed on.

"I thought it looked nice," I said quietly, my voice barely above a whisper.

Blake let out a frustrated sigh, crossing his arms over his chest. "Well, I'm the one who has to look at you. I'd rather not be seen with someone who looks like they just walked out of a trash heap."

He took a step back, shaking his head. "Get back in there and wash your face. I'm not going out with you looking like that. I'm doing you a favor. You're beautiful without all that crap."

I hesitated, feeling a lump form in my throat. I wanted to argue, to defend myself, but something about the way he spoke—almost as if he were trying to be helpful—made me second-guess myself.

"All right," I said, "I'll fix it."

Blake nodded, a crooked smirk on his lips. "Good. I don't understand why you need all that makeup anyway. You're naturally beautiful, you just can't see it."

As I walked back into the bathroom, I could hear Blake mumbling under his breath, the sound of his irritation mingling with a twisted sort of satisfaction. By the time I emerged, my face was bare. Blake nodded approvingly as he took in my refreshed look, though there was a cold edge to his smile.

"See? Much better," he said, almost as a compliment.

I forced a smile, trying to hide the hurt. "Thanks, Blake."

Blake grabbed his coat and headed for the door. The interaction was a harsh reminder of the power dynamics in our relationship, that despite my best efforts, my worth was often measured by his whims and judgments.

But I held on tight, hoping to hold us together. I wanted things to be OK. I kept telling myself we could find our way back—back to the nights under foreign stars, to sunrise hikes, to the version of us that crossed borders with nothing but backpacks and inside jokes. I missed that Blake—the blue-eyed, reckless dreamer who once made me believe love could be an adventure. I clung to the idea that he was still in there somewhere, waiting to resurface if I just held on long enough.

As summer continued, the atmosphere between us grew increasingly hostile. The piercing sound of Blake's verbal attacks were sometimes accompanied by the alarming thud of punches landing forcefully against the walls just inches above my trembling head.

I learned to cover the holes Blake punched in the walls, just as I tried to cover the holes punctured into my heart.

Each time Blake broke into his monster state of verbal and emotional abuse, that monster devoured his strengths. And mine. I was left diminished, like a flower robbed of its petals.

Blake was a strikingly handsome, charming, and talented musician; his reputation well-established throughout town. He was loved and adored by all. Our friends had inklings about the abuse, but Blake's outgoing personality and overwhelming talent made him impossible to hate. A shield of popularity. While Blake was burning in front of us, we all stood back, admiring the pretty flame.

After yet another wild night of partying, we stumbled back to our apartment. I fumbled with the key until the lock finally clicked open. Blake pushed past me. I let the door swing shut behind us. My purse slipped from my shoulder, landing in a heap on the floor. The dim light flickered above us, illuminating the cluttered living room— discarded cigarette butts scattered like forgotten confetti, and clothes strewn carelessly over the threadbare couch.

Blake turned on me suddenly, his voice sharp and venomous. "There you go, being a whore again."

"What are you talking about, Blake?" I slurred, attempting to stay steady on my feet.

"You know what I'm talking about, slut. I saw you." He attempted pointing a condescending finger my way, but in his drunkenness was pointing in the wrong direction.

"Saw me what, Blake? I haven't done anything wrong."

"Always so fucking innocent, are we? I saw you walking off with that guy to his car. What were you doing with him?"

"You're fucking psycho, Blake. That was Ben I was walking with, YOUR mate. He was lending me a sweater from his car."

"Sure he was. Along with his cock. No worries though, I can pass my cock onto other women too. Watch me, bitch." Blake staggered towards the door.

With the fear of abandonment greater than my instinct for self-preservation, I dove in front of Blake's exit. "Don't leave again like this. Please. I can't take this anymore."

"You deserve to be left for good." His bloodshot eyes bulged as he swayed. "I don't know why I bother staying with an ugly, loud-mouthed American anyways. I could have any woman in this town. And I will."

In my alcohol-induced rage I decided that this time he would not abuse me and leave immediately after. *This time I would stand up for myself.* This time, he would apologize for his painful words. "What the fuck, Blake? Why are you treating me like this? I don't deserve this. You can't keep acting like this, leaving me and then coming back like everything is OK."

Blake shoved me away from the door with brutal force, sending me staggering into the wall. The cheap plaster cracked under the impact.

Our first physical battle unleashed.

Desperation coursed through me, hot and choking, impossible to contain. "Blake, please!"

I hurled myself back into his path, clawing at his shirt, gripping his arms, anything to stop him from walking out and leaving me emotionally gutted and alone. But nothing I did made sense. My body moved before my mind could catch up, arms latching onto him with the last scraps of strength I had.

His rage only seemed deepened. He grabbed me by the shoulders and thrust me aside. My knees slammed into the floor.

Still, I scrambled back to my feet, blocking his way again.

"Get out of my way!" he roared, his face twisted with fury as he pushed me once more.

Tears blurred my vision, but I couldn't stop. I wouldn't. I threw myself in front of the door again and again, bruising my body with every blow. My mind was unable to fathom a world where he'd leave me like this.

Being bigger and stronger, Blake eventually got his way and fled from the house. "Jesus Christ, you're a crazy cunt. Don't you dare blame those bruises on me. You brought this on yourself."

The hurt I felt inside was a force stronger than the stinging on my cheek.

The police arrived soon after.

I scrambled to my feet, wiping my tear-streaked cheeks with quivering hands. A sharp stab of shame hit me as I stole a quick glance in the cracked mirror by the door. I stared at a woman I barely recognized—disheveled hair, a blotchy face. *How had I come to this?* I had to pull myself together. I smoothed my clothes, forcing a semblance of composure onto my battered frame.

When I opened the door, two uniformed officers stood there, their faces lined with concern. One of them leaned slightly forward, eyes darting past me into the apartment.

"Ma'am, are you okay?" the taller officer asked, his voice gentle but firm. "We received a noise complaint—concerns of a domestic disturbance."

I stiffened, gripping the edge of the door tightly. "I'm fine." I straightened my posture, gesturing at myself as if my unbroken body was proof. "It was just a little shouting match. It happens sometimes, you know? But he left, and it's all good now. Really."

The officers exchanged a look, clearly unconvinced, but nodded. The shorter one shifted, craning his neck to see more of the apartment's interior. "Are you sure?"

"I'm sure," I said, my voice firm, though my hands betrayed me by trembling on the doorknob.

The officers hesitated but finally nodded. "OK, ma'am. If you're sure. If anything changes, don't hesitate to call."

"Thank you," I murmured, closing the door softly. When the latch clicked into place, I sank to the floor.

I never imagined things would go this far.

That Blake was capable of such abuse.

I had now lived with over three months of verbal and emotional abuse, but physical violence was where I drew the line.

By morning, it felt as if every neighbor had been informed about our incident. The fact that my abusive relationship was now publicized and known within my community mortified me. It was as if a spotlight had been cast upon the delicate threads of my existence, laying bare my pain and suffering for the world to behold. Confusion gnawed at my core. How had I, once so vibrant and resilient, wilted to become a woman in such a vulnerable position? I had always considered myself a strong, educated, independent woman. The foundations of this self-perception trembled under the weight of my new reality.

The burning question echoed within me; *how could I allow such treatment?* Repeatedly. Over an extended period of time. The answer lay in a grim metaphor; if you put a frog in boiling water, it will jump out to save its life. But if you put a frog in room temperature water and gradually increase the heat, the frog will slowly cook to death. Why? Because it has been acclimatized to the heat and therefore loses its ability to sense danger. I was that frog. I had acclimated to the escalating mistreatment, its gradual progression deceiving my senses and eroding my ability to recognize the danger surrounding me.

No one intentionally hops onto the rollercoaster ride of an abusive relationship, but once you're there, it is hard to get off. That being said, I still decided to no longer be a bystander to my existence. The moment the police arrived at our doorstep was a "coming to Jesus moment." I realized I was on a collision course with myself, and that I could not keep it up. I had gradually changed into someone I didn't know, someone I didn't like.

I packed my bags.

I looked up plane tickets to anywhere but here.

Within days, I'd be gone.

I explained my plan to Blake.

"Shan. You have to forgive me. *Please.* You know this isn't my fault. You know I'd never intend to hurt you. I love you more than anything!! You're my everything." His eyes filled with tears as he continued to beg for forgiveness. "There's a monster inside of me, Shan. You know I'm trying to fight it. Sometimes I feel so out of control. All the partying here has just sent me into a bad place.... Don't leave me! I'll change. *PLEASE DON'T LEAVE ME.* We can claw ourselves out of this together. I'll stop drinking. We'll never fight like that again! We can go traveling together with the money I've saved. We are meant to be together, and you know it, Shan. We'll have our happily ever after. "

The sincerity in his tone made my chest tighten.

Blake leaned forward, elbows on his knees, his hands fidgeting with a lighter he'd picked up off the coffee table. "We could go to Morocco next."

"Morocco?"

"Yeah, it's close, a short flight from here. It's cheap, too, and—" he paused, biting his lower lip, "it's a Muslim country. Dry. No booze anywhere, you know? I could straighten myself out."

I studied his face, searching for cracks in his resolve. There were so many reasons I should say no, so many ways we could continue to unravel.

But his tone carried a glimmer of hope, something convincing.

"Things can't be like they've been, Blake. You can't keep treating me and speaking to me like you have this summer. I'm done."

"Shan. I love you." He leaned closer, his hands gripping his knees as if holding himself in place. "I love you more than I've loved another woman. *Please.* You know I'm sorry. I just have this anger in me. I'm working to control it. It's a process. Support me through this, Shan."

I wanted to believe him. He needed me. And how could I abandon him when he needed me? When he loved me? When he sincerely wanted to make things work? The vulnerability in his voice stirred something deep inside me—a mix of compassion and guilt. I wasn't perfect either. I had my own demons, my own temper that flared uncontrollably at times. I knew how it felt to wrestle with anger, to fight against the tide of emotion and fail. If anyone could understand, it was me. Surely, we could work through this together.

I swallowed hard. "Blake, I want to believe you. I really do. But how can I know this will really stop? You've told me this before."

"I know," he said quickly, his eyes locked on mine. "I know I've screwed up, Shan. I'll do better. I swear I'll do better."

Stripped of his bravado, pleading for my support, I felt a spark of that connection again. Maybe this was the turning point. Maybe Morocco could be the reset we both needed.

"OK," I said finally. "But Blake, if this happens again…I can't keep doing this. I won't."

He nodded, reaching for my hand. "I won't let you down."

As I looked at Blake, I clung to the hope that we could find pieces of ourselves in Morocco, pieces we'd lost along the way. Maybe, just maybe, we could fit them back together.

I was determined to overcome the obstacles, making them a gateway to a new beginning. With hope in my heart, we bought our tickets to Morocco to start anew. As American journalist Germany Kent once said, "We must never underestimate the power we have to take our lives into new directions."

26
WELCOME TO MOROCCO

MOROCCO

*S*urely a person can't give up all their vices in one go, *right?* Of course not. So Blake decided our Moroccan traveling jaunt would include a great deal of hash.

Hash is the oldest cannabis concentrate, usually more potent than cannabis buds themselves. It is made by first separating THC crystals (or trichomes) from the plant. In Morocco, this is done by gently rubbing dried cannabis over a mesh. This process produces a fine powder called kif. The kif is then heated and pressed together to make a dense and potent block of hash. The block can be soft or hard, and is usually brown.

There are many types of hash from all over the world; Afghani, Manali Cream (from India), and charas (from Nepal) are some key examples. However, the most well-known and beloved is Moroccan hash, because it gives a very chill and gentle high. In comparison to other types of hash, the user won't get "knocked out."

According to Blake, Moroccan hash could be used and enjoyed for almost any occasion. And thus, he led the way as we journeyed from town to town in what began to feel like a "hash tourism" affair.

I went along, curious more about the places and experiences than the smoke. There was something magnetic about the way Blake chased after each new experience. He approached travel like it was meant to be devoured. He was curious, bold, and reckless in a way that made the world crack open in front of us. Part of me admired it. Part of me hoped that if I just kept pace with him, I might repair whatever still lingered between us. Plus, I couldn't deny that hash mellowed him out—his temper dulled, his edges softened. And when he was calm, we worked.

"Why not?" he said, unwrapping a crinkled square of hash like it was some kind of sacred artifact. "The production and use of hash is an age-old story in Morocco. It's a cultural experience to enlighten myself by trying it!"

I rolled my eyes.

"Don't forget, Shan, Morocco's biggest foreign currency earner is tourism, but unofficially, *it's cannabis.* I have no choice but to follow the crowd, *right?*"

I shook my head and looked away. Still beside him—still trying, still holding on to the adventures we'd chased together, still hoping there were more to come. I wanted to believe love could weather the dips and turns, that it didn't mean reshaping someone, just loving them as they were. That was what I wanted too—to be accepted for all of me, without needing to be different to deserve it.

Hash helped Blake slip into that version of himself—the lighter one. It became his daily mission: to source it, roll it, smoke it, relax, and let go.

One afternoon Blake and I stepped out of the streets of Fes and into the dimly lit living room of yet another local man who offered hash. The air thickened with the scent of incense. Intricate tiles in shades of blue and green adorned the walls, each piece meticulously placed to form mesmerizing geometric patterns of stars and inter-locking diamonds. Colorful Moroccan carpets covered the floors, their vibrant hues of deep reds, rich blues, and warm golds adding warmth and life to the space. Around the room, embroidered fabrics draped over low, cushioned couches. The fabrics featured ornate calligraphy, interwoven with depictions of crescents. Our host,

Rachid, greeted us with a broad smile. "My friends, please sit. Welcome to my home! Please, make yourselves comfortable."

Blake and I settled onto the couches, sinking into the plush pillows as Rachid busied himself at a low, carved wooden table. He laid out an array of hash samples, each carefully wrapped and labeled.

"You will find, my friends, that each of these has its own character, its own strength."

As Blake began sampling, Rachid's wife, Fatima, entered the room. She carried a silver tray, laden with a traditional Moroccan teapot and small, delicately designed glasses. The aroma of fresh mint and the sweetness of sugar filled the room as she poured the tea. The liquid cascaded into the glasses from a great height, forming bubbles on the surface.

"Thank you," I said, taking a glass. The warmth seeped into my fingers.

Fatima smiled softly and nodded before retreating silently from the room.

Rachid raised his glass. "To friendship."

"To friendship," Blake and I echoed.

We talked about our travels, sharing stories of bustling markets in Marrakech, the desolate beauty of the Atlas Mountains, and the coastal charm of Essaouira. Rachid listened intently, nodding, and occasionally interjecting his own experiences.

"You must visit Chefchaouen, my friends," he said, his eyes lighting up. "The blue city. It is like no other place. This hash comes from there!" He reached out in Blake's direction, with a large ball of hash nestled inside his hand. "Very strong, very good for relaxation."

Blake inhaled deeply, exhaling slowly. "It does smell bloody strong."

Rachid beamed. "You try! I roll for you." His hands nimbly rolled a joint while I carried on our conversation.

"I've heard Chefchaouen is a picturesque city. Almost every house, building, wall, and street is painted completely blue, right? Why is that anyways?"

"Ah, that's a good question! If you ask local people in Chefchaouen, they tell you many answers." Rachid chuckled softly, leaning back in his chair while he lit the joint. He took the first slow, deep drag and held the smoke in his lungs for a moment before releasing it in a steady stream. He then passed it to Blake and continued speaking. "Some say the blue acts as a mosquito repellent. Mosquitoes like to live near water, but they don't like to be IN water, you see. The blues of Chefchaouen give the city a watery feel."

Blake's eyes narrowed as he listened to Rachid's explanation. He took a long drag, exhaling a thick cloud that hung in the air like a mist. "I guess that makes sense. There must be another reason though."

"Yes, my friend, of course! Others say the blue buildings help keep their homes cool. And of course, the blue buildings look nice and attract tourists, like you!"

"It definitely sounds like a great tourist attraction," I said.

Rachid's tone turned serious. "The real explanation is in history though." Smoke curled around his head, framing his face like a halo, though his eyes were sharp, calculating. "In 1920, many Jews went there. They wanted to escape killer Hitler. This was when parts of the city began to be painted blue."

I caught Blake's eye as he exhaled another plume of smoke. "What do Jews have to do with painting a city blue?" he asked, leaning forward with interest.

"For Jew people, the color blue represents the sky, like heaven, and God," Rachid explained. "They have strong tradition of painting things blue and using blue dye to color fabrics, like prayer mats."

"That's fascinating," I said.

"Yes, of course. Do not worry though. Not many Jew people there now. Most left for Israel in late forties and fifties" Rachid concluded, with a touch of pride in his voice.

My hands clasped together in front of me. "I can't wait to see it for myself."

"Yes, you will enjoy." And then, Rachid abruptly straightened his posture, as he pointed to the finished joint Blake was snubbing out in the ashtray. "Only the best for my friend, you see. So you will take? How much you want?"

Blake hesitated, his fingers tapping lightly on the side of his tea glass. "Just thirty dollars worth, mate. Thank you."

Rachid's face tightened, his eyes narrowing ever so slightly. "My friend, I thought we were closer than this. You come into my home, enjoy my hospitality, drink my tea, and this is how you repay me?" His smile, once genuine and warm, now seemed more calculated.

Blake and I exchanged a wary glance. We had encountered this tactic before, the pressure to buy more, the guilt trip that made me feel uncomfortable. It was a familiar play.

"We appreciate your hospitality, Rachid," Blake pointed in my direction, "but she doesn't smoke, and I only need a little for now."

Rachid's smile faded completely, replaced by a look of clear dissatisfaction. "My friend, I welcome you into my home, treat you as family, and this is what you do? This small amount? You need more. I give you good price."

The room suddenly felt smaller. I shifted uneasily on the cushions, feeling the pressure, but Blake, as always, remained determined to stand his ground.

"We really do appreciate everything, Rachid," Blake said, maintaining a calm and friendly tone. "But we're poor backpackers. This is all we can take for now."

Rachid sighed, but then nodded. "Very well. If this is what you want."

Blake quickly paid him, avoiding eye contact, and took the stash. The atmosphere remained heavy with unspoken words.

As we stood to leave, I offered a final, "Thank you, Rachid. You have a beautiful home."

Rachid merely nodded, his expression unreadable as his eyes followed us to the door.

Outside, the cool night air was a relief after the tension inside. Blake exhaled and gave me a faint lopsided grin. "Well...that wasn't awkward at all."

We walked away from Rachid's home, ready for whatever adventure awaited us next.

27

NAVIGATING THE SHADOWS

MOROCCO

"*Only those who risk going too far can possibly find out how far one can go.*" *T.S. Elliot*

After a week in Fes, Blake and I had enough of rambling through the medina—a maze of pedestrian streets with ornamented entryways, vibrant painted ceramics, and a lively market square of souk vendors selling specialized perfumes, spices, lamps, and leather goods.

Our new goal was to visit the famed city of Chefchaouen. By this point I'd heard many people gush about its attractive streets, rich history, lush food, and breathtaking hiking opportunities. The city was nestled among the Rif mountains, where most of the country's marijuana is grown. Blake wanted a marijuana farm tour, to experience the lifestyle of marijuana farmers, to learn how hash is made, and to buy some for personal use. So, we made our way to the station to catch a bus heading north.

Upon arrival, we navigated the chaos of the terminal until we reached the ticket window.

Blake stepped up first. "Two tickets to Chefchaouen, please."

The teller, a young man with dark hair and a weary expression, glanced at his computer and shook his head. "I'm sorry, but all the buses to Chefchaouen today are sold out, sir."

With no backup plan we stood there, blank.

I turned to Blake, searching his face for a hint of a solution, but he just exhaled, rubbing the back of his neck. Around us, travelers hurried by. Announcements echoed over the loudspeakers in rapid Arabic and French. We stepped aside, standing in a corner of the bustling station.

"What now?" I rubbed my forehead.

Blake shrugged. "We've always managed to figure things out. We'll find a way. Remember, we decided to embrace the flow of our travels."

Our carefree approach had served us well so far. We deliberately avoided excessive research about the countries we visited. Instead, we preferred to embrace spontaneity, allowing the flow to guide us on our adventures. This philosophy had led us to many unexpected treasures, often through the advice and recommendations of fellow travelers.

I sighed, leaning against the wall. "Yeah, I know. It's just...we had our hearts set on Chefchaouen."

"I know." Blake glanced around the station. "But something will come up. It always does."

Just then, two white foreigners walked past. They stood out against the Moroccan crowd. I assumed they were fellow tourists, heading somewhere intriguing. We quickly headed over to them.

"Hello!" I called out, trying to sound friendly and not too desperate.

The two young men turned to us, their expressions curious, but welcoming. They looked to be in their early twenties, with that scruffy, road-worn look of people who'd been living out of backpacks for a while. The blond one's face was dotted with sun-faded freckles and a few days of stubble. The other, more muscular and darker-haired, had a faded compass tattoo that crept out from under his shirt sleeve.

The taller one, with sandy blond hair sticking out in all directions, gave a wide smile that revealed a slight gap between his front teeth. "Hallo, yes? Can we help you?"

I have noted a phenomenon while traveling; it's common for foreigners seeing one another abroad to gravitate toward each other. Complete strangers readily extend warm welcomes and establish instantaneous connections. I suppose it's the shared experience of being outsiders in an unfamiliar place that creates an instant sense of camaraderie.

"We were wondering where you guys are heading. I'm Blake, by the way," he added, extending his hand.

"I'm Shannon," I said, doing the same.

The blond one stepped forward, extending a calloused hand. "Nice to meet you. I'm Honza, and this is Jakub."

Jakub reached his hand out as well. "We're from the Czech Republic."

"We're heading to a mountain town called Ketama," Honza explained. "We don't really have much information about the place, but we know that it's a big spot for growing marijuana in Morocco. That's why we want to check it out. Do you guys smoke?"

Blake nodded.

I shot him a side eye. The idea of heading off to a remote mountain town known for weed made me a bit apprehensive. But I didn't want to be the killjoy. Going with the flow had served us well so far, even if it sometimes led to strange detours. And truthfully, Blake was far more mellow when he had his hash—it beat his wild party self back in Portugal.

"All the tourists go to Chefchaouen," Honza continued, "but that's just another hotspot on the busy tourist trail. I think this place Ketama is the real deal, off the tourist track. You're welcome to join if you want. We're not sure what we're up for but...you're most welcome!"

"Sounds perfect," Blake said. "We're in."

I gave a half-smile. "Why not?"

The four of us headed back to the ticket counter and purchased seats on the next bus to Ketama. The bus was departing in one hour, so we sauntered outside to a shady spot to wait.

A local approached us, wearing a light-colored djellabah, the traditional dress for men in Morocco. It is a long-fitting outer dress with full sleeves. The qob, a baggy hood culminating in a point, hung loosely at his back. His head was adorned with a traditional fez or tarbush, the deep red headdress contrasting sharply with his salt-and-pepper hair. The tassel on top shifted with his movements. He had soft yellow babouche or balgha, heel-less slippers made from leather, on his feet. His eyes, a deep shade of brown, held a warmth that put me at ease. As he approached, he greeted us with a nod and a smile.

"As-Salam-u-Alaikum," the man said. This is the standard greeting used in many Muslim countries. The direct translation is basically "Peace be upon you."

We turned our attention to the man and replied in the respectful manner, "Wa-Alaikumussalam."

"Where are you headed?" the man inquired in surprisingly good English.

"Ketama," we replied in unison.

His eyes perked up. "Oh, Ketama! An interesting place. I am sure you will have a good time, inshallah. Where will you stay?"

"Not sure yet," Blake replied.

"You must be careful. Many people will hassle you upon arrival. You should stay with my brother, Mustaffah. He has a beautiful cannabis farm. He can show you his crops and how he turns the cannabis into hashish. His wife is a wonderful cook. His children are respectful. You will enjoy your stay!"

A genuine homestay experience had just fallen into our laps! Going with the flow as we tended to do, this seemed like a lovely idea, and we promptly agreed to it.

"Excellent!" our new friend declared. "I will call my brother and tell him you will be arriving. When you arrive at Ketama, you need to get off at the second bus stop. Mustaffah will be waiting there for you. Be careful, don't go with anyone but Mustaffah."

His directions seemed easy enough, but his emphasis on avoiding anyone but Mustaffah puzzled me. We thanked the man for his offer and looked forward to the experience as we boarded the bus.

I stared out the window as the bus rumbled out of the station in Fes and began its journey to the Rif Mountains. The scenery transformed from the urban sprawl of Fes to fertile plains cross-hatched with fields of wheat and barley swaying gently in the breeze. Their golden colors glowed under the warm Moroccan sun. The landscape gradually shifted from flat plains to rolling hills dotted with olive groves and the occasional cluster of whitewashed houses.

As the bus climbed higher into the Rif Mountains, the terrain became more rugged. Steep, rocky slopes covered in dense forests of pine and cedar rose on either side of the winding road. The occasional burst of wildflowers added splashes of red, yellow, and purple to the verdant landscape. Each bend in the road opened onto wide, sunlit valleys below, where terraced farms clung to the hills, tracing soft lines across the land like the earth had been combed with careful fingers.

The higher we climbed, the more remote and untouched the landscape became. Herds of goats, tended by shepherds, grazing on the steep hillsides. With the bus windows open, the sounds of their bells tinkling softly in the crisp mountain air could be heard.

A few hours into the trip, I glanced out the window and did a double take. Row after row of marijuana plants stretched across the hillsides, openly basking in the sun like any other crop. I knew cannabis grew abundantly in this region—that was the whole reason we were headed there—but I hadn't expected to see it so boldly displayed along the roadside. I'd assumed it would be tucked away on hidden farms, kept discreet given its illegal status. But there it was, out in the open, unguarded and unapologetic.

The plants stood about chest-high, their bushy forms packed tightly together. Each one was covered in distinct jagged leaves shaped like elongated fingers, with serrated edges and a network of fine veins running through them. The shades of green varied subtly, giving the plants a rich, layered texture. The scent of earth and resin infused the air, hinting at the potency and richness concealed within those luscious leaves.

As the bus kept winding its way through the mountains our cellphones went out of range. Without any service, we had no way of knowing when we would actually reach Ketama. But I'd grown used to disappearing from the map. I didn't think twice—*though maybe I should have.*

After another hour the bus stopped and a mass of people flooded in. They ignored all the locals on the bus and stampeded straight to the back where my new friends and I sat.

"Come, come, my friend! Welcome to Ketama! Best farm, you see! Very good, very good!" one man urged, his face inches from mine. The smell of sweat was strong on his clothes.

"You not go with him, come with me! I show you real deal! Cheap price!" one insisted, waving a hand frantically in front of Jakub's face.

"You tourists, yes? You want best stuff? My farm best farm!" said another, his eyes wide and insistent, as if sheer willpower could compel us to follow him.

"We friends, yes? I help you! You must come with me!" Yet another man added, his tone a mix of pleading and command.

The cacophony overwhelmed me. The intensity of their approach left us with little room to breathe, let alone think. I was thankful that we already had a plan, which felt like a safety net.

"No thank you, no thank you. We already have a place to stay," Honza countered the crowd.

"But where will you stay?!" One man screamed. "You MUST come with me!"

"Again, no thank you," Blake retorted. "We have a friend, Mohammad, coming to pick us up at the next bus station." Blake had got the name wrong, but that didn't matter. What mattered was getting this throng of people to leave us alone.

"Mohammad?" one of the men answered. His face suddenly brightened with a cheeky, mischievous glint.

We nodded in response.

"I see," he said. "Goodbye." With a short wave of his hand, he and the others abruptly disembarked the bus as fast as they had entered.

I was surprised by their sudden departure; after all the hassling, the abrupt shift felt surreal. One moment we were surrounded, their voices a relentless tide; the next, they were gone, leaving behind only the echo of their pleas. The bus felt eerily quiet.

Jakub let out a breath. "Well, that was intense," he muttered, shaking his head.

A few minutes later, we rolled up to the second bus station. The moment the bus screeched to a halt, another aggressive mob of pursuers swarmed on board, like an army of determined ants, zeroing in on us at the back of the bus with alarming speed. Each of them vied for our attention and fiercely advocated for us to choose their farm as the ultimate destination. They created an unyielding human wall, a dense and suffocating barrier that left no room for us to exit. The air reverberated with a mixture of competing voices, each clamoring louder than the next, in a desperate attempt to persuade us.

Blake quickly lost his patience. "NO! We will not be staying with you! LEAVE US ALONE. We have a friend coming to pick us up!"

"Oh, hello," came a voice. A man effortlessly weaved his way through the crowd. Upon seeing him, the crowd retreated, which I was ever so grateful for at that moment. The man held his hand out to Blake. "My name is Ahmed. I am a friend of Mohammad. He sends his apologies for not being able to personally pick you up. He has asked me to come and retrieve you. Please, follow me."

Blake had mentioned the wrong name back at the first stop. Someone had heard that one slip of the tongue and spun it into a trap. And now we were standing in it.

Our contact wasn't Mohammad. It was Mustaffah.

We didn't know who this man was, but we were sure he was not the man we wanted to go with. He was lying, trying to trick us into joining him.

Ahmed turned to get off the bus and we followed at a safe distance. Once outside, we looked around—no one was searching the crowd for us. No Mustaffah. Dread pooled at the base of my spine.

As we reached the curb, a sleek black BMW 7 series, with no license plates, pulled up beside the bus. The completely tinted windows concealed the occupants within. Ahmed opened the door to reveal three huge men sitting inside. My eyes darted from one to the other. A glint of steel caught my attention. One of the men had a machete resting by his feet. A gun snugly holstered in another's belt.

There was no way we were getting in that car.

"It's actually been a really long journey," I said to Ahmed. "We're going to go to the tea shop across the road and relax for a bit. Then we'd like to stay at a hotel in town. Thanks anyways." I motioned for Blake and our friends to follow me.

Ahmed gave a small, almost indifferent shrug, as if our departure was no more significant than a minor interruption to his day.

As we approached the tea shop and took seats at a corner table, a swarm of locals engulfed us once again.

"Come, come, my friend! You must visit my farm! Best quality!" one man said. His eyes were wide, filled with an earnest desperation.

"Why you not come with me? My farm is closest!" Another man grabbed at Jakub's sleeve, his grip firm.

"You must see my farm! We have the best! No one else offer such good price!" a third man shouted over the din. He leaned in so close I could smell the faint hint of spices on his breath.

The crowd closed in around us, their gestures increasingly frantic as they shouted over one another, each trying to outdo the others with promises of unparalleled quality and unbeatable prices.

My shoulders tensed, and my head felt heavy as their voices piled one on top of the other in a roar. A wall of noise pressed in from all sides, leaving me rooted to the spot with no clear way to escape. Trapped. Suffocated.

"I can't take this anymore!" Blake yelled. He thrust his arms out in a desperate gesture of defiance. His face flushed with anger. "Leave us alone! We're not interested in your farms!"

"We're not going anywhere with you! Just give us some space!" Honza yelled out, his jaw tight.

The crowd seemed momentarily taken aback, but quickly regrouped, their persistence undeterred.

"We're trying to help you! Why you refuse?" one man argued.

My heart pounded in my chest. Anxiety surged through me.

And then, Ahmed and his men sauntered up with an air of nonchalance. Uninvited guests, they casually pulled up chairs to sit around the table with us. Ahmed was a big man, with a deep black beard. He chewed a toothpick and didn't blink. His eyes were like coal, dark and hard. The man beside him looked like he could lift a fully-grown cow over his head. He stretched out in his chair, in the way anacondas do after they've finished consuming an adult goat.

The once boisterous crowd immediately grew silent and dispersed. A hush blanketed the surroundings, leaving an eerie stillness in its wake. At that moment, we were caught between conflicting emotions. Gratitude welled up within us, for the sudden respite from the overwhelming crowd. Yet, beneath the surface of our relief, a disconcerting unease simmered. The ease with which Ahmed and his men had established their dominance among the crowds of people unsettled us, hinting at an underlying power dynamic.

Ahmed raised his hand to signal a passing waiter, summoning him with a flick of his wrist to attend to our tea needs, a staple of daily life in Morocco. When the fragrant mint tea arrived, Ahmed seized the opportunity to scoop spoonful after spoonful of sugar into the teapot. Moroccans are known to luxuriate in an ungodly amount of sugar in their tea. Then, Ahmed aerated the tea. I was hypnotized by the way he stretched his arm high, as he proceeded with the standard Moroccan ritual of "pulling" the tea back and forth between the pot and the glass. It was a sight to behold, witnessing the stream of tea rise to astonishing heights without a single drop spilling, as if defying the laws of physics.

Once the tea had been properly aerated, and the sweetness perfected, Ahmed poured each of us a glass with practiced precision. "You will come to the farm with us," he said, his voice resonating with confidence and authority. "You will love it. It is a very remote and peaceful place. Completely off grid. No cell service. We can show you our farm. It is a very successful business. We look forward to doing business with you."

His words hung in the air, pregnant with possibility, while the bitter steam from my tea clouded my mind. Unease gnawed at my gut. Ahmed's casual smile didn't reach his eyes. My intuition screamed at me to stay away. In fact, there was something off about everyone here. Despite just arriving, I was already loathing the town.

"We appreciate your invite, mate," Blake replied, "but we're not here to do business. We're just here to look around, and we'd prefer to stay at the hotel, thanks."

Ahmed scrunched his eyebrows in apparent disappointment but continued to sip his tea casually without a response. His men sat motionless, their gazes fixed on us with piercing scrutiny. The atmosphere had grown into jagged shards of glass, waiting to cut, dangerous to cross.

We intended to leave the awkward situation as soon as possible. The four of us gulped down our tea and stood to leave. There was a hotel just down the street from the tea shop; it was the only hotel in town. We scurried off in that direction. Ahmed and his men's eyes followed us with a lazy, detached interest. Their relaxed demeanor was a stark contrast to our frantic movements.

Upon entering the hotel, a receptionist welcomed us in English, addressing the men first, as is customary. "Hello, sirs, how can I help you?"

"Good afternoon," Jakub said. " We're looking for two hotel rooms, please."

"Certainly. Do you want two single beds or one queen bed to share in the room?"

"In our room a queen please," Blake butted in. "The lads will have two singles. Thanks. What's the price?"

Before the receptionist could answer, a voice cut in, speaking in Arabic. Startled by the unexpected sound, I turned around. Ahmed had followed us into the hotel.

From that point forward, the receptionist turned his gaze to the ground and refused to speak directly with us.

"I will help check-in for you," Ahmed announced firmly.

My throat tightened.

"This gentleman was helping us just fine, thanks," Blake rebutted, with equal firmness. He turned back to the receptionist. "So, mate, can you please tell us the costs of the two rooms and show us where they are? We're buggered."

Ahmed shot a stream of Arabic words at the receptionist once again. The receptionist shook his head no and continued to stare at the ground.

"It's much easier for me to help you," Ahmed carried on. The receptionist handed Ahmed the keys. "It costs ten dollars a night. You can pay when you check out to come visit my farm. Follow me."

He led us down a dimly lit hall, his three henchmen in tow. My skin prickled, breath caught in my throat. *They knew our room numbers.* We were exposed. But saying anything felt useless—like screaming underwater.

Upon arrival at our meager rooms we awkwardly "thanked" Ahmed and his men for helping us.

"My friends will be with you until you decide to visit the farm," Ahmed dictated.

"My friend, we really don't have an interest or need to visit your farm, but thank you for the invite," Honza replied.

"You will change your mind," Ahmed countered with an eerie smirk. And at that, he turned to leave. We promptly closed the door to this strange world we had stepped into.

After a lie-down, it was time for a much needed shower. I walked through the hallway to find the shared bathroom. The women's was locked, and the receptionist was nowhere to be found. Blake stood guard for me outside of the men's while I washed away the stress of the day.

Fresh and rested, Blake and I then decided to stroll through town with Honza and Jakub to find some tajine, a slow-cooked Moroccan dish typically prepared in a cone-shaped clay pot, with tender meat, vegetables, and a fragrant blend of spices like cumin, coriander, turmeric, cinnamon, and paprika. We were shocked to find Ahmed's men sitting outside the hotel waiting for us.

"Hey, what are you guys doing here?" Honza asked.

"What you want?" one of the men uttered in broken English.

I tried to answer in a light and casual manner. "We're just going to grab a bite to eat."

We brushed past the men and marched down the street at a brisk pace. They followed.

As we walked along the road, a constant stream of eyes stared holes through us. These were not friendly or curious gazes of innocent intrigue, but glares of contempt, casting a shadow of disdain upon our every step. I couldn't fathom the reason behind their animosity, but it seeped into the atmosphere.

Every stare, every person who passed, was a man. I had not seen a woman anywhere since we arrived. Was that why the women's bathroom in the hotel was locked? Were there only men in this city farming and selling drugs? It seemed likely. I was out of place, vulnerable in a world of seedy men. An easy target waiting to be singled out.

The vibe on the street was dark, pained, violent. Every man roaming looked weathered and worn. The majority of them had huge cuts and scars scattered over their bodies, as if machetes had sliced through their faces. Some walked with noticeable limps, their gaits likely marred by past battles. Others missed pieces of their ears or had only one working eye. I hated this place and regretted ever coming.

After following us down the road for a few minutes, one of Ahmed's thugs pointed to a nearby cafe. "You eat here."

Honza, Blake, Jakub, and I all stared quizzically at one another, unsure what to do. We wanted to ditch these guys, but that clearly wasn't going to happen, so we turned into the restaurant, with the men following.

We ordered tagine and couscous. It was hard to enjoy the food as the men sat there, their backs straight in their chairs, glaring. We ate in silence, shoveling the food in quickly, barely chewing, desperate to finish the awkward meal. All we wanted was to retreat to the hotel, away from the watchful eyes of the men.

It was sunset when we walked back to the hotel, which was traditionally one of the times that "the call to prayer," or adhan, would blast through a nearby mosque speaker, reminding Muslims to come to mandatory prayer and leave worldly matters behind. The word *adhan* itself means "to listen." It is delivered five times a day, repeating phrases such as "Allahu Akbar" (God is great), "Hayya ʻala-s-Salah" (hurry to the prayer), and "Assalatu khairum-minan-naum" (prayer is better than sleep). In every single city, village, and Moroccan town, no matter how small, the call to prayer can be heard every day, five times a day.

A chill slithered down my spine when I realized I hadn't heard a single call to prayer in Ketama. *This place was so awful not even God came here.*

That evening, the four of us huddled in Honza and Jakub's hotel room. Unease filled the space, thick gnawing fear of what might come next.

"We can't just sit here and do nothing," Honza said, his brow furrowed.

Jakub nodded, his fingers tapping anxiously on the table. "We need to figure something out."

Blake leaned back in his chair, crossing his arms. "We definitely can't trust Ahmed and his men. That's for sure."

I fiddled with the hem of my shirt. "Agreed. It just doesn't feel safe to hop into that unmarked car with them and go to a remote farm where there is no cell service, police, or any chance of being heard screaming out for help."

"But we can't give up on Ketama," Honza insisted, his voice tinged with determination.

Jakub sighed, running a hand through his hair in frustration. "Maybe we can find another farm. One that doesn't give off such sketchy vibes."

Honza's eyes lit up with a glimmer of hope. "That could work. We could wake up early, before those stupid men come to the hotel, ask around town, see if anyone knows of a more trustworthy farmer. Hell, maybe we could find Mustaffah."

Jakub nodded. "I like the sound of this. We can organize a little day tour, and then head to Chefchaouen the next day!"

Blake clapped his hands together. "Cool with you, Shan?"

"Sure, why not? It would be nice if we could get out of here accomplishing our original mission."

At 8 a.m. the next day, the boys and I opened our hotel room doors to find two men leaning against the hallway walls with guns in their laps.

"Going somewhere?" one of the men asked with a wry smile on his face.

His expression churned my stomach. The weight of his gaze lingered heavy with unspoken intentions.

"Just to get some breakfast," Blake shot back. "You are not invited."

He grabbed my hand and dragged me out of the hotel and down the front steps. Heads down, Honza and Jakub followed. I felt a rush of relief as Blake pulled me away, desperate for a moment's respite from the oppressive weight Ahmed's men brought.

This comfort was short-lived as the men stood up and casually followed.

Anywhere we went for the entire day the henchmen followed, eyes on the prize (us) and hands on their holsters. No one dared to speak to us in the presence of these men. It scared me to see how fearful every member of the town appeared in their ominous presence. It scared me even more how it seemed every man we walked past undressed me with shifty eyes. I felt like meat on a plate, the only woman in sight, a prize to be taken.

That night I cried in Blake's arms. I was convinced I would be raped in this hungry town. No part of it felt safe, not even the room we sat in. Gunmen waited outside, free to bust through the door and attack any moment they pleased. And what if something did happen? I imagined the story of my rape making headlines; that every person who saw it would merely laugh at my stupidity, exclaiming that I bloody well deserved it for being such a naive tourist wandering into a drug town of violent international smugglers.

We made our way past the guards and into Honza and Jakub's room to have another discussion.

"We can't keep risking our safety like this. This mission is failed and I want to give up," I said, my voice laced with frustration as I collapsed onto the bed.

Honza nodded solemnly, his attention fixed intensely at the floor. "Agreed. It's just not worth it anymore."

Blake leaned against the wall, arms tight across his chest. "We need to get out of here as soon as possible."

Jakub glanced at the bus schedule posted on the wall, a hint of optimism brightening his expression. "Look, the first bus to Chefchaouen leaves at 5:30 tomorrow. Surely Ahmed's henchman won't be here that early. We can use that to our advantage."

I nodded, relief loosening my muscles. "Please!"

With our minds made up, we settled in for the night, hoping that tomorrow would end our misadventures in Ketama.

Blake and I cautiously creaked open our door at 5 a.m. to find two men hunched against the wall with their eyes half closed. They instantly stiffened, rising to their feet in one swift motion, eyeing us maliciously.

"Where you going?" One of the men demanded.

"We need to leave. We have plans to meet friends in Chefchaouen today."

The man towered over us both, his hand gently holding on to the gun hanging from his belt. "You must come to our farm before you go. That is the agreement. Ahmed will come to speak with you and make plans."

Despite the fact that we'd made no agreement, we knew that catching the morning bus was not an option. We retreated to our room instead.

Someone knocked loudly an hour later. Tension prickled at the back of my neck.

As Blake cracked open the door, Ahmed busted his way inside. He pulled out the only chair in the room for himself to sit on, leaving us awkwardly perched at the end of the bed.

I sat quietly, willing a forcefield around myself.

"My friends, every foreigner who comes to this town comes to do business. We are one of the world's largest hashish exporters. I know why you are here, for hashish. I can help you."

"OK, sure, mate, we'll get a bit of hashish off you, but then we really need to leave. We need to get to Chefchaouen," Blake said, arms crossed over his chest.

"Yes, OK." Ahmed's face lightened up. "I have a very good business record. I have many connections. I can help you to fill a boat to go across to Europe. I've done this many times."

A shocking realization set in. Ahmed thought we were big-time smugglers. Why else would we have come to the place where seventy percent of European hash and half of the global production comes from? We hadn't stumbled into a touristic, weed friendly town. We'd fallen head first into a land of serious drug business, where hundreds of millions of dollars flood through yearly.

I felt dizzy, my breath quickening in short, shallow gasps. We couldn't—and wouldn't—play out Ahmed's request, but the terrifying question was whether he would accept our refusal. *What would he do if we said no?* He appeared too well-connected, too powerful. How could we convince him we were just a group of clueless travelers? *What if he didn't care?* A single misstep, and we could be in deeper trouble than I could comprehend. I glanced at Blake, hoping he had a plan.

Blake cleared his throat. "My friend, I'm sorry, I think you misunderstand the kind of people we are. We are just backpackers. We don't have a lot of money. We were looking to buy maybe twenty dollars worth of hash, no more."

Ahmed burst into laughter. "My friend, the only foreigners who come to Ketama come to do big business. You can pretend you are someone else, but I know who you are, and we will do good business together. When you decide you're ready, you tell my men." He continued, "Your woman can help too."

My stomach twisted as he eyed me up and down.

"She can carry around one kilo of hashish. She just needs to swallow the packets."

My lips parted to respond, but no sound came out. I swallowed hard, my throat suddenly dry and tight as if it had closed up in protest of the absurd reality unfolding before me. Ahmed wasn't just suggesting we transport drugs; he was talking about *me—my body—* being the vessel to carry his product across borders.

Body packing. The term surfaced in my mind like a nightmare. Swallowing tightly wrapped packets of drugs, layer upon layer of polyethylene or latex, sometimes coated with wax. Then waiting— agonizingly waiting—for the capsules to pass through my intestines so they could be retrieved, cleaned, and sold. The taste of bile rose in the back of my throat, but I forced it down, praying Ahmed couldn't see the tremor that had started in my hands. I rubbed the back of my neck, the muscles taut and stiff. *I was never going to be on board with this plan.*

Blake's eyes narrowed. He clenched his fists. "Mate, that is *never* going to happen. We really aren't the type of people you think we are. We're penniless travelers, and we need to leave this place."

Ahmed squared his shoulders, his voice low. "Yes, and you will, after you visit my farm and we do business."

Before we could get another word in, he stood and strode out of the room without a glance back.

When the door closed I screamed at Blake in dismay. "What are we going to do!? They're holding us hostage! We are guarded twenty-four hours a day, and there is literally no escape except for agreeing to do business with them! **We're completely fucked.**"

"We're going to find a way out of here." Blake, ever the macho protector, tried to calm me. "Let's go talk to the guys."

We collapsed onto the floor of our friends' room. We needed to come up with an immediate plan of escape. Thankfully, the guys and I agreed that I was particularly vulnerable, being a lone female caught amongst a dark world of drug lords.

The guys felt so strongly about the need to prioritize my escape that Honza and Jakub made the kindest and most heroic offer, one which I will remain thankful for the rest of my life.

"Listen, Shannon needs to get out of here," Jakub stated matter-of-factly. "Why don't Honza and I just agree to go to the farm with Ahmed, if he agrees to let you two go? You should obviously stick with her for safety's sake, Blake. Ahmed's not going to let us all leave without visiting the farm. Honza and I can do it. We're the ones who had the idea to come here in the first place. We got you into this situation. We want to help get you out."

"Jakub, you guys don't have to do that for us," I mumbled, uncomfortable with the idea of putting my new friends into potential danger on my behalf. "We can think up another plan."

"There's no other way, Shan," Honza interrupted. "Let's do it, Jakub. I'm sure they're not going to fuck with us. We can just take a look around the farm, which we wanted to do anyways. We'll buy a couple hundred euros of product, and be on our way. Maybe we'll tell them it's a sampler or some shit, that we'll come back for more."

"Are you sure about this, guys?" Blake interjected. "They might not accept a small offer. Once you're stuck on the farm alone with them you have lost all control of the situation. You're in their grasp. Seems pretty sketchy."

"The lot of us have no other choice, Blake. We're doing it." Honza looked at me apologetically. "You need to get Shannon out of here. I'm sorry we got you guys in this mess."

My sight focused on the floor while my heart raised to the roof. I was overwhelmed by a tidal wave of gratitude. I marveled at the magnitude of love and courage displayed by these individuals who had been complete strangers a few short days ago.

"Thanks, guys. I appreciate your offer so much," I managed to utter, my eyes brimming with tears at the idea of escaping the situation unscathed.

"Stop, Shan, it's fine. We'll meet you in Chefchaouen in a couple days, OK? We'll smoke a fatty and laugh about the absurdity of this whole thing."

"Deal."

Ahmed's crooks were, of course, still sitting outside the hotel room door when Blake and I emerged from the boys' room. Blake told them we needed to speak with Ahmed. Their eyes twinkled, as they must have thought this was finally the moment we would crack.

Ahmed's commanding presence filled the confines of our hotel room within the hour. In his characteristic power move, he claimed the solitary chair, a throne of dominance that amplified his control over the space. Blake, compelled to assert his own sense of strength, stood alongside Ahmed, a towering figure projecting an aura of machismo. Meanwhile, I sought refuge on the edge of the bed, its soft surface offering a modest sanctuary amidst the charged atmosphere. Ahmed's piercing gaze bore down upon me, a frown etched upon his face. My instinct was to avert my eyes, fearful of the raw power that emanated from him.

"Ahmed," Blake began, "my girlfriend is very uncomfortable and she wants to leave this place..."

Ahmed quickly interjected. "Yes, why did you bring your woman here? This town is no place for a woman." The words pierced my heart as Ahmed went on, "It is very dangerous for your woman here. Many hungry men. We work so hard on the farms and never get chances to experience women. Your white woman, *many would love to experience her.*"

My stomach churned as Ahmed's hungry eyes lingered over me.

"Yes," Blake said, "I need to get her out of here, Ahmed. **Today.** Honza and Jakub have agreed to go to your farm with you and do some business, but my woman and I need to go. We need to leave for Chefchaouen. **Today.** That is the deal."

Ahmed paused for a moment, as if considering the proposal. He thoughtfully twisted his long, wiry beard. "Yes," he slowly responded. "Yes, we can arrange for that. This is no place for a woman."

"I understand that now, mate. It was a mistake. Thank you."

Ahmed continued, "You and your woman can go in my car to Chefchaouen. Your friends will come to do business at my farm."

"We don't need to take your car, Ahmed," Blake insisted. "We prefer to take the bus, thank you."

"You will take my car," Ahmed said again, malice in his voice. "There is no bus until tomorrow morning."

My mind raced, trying to conjure some alternative, but there was none. Desperation drove me to accept any means of departure. We didn't have the luxury of choice. Whatever doubts gnawed at the edges of my thoughts, I knew this was my only shot at getting out. I bit the inside of my cheek, the sharp sting grounding me as I stared at the worn carpet beneath my feet.

Ahmed abruptly stood, opened the door, and held it for us to leave. "Grab your things. My car will be waiting outside."

Everything moved at warp speed. Now was our moment, and we could not risk faltering for a second or Ahmed might change his mind. We grabbed our packs. We'd left them packed the entire time, as we intended to escape as soon as possible. The boys, hearing the commotion in the hallway, opened their door as we emerged.

"Everything OK?" Jakub questioned. "Our plan going through?"

"Yes, Jakub!" I ran into his chest for a deep embrace. "We're leaving now, in Ahmed's car, to head to Chefchaouen. Come meet us right when you leave here, OK? We'll be at the Hostel Baraka." Jakub nodded solemnly as Honza came up for a hug too. "I could never thank you guys enough."

"Seriously, mate," Blake jumped in, grasping them both for a tight hug. "See you on the other side, guys. **Stay safe.**"

Our farewell was cut short as Ahmed's men hurried us out of the hotel and into their vehicle. I didn't have time to think of exchanging emails or contact details with Honza and Jakub.

As I squeezed into the car, trapped between Blake and the armed men on either side, I realized we were still in danger. But this was our only chance to escape, and I clung to the hope that it was really happening.

I shifted in my seat, the fabric of my pants damp against my skin. Sweat was pooling beneath my arms, trickling down my back in tiny rivulets that only added to the suffocating heat in the car. Every muscle in my body screamed to run, but where could I go? He ran the town, the roads, the people outside the hotel. There was no escape.

The six of us sat crammed into the car, enveloped by silence. The pervasive stench of body odor permeated the cramped space, thick and stifling. The engine hummed, its vibrations reverberating through our bodies as we navigated the winding roads through the Rif Mountain Range and into the famous blue city of Chefchaouen.

When the car finally pulled up to the side of the road, the heavy silence of our journey was broken by the soft rustling of seats as we began to gather our belongings.

"Thanks, guys," Blake said as he pushed open the car door and stepped out. I silently nodded in agreement.

The men remained straight-faced, offering little more than a slight nod of acknowledgment.

When my feet touched down on Chefchaouen, it felt like shedding a heavy coat on a scorching summer day, leaving me lighter and freer than ever before. I had spent days trapped in a cycle of fear and uncertainty, and now, as I stood there, in this peaceful town, it was hard to believe we had actually made it.

For a long moment, I just stood there, trying to process everything that had happened. The blue-washed buildings rose around me like something out of a dream. It was too quiet, too calm. My mind struggled to catch up. Harrowing images surged forward: Ahmed's raised voice, Jakub's pale face. Fear clung to me still, like smoke in my hair.

I closed my eyes and exhaled. A long, trembling breath.

Over the next week, Blake and I wandered the town's narrow, cobbled streets. The shades of sky and sea sunk into us, and the static in my mind began to clear. The tightness in my shoulders gave way to something softer as the tension that clung to my body let go.

But the calm was only surface-deep.

Each day felt borrowed. Each moment was haunted by the absence of Honza and Jakub.

Blake and I sat on the rooftop terrace of our guesthouse one afternoon, legs stretched out under a low table scattered with peanut shells and half-drunk tea. I caught Blake glancing at the alley below for the third time in five minutes.

"They're not coming today," I said.

He didn't answer, just rubbed his palms on his jeans and leaned forward, resting his elbows on his knees.

"What if something went wrong?" I said quietly. "What if they're still being kept there?"

Blake's jaw tightened. "They're OK. They have to be."

"I just... I feel like we abandoned them."

"Don't." Blake shook his head. "They made that decision. It was their idea. They chose to stay so you could leave."

I nodded, blinking against the sting behind my eyes. Below us, a man selling leather belts shouted into the street. Someone's scooter backfired. Everything around us kept moving.

But I kept seeing Honza's tense expression as he said, *go*. Jakub's forced grin.

I hugged my knees to my chest. "Heroes."

Blake didn't argue. He just stared down at the road, waiting.

They never showed up.

Without last names, contact details, or a way to trace them, they vanished into the unknown. We tried searching online. We asked around. Scoured the town. Nothing. Eventually, we had to admit what neither of us wanted to say aloud: we might never know what happened to them.

The weight of that truth still lingers.

As we departed from Chefchaouen, I was left to reflect about my choices. I promised myself to be more thoughtful next time—more aware of the risks I take. I liked to think of myself as adventurous and eager for experience—but I was learning that those traits, while valuable, needed to be balanced.

In the aftermath, I felt humbled. I vowed to approach future travels with a deeper respect for the boundary between exploration and recklessness. To recognize that not every opportunity is an invitation. *Not every risk is worth the story.* The world is wide and full of wonder, but it's not mine to treat like a personal playground.

Curiosity and courage had carried me far, but I was learning that real wisdom lies in knowing when to pause, to ask questions, to recognize the edges of what I don't yet understand. And while I still believe in taking chances, I now know that the boldest kind of bravery can sometimes look like caution. Or stillness. Or walking away.

28

THE PROMISE OF THE
OPEN ROAD

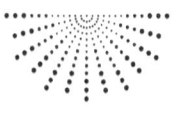

MOROCCO

*T*he sun slipped lower in the sky, tinting the indigo walls of Chefchaouen with a watercolor haze. Every surface a different shade of blue—like the city was holding its breath underwater. I was too. Lungs shallow, bracing for a conversation I wasn't ready to have.

Blake and I sat tucked into a corner table of a small rooftop café that overlooked the medina, where laundry flapped from balconies like surrender flags and the call to prayer echoed softly off the hills. The scent of grilled lamb and burnt sugar wafted from the kitchen behind us, mingling with the tang of spiced olives laid out on the ceramic plate between us.

Blake pushed aside his empty bowl of tagine, then swept his arm toward the glowing horizon, like a game show host revealing the grand prize. "So, you still hate Morocco?"

I didn't answer right away. My fingers picked at the edge of a flatbread, pulling it apart like I could undo the past week if I unraveled it just right. "I don't hate it," I said finally. "But I'm done. Done with the fake smiles. The constant push of every interaction. Like...everyone wants something. Every 'hello' is just a setup for a sale. It's exhausting."

Blake nodded, tracing his thumb around the lip of his tea glass.

"Yeah," he said, "sometimes it does feel like the whole country is playing a game you never agreed to be in."

I glanced at him, then out at the fading light washing over the Rif Mountains. My chest still felt tight when I thought about Ahmed. About Jakub and Honza and the silent question mark that hung over their fates.

"Portugal didn't exactly help my bank account either," I muttered. "Five euros an hour. What a joke."

Blake snorted. "You didn't complain when you were dancing on tables."

I rolled my eyes. "Yeah, well. We both know that glamour faded. And now I'm counting coins for dinner."

"All right. New plan. Hear me out. New Zealand."

I raised an eyebrow. "What?"

"New Zealand," he repeated. "Working holiday visas. Americans can get one for a year. Wages are decent. Like sixteen bucks an hour minimum. And it's stunning. Mountains, fjords, beaches, sheep. The whole damn Hobbit package."

"Ah, yes. Nothing screams stability like fleeing to Middle Earth with a sunburned musician."

"Come on. Have a sense of adventure. We could live in Wellington for six months working. It's the capital. Artsy, ocean on one side, hills on the other. Good coffee. Chill people. We stack some cash, and while we work, we buy a van, fix it up. Then, we hit the road for six months of van-life. Campsites, hiking, hot springs, glaciers, all of it."

A man in a red fez tugged a reluctant donkey through the narrow street below, its cart piled high with oranges. The donkey planted its hooves and refused to move, so the man threw up his hands and shouted into the sky, as if scolding fate. I surprised myself by smiling. The absurdity felt like an invitation—to not take everything so seriously. To move, even if clumsily, toward whatever came next.

After Morocco, fear would've made sense. After everything with Blake, hesitation would've been natural. But instead, my mind drifted to pine-scented mornings and steaming mugs of coffee high on a mountaintop. I saw Blake humming softly while running his hand along the van door, checking for dings and tightening a loose hinge. I pictured a different kind of challenge. A different kind of freedom.

"That sounds...awesome." The words landed in my chest like an anchor.

Blake smiled wide. Relief, or maybe victory, flickered in his eyes.

Down below, lanterns flickered to life. Shopkeepers packed up vibrant rugs. A toddler wailed in the alley. The distant hum of a call to prayer sliced through the evening haze holding a promise of something beyond.

I didn't know what would come next—but I knew I couldn't stay still. Not yet. *Would I ever?* It felt impossible to imagine being the kind of person who settles down and calls a place home without itching for something more.

The adventure would continue—me, Blake, and a van full of restless dreams, chasing horizons that shifted with every mile. I would take the lessons I'd learned on the road so far.

No doubt, more lessons lay ahead.

I thought I was as ready as I'd ever be.

AUTHOR'S NOTE

"The older I get the more I believe the only thing we have to offer is what we have been through." —Jeffrey Gettleman, *Love, Africa*

I never thought of myself as a particularly creative person, but loved ones have reminded me that writing is its own form of art.

A memoirist, like any storyteller, wants to craft a compelling narrative. Real life, of course, is messy and often resists neat arcs or tidy endings. That's the inherent tension in creative nonfiction: we strive for truth, but we also make choices about what to emphasize, what to compress, and what to leave unsaid.

The stories in this book are drawn from my real experiences. They are as accurate and honest as I can make them. However, the events in these pages are drawn from memory—and I'll be the first to admit that memory can be an unreliable narrator. What we remember most clearly often says more about what mattered to us than the precise way an event unfolded.

Writing from memory also means writing from a place of hindsight. Time gives us perspective, and with that perspective comes the temptation to reinterpret the past—to smooth out emotional rough spots, to assign meaning that might not have been there in the moment. The past, it turns out, is as pliable as wet clay.

The challenge for any memoirist is not to pretend this limitation doesn't exist. Perhaps the most honest thing a memoir writer can say is that truth is layered, memory is biased, and our life stories are, in part, interpretations. My aim has been to shape those interpretations into something that feels true.

For this reason, I relied heavily on the journals I kept while traveling—pages filled not just with big moments and emotional turning points, but with everyday details: the way someone adjusted their shirt collar before speaking, the slant of light across a kitchen table, the sound of a market at dusk. These records helped me stay true to what was actually happening while I was living it.

The names of people in this book have been changed to protect their privacy. The emotions, the relationships, and the journeys described here remain as I experienced them. The conversations you'll read aren't word-for-word transcripts, but they hold the tone, rhythm, and heart of what was said. My aim isn't to document every fact with scientific precision, but to share the truth that mattered most: how it felt to be there, what I learned, and how those moments changed me.

I hope as you read about my experiences that you find personal connections, feel entertained, and catch sparks of motivation. I hope you feel encouraged to get out and experience the world more fully, reflecting and learning from your experiences as you go. More importantly, I hope you feel empowered to live the life you dream of. It is a revelation to realize that we have the power to create different versions of our lives again and again, learning from every hiccup, laughing at outcomes, connecting deeply with others, and interacting with the strangest of things, all with an open mind. There is no "normal path" to life after all—only the one you create, revise, and recreate. That reinvention is not just possible—*it's necessary.*

This book took four years to write—and many more to live. The travels, the misadventures, the moments of connection and loss—

they've all led to these pages. I've poured my heart into them. It's an honor to share this story with you, and I hope somewhere in these words, you find something that stays with you long after the last page.

ACKNOWLEDGMENTS

First and foremost, I want to thank my mother—my forever rock of support and my model for resilience. I honestly don't know what I'd do without her. The poor woman has had to live on the sidelines, biting her nails with worry through all my adventures. I made it, Mama! (And sorry in advance—I know you'll hate reading some of these harrowing and, let's face it, irresponsible stories.)

To my big sister, Tara—*thank you*. You've listened to far too many rants and offered encouragement, perspective and the sage wisdom that only an older sister can. Your presence in my life is a gift.

To my husband, Mat—thank you for your endless patience and love. You've sat through every draft of this book, endured three years of my obsessive rambling, and never once stopped cheering me on. Your unwavering belief in me keeps me going every single day. I am so grateful to have found you on this journey.

A huge thank you to the Scribophile community. You helped me edit, re-edit, and polish this story countless times. You challenged me, pushed me, and ultimately made me a better writer. I'm deeply thankful for your time, honesty, and encouragement.

To my editor, Eldes Tran—thank you for your sharp eye and professionalism. You helped me work out all the kinks to make this book polished and ready for the world. It was a joy to collaborate with you.

To all the incredible humans I've met along my travels—you've touched and influenced my life more than you'll ever know. What a blessing it's been to share these adventures with you.

And to all my friends who've been cheering me on from the sidelines—offering advice, opinions, kind words, and encouragement—thank you from the bottom of my heart.

Finally, thank **you**, dear reader, for taking the time to read this book. I hope it leaves you inspired, and I hope you'll share it with someone you know.

ABOUT THE AUTHOR

For over 15 years, Shannon O'Brien has made the world her classroom—traveling widely, immersing herself in new cultures, and chasing stories that reveal how journeys transform us. A writer, educator, and lifelong adventurer, her work explores themes of identity, resilience, and the emotional landscapes of travel. Originally from California, she has lived across the globe, weaving her experiences into vivid, character-driven storytelling. Her debut travel memoir, *Stray: Breaking Free, Falling Hard and Growing Stronger*, blends raw honesty with rich cultural detail, capturing both the external journey and the inner one. She now lives in Malta, where she teaches at an international school and continues to write with an intention to inspire others to live courageously, embrace their authentic selves, and explore the world with open-minded curiosity. Discover more of Shannon's adventures and stories on her website.

www.shannon-obrien.com